T0300331

*Routledge Revivals*

# Social Democracy in Capitalist Society

First published in 1977. This book considers the nature of industrial society, contemporary capitalism and the impact of political ideas on social structure. These ideas are discussed by reference to the impact of social democracy on the structure of capitalist society in a comparative analysis of Britain and Sweden — including an interview survey of industrial workers socio-political attitudes. The study is concluded by a general discussion of the role of social democracy in capitalist society. It is argued that the development of social democracy generates 'strains' which, in the long term, question the legitimacy of capitalism among industrial manual workers.

# Social Democracy in Capitalist Society

## Working-Class Politics in Britain and Sweden

Richard Scase

Routledge
Taylor & Francis Group

First published in 1977
by Croom Helm

This edition first published in 2016 by Routledge
2 Park Square, Milton Park, Abingdon, Oxon, OX14 4RN
and by Routledge
711 Third Avenue, New York, NY 10017

*Routledge is an imprint of the Taylor & Francis Group, an informa business*

© 1977 Richard Scase

**Publisher's Note**
The publisher has gone to great lengths to ensure the quality of this reprint but points out that some imperfections in the original copies may be apparent.

**Disclaimer**
The publisher has made every effort to trace copyright holders and welcomes correspondence from those they have been unable to contact.

A Library of Congress record exists under LC control number: 76030344


ISBN 13: 978-1-138-64875-3 (hbk)
ISBN 13: 978-1-315-62624-6 (ebk)

# Social Democracy in Capitalist Society

WORKING-CLASS POLITICS IN
BRITAIN AND SWEDEN

RICHARD SCASE

CROOM HELM LONDON

ROWMAN AND LITTLEFIELD

Croom Helm Ltd.,
2-10 St John's Road, London SW11

ISBN 0 85664 657 1
Reprinted 1977

Printed and bound in Great Britain by
REDWOOD BURN LIMITED
Trowbridge & Esher

# CONTENTS

# PREFACE

This study assesses the role of social democracy in capitalist society. More specifically, it seeks to find out whether the development of social democratic parties and labour unions has had any noticeable impact upon class inequalities and political attitudes. This is investigated by comparing political and industrial developments in Britain and Sweden. Particular attention is given to Sweden since no other capitalist country has had such a long tradition of social democratic governments and few, if any, have had as influential a trade union movement. This analysis claims that although the egalitarian goals of the Swedish Social Democratic Party and labour unions have been constrained by the forces of industrial capitalism, tensions have been generated which are reflected in the socio-political attitudes of rank-and-file supporters. Consequently, the legitimacy of Swedish capitalism as a long-term socio-economic system could be questioned among industrial manual workers.

This is a revised and edited version of my Ph.D. thesis, 'Social Democracy in Sweden: A Comparative Analysis', University of Kent, 1974. Sections of Chapters 4 and 5 have earlier been published as 'Conceptions of the Class Structure and Political Ideology: Some Observations on Attitudes in England and Sweden', in F. Parkin (ed.), *The Social Analysis of Class Structure,* Tavistock Publications, 1974; and 'Relative Deprivation: A Comparison of English and Swedish Manual Workers', in D. Wedderburn (ed.), *Poverty, Inequality and Class Structure,* Cambridge University Press, 1974.

I am grateful to John Westergaard for his most detailed and helpful advice and to Rolf Andersson, Robert Erikson, Roland Spånt and other members of the Swedish Institute for Social Research for their various comments. I am also thankful to Anita Ehn-Scase and the Respondents for the interviews, Joan Dolby for computing assistance, and Tricia Pike for typing. Finally, and above all, I am indebted to David Donnison for his untiring help and encouragement. This book is for him.

Spring, 1976.                                                                                 *Richard Scase*

# INTRODUCTION: THE COMPARATIVE STUDY OF SOCIETIES

The early sociologists emphasised the need for the comparative method. Comte,[1] Durkheim[2] and Weber,[3] for example, argued that the comparative study of societies should be an integral part of sociological analysis, not only for the investigation of specific empirical variables, but also for the study of large-scale social processes. Therefore, they claimed, it was only by the comparative method that it was possible to identify patterns of human development and to understand social structures. However, during the inter-war years there were few attempts to investigate the social structures of two or more societies. Instead, sociological enquiry tended to focus almost exclusively upon the documentation of social variables as they were found to exist within specific societies. This was partly a result of sociologists ignoring the 'grand theories' of the earlier writers and also because the major locus for sociological research during this period was in the United States where, until the late 1930s, the 'Chicago School' was one of the major influences, defining what was appropriate for empirical investigation.[4] Thus, there was a tendency for investigators to concentrate upon those areas which they felt were appropriate for precise measurement and statistical quantification. These included the ecological structure of cities, demographic differences between rural and urban communities, patterns of migration and a wide range of 'social problems'. Similarly in Britain, where the tradition of sociology was empirical, practical and problem-orientated, the comparative perspectives of such writers as Weber and Durkheim were largely disregarded and sociological research tended to focus upon describing particular aspects of the social structure. Hence, British sociology during the inter-war years studied almost exclusively the distribution and causes of such 'problems' as urban poverty, bad housing, crime, illness and other aspects of social and economic deprivation.[5] Consequently, it was not until after the Second World War that more attention was devoted by sociologists — both in Britain and in the United States — to the comparative study of social structures. The reasons for this would appear to include the following.

First, there seems to have been some scepticism among sociologists about the validity of developing a subject which, although heavily laden with empirical data, was highly limited in its theoretical perspectives.[6]

9

Thus, there was a search for theories and a renewed interest in the ideas of the nineteenth-century writers. Consequently, much of the research in the sociology of deviance was related to the ideas of Durkheim — particularly to his discussions about anomie and social control — while discussions of social class and of social change were often linked to the writings of Marx. But, in addition to providing hypotheses for empirical research, the ideas of the 'Founding Fathers' generated a recognition among investigators that sociology should study large-scale structural changes, and in doing so, adopt perspectives which were both historical and comparative.[7]

Secondly, there was a growing interest in the sociology of development. After the Second World War, sociologists, economists and other social scientists began to investigate the social structures of developing countries, using approaches and methodologies which had been used for the study of industrial societies. Consequently, there were attempts to formulate theories of social change; all of which were conducive to the development of a comparative sociology of the kind which the earlier social theorists had advocated.[8]

Thirdly, the emergence of a number of socialist states in Europe stimulated an interest in the comparative study of industrial societies. A number of writers, interested in the interrelationships between political ideology and social structure, investigated differences and similarities in the social structures of capitalist and socialist countries. Within this context, an issue which received special attention was the degree to which socialism, as a political ideology and an economic and political system, would lead to the emergence of societies with important structural differences to those of capitalist countries.[9]

These, then, are three of the major influences which were conducive to the development of a comparative study of societies. While the perspectives of nineteenth-century social thinkers provided the more important theoretical orientations, developments in non-industrial societies and in socialist states became major areas of enquiry. It was the study of these issues which led to the formulation of the 'convergence thesis'.

The 'convergence thesis' is frequently regarded as consisting of a set of interrelated propositions about the dynamics of social change. However, there is no single 'convergence thesis', and at best the term can only be used to refer to those claims which have suggested that as societies industrialise they will become increasingly similar in terms of a wide range of institutional and cultural features.[10] Thus, it is often suggested that industrial technology imposes a set of 'uniform' charac-

teristics upon the social structures of developing countries,[11] and that
different capitalist and socialist societies are adopting a number of
common features which largely transcend diversities created by their
respective political and economic systems.[12] It would be redundant to
give a detailed account of these features since this can be found elsewhere,[13] but briefly they are often seen to be as follows.

First, with industrialisation and the utilisation of inanimate sources
of power, it is claimed that the division of labour becomes more complex and that specifically defined occupational roles emerge which are
— to a considerable degree — institutionally separated from other
relationships within social structures.[14] Secondly, because of the
imperative demands of modern technology, different industrial societies
develop similar occupational structures.[15] These, in turn, are often seen
to be conducive to the development of educational systems which are
primarily orientated to the production of technically skilled manpower.[16] Thirdly, it is argued that industrialisation generates changes in
systems of social stratification so that the significance of traditional
systems of ranking based on 'ascribed' characteristics declines, while the
role of educational qualifications for the determination of socio-
economic positions becomes more important. Consequently, it is often
suggested that different societies at similar levels of industrialisation
have comparable systems of social stratification; measured, that is, in
terms of the distribution of economic rewards, patterns of social recruitment, and the prestige accruing to different occupational roles.[17]
Fourthly, it is claimed that the 'logic' of industrialism imposes constraints upon the exercise of power in society. Clerk Kerr and his associates, for example, claim that traditional class antagonisms are super-
seded by pressure groups which operate within power structures regu-
lated by 'omnipresent' states; these establish 'webs of rules' within
which conflicts are resolved. As a result, the power structures of all
industrial countries — both socialist and capitalist — become similar, if
only because of the emergence of 'pluralistic industrialism'. Finally, it is
often suggested that industrialism leads to the breakdown of 'traditional' attitudes and values and to the development of ideologies and
social perspectives common to all countries.[18]

These, then, are some of the ideas as expressed in the statements
of those writers who claim that industrialisation leads to the development of similarities in the social structures of different countries. Even
the briefest summary of the argument is sufficient to indicate the lack
of sociological sophistication which it displays, despite the fact that it
has been the basis for most discussions about the nature of industrial

society. Therefore, only three points need to be made.

First, the terms 'industrialism' and 'industrialisation' tend to be vaguely defined. In some writings they refer to inanimate, technological processes,[19] while in others they are more embracing concepts, incorporating not only technology but a range of social and economic variables.[20] In other words, there is little agreement about the definition of terms. At the same time, it is often unclear which socio-economic variables constitute the causes of industrialisation, which the effects and which the components of the process itself.[21] Consequently, many discussions appear tautologous. Secondly, there are often implications of a form of technological determinism. Hence, technology is often considered to be an independent variable which determines most features of a society. Studies of the impact of industrialisation in 'developing' societies often regard technology as a source of social change which by itself has important repercussions for 'traditional' social structures. 'Problems' of development are then regarded as relating to those features which are resistant to forces of change brought about by the introduction of 'modern' technological systems.[22] Thirdly, societies are often conceptualised as highly integrated social systems; changes in one aspect are expected to bring about changes in all others.[23] However, the degree to which this is the case must be regarded as problematic, in precisely the same manner as the direction of changes must be seen as uncertain. As Dunning and Hopper have suggested, it is quite possible for societies to converge in some respects, but to diverge in many others.[24] Fourthly, an over-emphasis upon the 'logic' or 'dynamics' of industrialism has meant that a number of writers have given insufficient attention to the role of ideology and purposive political action in shaping the development of social structures.[25] Goldthorpe makes this point in a discussion of the stratification systems of capitalist and socialist countries.[26] He argues that there are important generic differences between these types of society in terms of the forces which shape their stratification systems; in the former, the structure of inequality is more or less determined by the operation of market forces and the private ownership of the means of production, while in the latter it is heavily influenced by the explicit objectives of political leaders. Consequently, a 'logic' of industrialism cannot be seen to have the same and inevitable consequences for all social structures. An increase in the level of technological complexity may create more economic wealth but the distribution of this will be determined by various social, economic and political factors; in the case of socialist and capitalist countries, by different political institutions and property relationships. Finally, the whole debate has been hindered by a lack of comparative empirical data and by the absence of social indicators which can be used to measure variables over time and between societies.[27] Until such indicators have been established, discussions about variations and similarities in the development of different societies will continue to be based more upon assumptions than the testing of ideas by the collection and analysis of empirical data.

Despite these criticisms, the convergence thesis has generated wide-spread discussion among those interested in the comparative study of societies. The present study has been similarly motivated by these ideas. Generally speaking, the comparative study of industrial societies has tended to concentrate upon similarities and differences between capitalist and socialist countries. But if the dynamics of contemporary social structures are to be better understood, it is necessary to investi-gate developments within each of these societal types.[28] This study, therefore, attempts to describe for two capitalist countries — Britain and Sweden — patterns of industrialisation and political change. It then investigates the consequences of these processes for the respective class structures. More specifically, it seeks to find out whether the development of the working-class movement and a social democratic ideology of egalitarianism in Sweden has, compared with Britain, led to important differences in the class structures of the two countries.

This, then, is a study in comparative sociology. Chapters 1 and 2 are heavily dependent upon secondary sources of data. These should be interpreted with extreme caution if only because the systems of classif-ication used for describing trends in Sweden and Britain are rarely the same; this is particularly the case in the discussion of industrialisation. Similarly, Chapter 2 refers to a number of sociological investigations, many of which differ in terms of their samples and the dates when they were undertaken. Great care should be taken in regard to the compara-tive generalisations which can be made on the basis of these. The remainder of this study discusses workers' attitudes in the two coun-tries and for this, secondary sources of data were either unavailable or not assembled in a form useful for the purposes of comparison. Conse-quently, a comparative study of two groups of English and Swedish manual workers was undertaken, the results of which are produced in Chapters 4, 5 and 6.

In conclusion, it should be stressed that although the data used in the present study — both primary and secondary — are subject to limit-ations of interpretation, they are, more likely than not, *indicative* of trends within each of the two countries. Certainly they warrant an attempt to compare developments and processes of change within the class structures of Britain and Sweden.

## Notes

1. A. Comte, *Cours de Philosophie Positive*, Paris, 1830-42. For a discussion of his work, see R. Fletcher, *The Making of Sociology*, Vol. I, London, 1971, pp. 165-91.
2. E. Durkheim, *The Rules of Sociological Method*, Chicago, 1958.
3. M. Weber, *The Methodology of the Social Sciences*, Chicago, 1949.
4. For a detailed discussion of the 'Chicago School' during the 1920s and 1930s, see R. Faris, *Chicago Sociology, 1920-1932*, California, 1967.
5. See, for example, G. Mitchell, *A Hundred Years of Sociology*, London, 1968, Ch. 10; and J. Rex, *Discovering Sociology*, London, 1973, Ch. 5.
6. For some critical comments on 'abstracted empiricism', see C. Wright Mills, *The Sociological Imagination*, New York, 1959.
7. One of the best examples of such a study conducted during the 1950s is R. Bendix, *Work and Authority in Industry*, New York, 1956.
8. For an early attempt, see D. Lerner, *The Passing of Traditional Society*, New York, 1958. For more recent discussions, see B. Hoselitz and W. Moore (eds.), *Industrialisation and Society*, Paris, 1963; C. Kerr, J. Dunlop, F. Harbison and C. Myers, *Industrialism and Industrial Man*, Cambridge (Mass.), 1960; M. Levy Jr., *Modernisation and the Structure of Societies*, Princeton, 1966; W. Moore, *The Impact of Industry*, Englewood Cliffs, 1965; and W. Moore, *Social Change*, Englewood Cliffs, 1963.
9. For two early discussions, see R. Bauer, A. Inkeles and C. Kluchhohn, *How the Soviet System Works*, Cambridge (Mass.), 1956; and A. Inkeles and R. Bauer, *The Soviet Citizen*, Cambridge (Mass.), 1959.
10. The literature is vast. For a major statement, see A. Feldman and W. Moore, 'Industrialisation and Industrialism; Convergence and Differentiation', *Transactions of the Fifth World Congress of Sociology*, Vol. 2 (1962); C. Kerr *et al.*, op. cit.; M. Levy Jr., op. cit.; and W. Moore, op. cit., 1965. For two major reviews of the literature on convergence, see A. Meyer, 'Theories of Convergence', in C. Johnson (ed.), *Change in Communist Systems*, Stanford, 1970; and I. Weinberg, 'The Problem of Convergence of Industrial Societies: A Critical Look at the State of a Theory', in *Comparative Studies in Society and History*, Vol. II (1969).
11. C. Kerr *et al.*, op. cit.
12. A. Inkeles and R. Bauer, op. cit.
13. C. Kerr *et al.*, op. cit; M. Levy Jr., op. cit; and W. Moore, op. cit., 1965.
14. W. Moore, op. cit., 1965.
15. C. Kerr *et al.*, op. cit.
16. C. Kerr *et al.*, op. cit.
17. C. Kerr *et al.*, op. cit.
18. A. Inkeles, 'Industrial Man: The Relation of Status to Experience, Perception and Values', *American Journal of Sociology*, Vol. 66 (1960-1).
19. W. Moore, op. cit., 1965, p. 4.
20. W. Faunce and W. Form, "The Nature of Industrial Society' in W. Faunce and W. Form (eds.), *Comparative Perspectives on Industrial Society*, Boston, 1969, p. 3.
21. This is particularly evident with the definition used by C. Kerr *et. al.*, op. cit.

22. See, for example, C. Kerr *et al.*, op. cit.
23. See, for example, N. Smelser, 'Mechanisms of Change and Adjustment to Change' in W. Faunce and W. Form (eds.), op. cit.
24. E. Dunning and E. Hopper, 'Industrialisation and the Problem of Convergence: A Critical Note', *Sociological Review*, Vol. 14 (1966).
25. See, for example, W. Moore, op. cit.; N. Smelser, op. cit., and W. Faunce and W. Form, op. cit.
26. J. Goldthorpe, 'Social Stratification in Industrial Society', *Sociological Review Monograph*, No. 8 (1964).
27. This point has been emphasised by E. Dunning and E. Hopper, op. cit.
28. For a discussion of the need for such studies see W.G. Runciman, 'Towards a Theory of Social Stratification', in F. Parkin (ed.), *The Social Analysis of Class Structure*, London, 1974.

# 1 THE SOCIAL STRUCTURES OF BRITAIN AND SWEDEN: 'AN OVERVIEW'

Two social structures as complex as those of Britain and Sweden create problems for any comparative analysis. In order to provide a background to the study of class inequalities in the two countries, it is difficult to decide which factors to include; sociologists are unlikely to agree about the criteria and any selection of issues will almost certainly incorporate personal prejudices and interests. Therefore, the present analysis will only consider developments which the investigator feels to be the most important for the study of their contemporary class structures. In this, more attention will be devoted to Sweden on the grounds that information for that country is generally less known than the material for Britain; for the latter, references will be given to the relevant discussions.

To investigate aspects of class inequality in the two countries it is necessary to describe historical developments in terms of (i) patterns of industrialisation – together with the related processes of urbanisation – and (ii) patterns of political change. For a more comprehensive analysis it would be necessary to consider other factors. But this study only focuses upon industrialisation and political change, since these are considered by many to be among the more important determinants of class inequalities.[1]

## (i) Patterns of industrialisation

Sweden was predominantly an agricultural country until the early part of the twentieth-century. The first reliable statistics for the occupational structure describe the situation in the late eighteenth century. These were collected by the clergy and have been interpreted by Heckscher. According to these, 5 per cent of the Swedish population in 1760 consisted of the nobility, the clergy and other 'gentlefolk', 10 per cent of soldiers and state employees, 6 per cent of traders, craftsmen and merchants and 79 per cent of rural craftsmen, cottagers, crofters and farmers.[2] There were few signs, therefore, to suggest that Sweden in the latter part of the eighteenth century was at the beginning of any 'take-off' in industrialisation – a process which, in fact, was not to occur until a century later. But there was some commerce at this time; copper and iron ore were exported while burghers were allowed to manufacture and trade goods within terms stipulated by the state. However, despite the fact that some of these became extremely wealthy, their impact on the social structure was very limited, if only because of the predominantly agrarian economy. But like their counterparts elsewhere, the capital which they accumulated was to play a significant role in the later industrialisation of the country.[3]

It is difficult to compare the social structure of Sweden with that of Britain in the middle of the eighteenth century because of the absence of comparable statistical evidence. The only material which can be used for the purposes of comparison is Joseph Massie's estimate of the social structure in 1760. Massie's figures have been analysed by Mathias and these suggest that the social structure of Britain was much less agrarian than that of Sweden.[4] They indicate that a higher proportion of the population in Britain was engaged in trading and manufacturing; perhaps something like 40 per cent compared with much less than 10 per cent in Sweden. But despite this, there were a number of common features in the social structures of the two countries. Both were agrarian economies and it seems very likely that the life chances and life-styles of the greater majority of the two populations were similar; in the rural areas most of the agrarian populations existed at subsistence levels with poor diets. Mortality rates were high and there were periodic outbreaks of famine. Samuelsson claims that in Sweden, only hunting and fishing supplemented a drab diet which for the agrarian population consisted mainly of bread.[5] Conditions for the English rural population were probably not much better and whether or not early industrialisation raised living standards for this sector of society has been the subject of dispute among economic historians.[6]

However, from the end of the eighteenth century until the beginning of the twentieth, the social structures of the two countries were characterised by distinctive differences. While Britain rapidly industrialised throughout the nineteenth century, Sweden remained an almost completely agrarian society. Differences in the development of the two social structures during this period are illustrated in Tables 1.1 and 1.2.

It is clear from Tables 1.1 and 1.2 that Sweden in 1900 was less industrialised than Britain in 1801. Whereas the period of most rapid industrialisation in Britain was before 1831, the comparable era in Sweden was after 1880. But this is not the only difference; there were also variations in the processes whereby industrialisation occurred. While it led to rapid large-scale urbanisation in Britain, this did not happen to the same extent in Sweden. Instead, industrialisation tended to be much more dispersed, mainly because of the key importance of iron mining

The Social Structures of Britain and Sweden

Table 1.1: The percentage distribution of the total Swedish population according to main industrial groups, 1790-1900[7]

| Date | Agriculture Forestry & Fishing | Manufacturing & Industry | Trade & Communication | Public Service & Professions |
|---|---|---|---|---|
| 1790 | 79.6 | 11.0 | 1.5 | 7.9 |
| 1810 | 82.4 | 6.7 | 2.8 | 8.1 |
| 1830 | 82.1 | 7.4 | 2.1 | 8.4 |
| 1840 | 80.9 | 8.5 | 2.2 | 8.4 |
| 1850 | 77.9 | 9.2 | 2.0 | 10.9 |
| 1870 | 72.4 | 14.6 | 5.2 | 7.8 |
| 1880 | 67.9 | 17.4 | 7.3 | 7.4 |
| 1890 | 62.1 | 21.7 | 8.7 | 7.5 |
| 1900 | 55.1 | 27.8 | 10.4 | 6.7 |

Source: Extracted from A-L. Kälvesten, The Social Structure of Sweden, Stockholm, 1966, Table 4.

Table 1.2: Estimated percentage distribution of the British labour force, 1801-1901[8]

| Date | Agriculture Forestry & Fishing | Manufacture, Mining, Industry | Trade & Transport | Domestic & Personal | Public, Professional & all Other |
|---|---|---|---|---|---|
| 1801 | 35.9 | 29.7 | 11.2 | 11.5 | 11.8 |
| 1811 | 33.0 | 30.2 | 11.6 | 11.8 | 13.3 |
| 1821 | 28.4 | 38.4 | 12.1 | 12.7 | 8.5 |
| 1831 | 24.6 | 40.8 | 12.4 | 12.6 | 9.5 |
| 1841 | 22.2 | 40.5 | 14.2 | 14.5 | 8.5 |
| 1851 | 21.7 | 42.9 | 15.8 | 13.0 | 6.7 |
| 1861 | 18.7 | 43.6 | 16.6 | 14.3 | 6.9 |
| 1871 | 15.1 | 43.1 | 19.6 | 15.3 | 6.8 |
| 1881 | 12.6 | 43.5 | 21.3 | 15.4 | 7.3 |
| 1891 | 10.5 | 43.9 | 22.6 | 15.8 | 7.1 |
| 1901 | 8.7 | 46.3 | 21.4 | 14.1 | 9.6 |

Source: Extracted from P. Deane and W. Cole, British Economic Growth 1688-1959 (2nd ed.), Cambridge, 1967, Table 30.

and forestry in Swedish economic growth. Iron ore had been exported from as early as the thirteenth century and by the eighteenth century Sweden dominated the world market.[9] It was the mining of ore which led to one of the principal features of early industrialisation in Sweden — the 'bruks'. These were essentially mining villages which had developed within the context of the rural economy. They were usually controlled by a single family, who owned the mines, the land and the employees' houses. They were structured in a very hierarchical manner, so that social relationships between employer and employee were often paternalistic, with the owners providing not only employment but also rudimentary forms of 'social welfare' such as care of the sick, the old and the widowed. 'Bruks' were significant for the early industrialisation of Sweden because they avoided many of the social conflicts found in the few densely populated urban areas. The origins of organised labour, therefore, are not to be found in the 'bruks' but among the craftsmen of Stockholm, who had often obtained their training abroad and gained first-hand experience of industrialisation in other countries.[10]

During the nineteenth century the signficance of the 'bruks' declined because of growing international competition; this was mainly because competitors started to use coal instead of charcoal in the production of iron. Consequently, there was a concentration of output in the Swedish industry so that while a few of the 'bruks' developed into steel towns, most of them either stagnated or ceased production. Nevertheless, the iron industry, in a more 'rationalised' form, continued to be one of the major bases of Swedish industrialisation; during the 1870s it led to the growth of the machine and shipbuilding industries, while in the 1890s its products were used for the manufacture of electrical goods. It was these developments which, in the earlier years of the twentieth century, contributed to the expansion of such urban areas as Stockholm, Gothenburg and Malmö. At the same time, the rapid exploitation of iron ore in the north of Sweden generated the growth of such urban settlements as Kiruna and Lulea.[11]

In addition to the production of iron and the manufacture of its various products, the other major factor in Swedish industrialisation was the exploitation of forests, a process which had two major consequences. First, there was the growth of saw-mill communities on rivers in northern Sweden. Secondly, the development of forest-based industries led to the growth of small carpentry workshops which specialised in the manufacture of furniture and other components for house construction. But neither of these processes brought about the concentration of populations in urban areas. Even the largest saw-mill towns in the north of Sweden had relatively small numbers; Sundsvall in 1890, for example, had a population of only 13,215 and this was scattered over a large geographical area.[12]

As a result of these developments Sweden had, by the 1870s, reached what Rostow has termed the 'take-off' stage of industrialisation.[13] The rate of gross capital formation, expressed as a percentage of gross national product, was 6 per cent during the 1860s, 9 per cent in the 1870s, 11 per cent in the 1880s and 18 per cent by the turn of the century.[14] Consequently, the social structures of Britain and Sweden, which were so different for the greater part of the nineteenth century, came to share a number of common features. Indeed, during the first half of the present century Sweden caught up; thus, by the 1950s the two countries had similar industrial profiles. The patterns are shown in Table 1.3.

Table 1.3 suggests that whereas in Britain there was little change in the percentage of the population engaged in industrial and manufacturing activities between 1911 and 1961, the proportion in Sweden continued to increase; from approximately one-third in 1910 to more than 45 per cent in 1960. Furthermore, there was a decline of more than two-thirds in the proportion of the Swedish population working in agricultural and allied occupations. By the 1950s, and certainly by the 1960s, Britain and Sweden were both highly industrialised countries with almost one-half of their respective labour forces engaged in industrial occupations. They both produced a wide range of engineering, electrical, metallic and chemical goods; indeed, the distribution of employees between different sectors of industry within the two countries was remarkably similar. In 1969, for example, 49 per cent of industrial workers in Britain were engaged in the manufacture of fabricated metal products, electrical goods and vehicles compared with 53 per cent in Sweden. A further 9 per cent of the two industrial labour forces were employed in the food, drink and tobacco industries, and 6 per cent in chemical processing and allied industries.[15] By 1971 the distribution of workers between different sectors of the Swedish and British economies was almost identical. As Table 1.3 shows, about 40 per cent were engaged in industrial occupations, 20 per cent in trade and communications and roughly one-third in 'service' activities. The only major difference between the two countries was in the proportions in agricultural and allied occupations; this was 3 per cent in Britain compared with 8 per cent in Sweden. The common structure of industrialism within the two countries has had important implications for their occupational structures; as Table 1.4 suggests, these appear to be very similar.

Although the occupational structures of the two countries are not identical, there are no fundamental differences between them: in each, 'craftsmen and production workers' constitute between 34 and 40 per cent of the economically active population. The only major variations are in terms of the proportions of professional and technical workers, and of farmers and fishermen; in each case Sweden has a higher percentage than Britain. But these do not override the common features

Table 1.3: Percentage distribution of the British and Swedish labour forces, 1910-1970

| Date | Agriculture, Forestry and Fishing | | Manufacture, Mining and Industry | | Trade and Communications | | Public, Personal and Professional Services | | Total | |
|---|---|---|---|---|---|---|---|---|---|---|
| | Britain | Sweden | Britain | Sweden | Britain | Sweden | Britain | Sweden | Britain | Sweden |
| 1910/11 | 8.3 | 48.8 | 46.4 | 32.0 | 21.5 | 13.4 | 23.8 | 5.8 | 100.0 | 100.0 |
| 1920/21 | 7.1 | 44.0 | 47.6 | 35.0 | 20.3 | 15.2 | 25.0 | 5.8 | 100.0 | 100.0 |
| 1930/31 | 6.0 | 39.4 | 45.3 | 35.7 | 22.7 | 18.2 | 26.0 | 6.7 | 100.0 | 100.0 |
| 1940/41 | – | 34.1 | – | 38.2 | – | 19.5 | – | 8.2 | – | 100.0 |
| 1950/51 | 5.0 | 24.6 | 49.1 | 42.7 | 21.8 | 22.6 | 24.1 | 10.1 | 100.0 | 100.0 |
| 1960/61 | 3.8 | 13.8 | 46.0 | 45.1 | 22.5 | 21.0 | 27.7 | 20.1 | 100.0 | 100.0 |
| 1970/71 | 2.5 | 8.1 | 42.3 | 40.2 | 21.1 | 21.6 | 34.1 | 30.1 | 100.0 | 100.0 |

*Sources:* Extracted from Central Bureau of Statistics, *Historical Statistics for Sweden, Vol. 1,* Stockholm, 1955, Table A21; P. Deane and W. Cole, *British Economic Growth, 1688-1959* (2nd ed.), Cambridge, 1967; and International Labour Office, *Yearbook of Labour Statistics,* Geneva, 1967, Table 2A, and 1975, Table 2A.

Table 1.4: The structure of the economically active population in
Sweden (1970) and Britain (1971)

| Occupation Category | Britain % | Sweden % |
|---|---|---|
| Professional, Technical and Related Workers | 11.1 | 19.2 |
| Administrative and Managerial Workers | 3.7 | 2.3 |
| Clerical and Related Workers | 17.9 | 17.1 |
| Sales Workers | 9.0 | 9.0 |
| Service Workers | 11.7 | 9.6 |
| Agricultural, Forestry Workers and Fishermen | 3.0 | 8.0 |
| Production Workers, Craftsmen and Related Workers | 40.0 | 34.1 |
| Workers not Classifiable by Occupation | 2.6 | 0.2 |
| Members of the Armed Forces | 1.0 | 0.5 |
| Total | 100.0 | 100.0 |

Source: International Labour Office, Yearbook of Labour Statistics, Geneva,
1975, Table 2B.

between the two countries. Indeed, similarities in industrial profiles are
reinforced by the distribution of their labour forces between enterprises of different sizes. This is shown in Table 1.5.

Table 1.5: The percentage distribution of employees among enterprises
of different sizes in manufacturing industry in Britain and Sweden

| Size of Enterprise (Nos. of Employees) | Percentage of Employment | |
|---|---|---|
| | Britain (1958) | Sweden (1964) |
| - 99 | 15.8 | 28.9 |
| 100 - 499 | 20.1 | 20.3 |
| 500 - 999 | 9.2 | 8.6 |
| 1000 + | 54.9 | 42.2 |
| Total | 100.0 | 100.0 |

Source: Extracted from M. Utton, Industrial Concentration, Harmondsworth,
1970, Table 3; and Statens Offentliga Utredningar (S.O.U.), Agände och
Inflytande inom det Privata Näringslivet (Ownership and Influence in the
Private Economy), Stockholm, 1968, Table 2:4.

Despite the Swedish population being only one-seventh the size of that
in Britain, Table 1.5 shows that comparable proportions of their industrial work-forces in manufacturing industry are employed by enter-

prises with at least 1,000 employees. Among those working in Swedish industry, 42 per cent are employed in enterprises of at least this size compared with 55 per cent in Britain. At the same time, similar proportions work in enterprises with between 500 and 999 employees.

Clearly this discussion suggests, despite a number of differences in the development of industrialisation in Britain and Sweden,that there are many similarities in their contemporary industrial structures. They have comparable industrial profiles, common occupational structures and similar proportions of employees engaged in large industrial enterprises. Despite these factors, however, there are differences in their trajectories of industrialisation and population sizes which have produced an important contrast between the social structures of the two countries; in Sweden urbanisation has been more recent and on a smaller scale.

In 1880, somewhat less than 10 per cent of the Swedish population lived in what were 'administratively' defined as towns and it was not until the more rapid industrialisation of the 1870s that the urban population began to increase.[16] This was mainly a consequence of the highly diffuse nature of Swedish industrialisation, which led to the growth of a large number of relatively small-scale urban communities — that is, with between five and ten thousand inhabitants — rather than the concentration of populations in large urban areas. In fact, by 1930 only five Swedish towns had more than 50,000 inhabitants and even in 1963 there were only three with populations of more than 100,000, compared with the 62 in Britain in 1969.[17] In 1963 no more than 37 per cent of the Swedish population lived in towns of 100,000 or more compared with 78 per cent in Britain.[18] This, of course, has had implications for the ecological structure of towns in the two countries and for the development of urban life-styles. The smaller size of Swedish towns, for example, together with their more recent growth, has possibly restricted the development of working-class subcultures and life-styles of the kind which have been found to exist in many urban areas in Britain.[19] Hence, the more recent migration to Swedish towns may have limited the emergence of three-generational, 'extended' family systems within the context of traditional community structures. The Swedish urban dweller is generally either the son of a migrant, or a migrant himself; perhaps the only exceptions are the inhabitants of the older areas of Stockholm, Malmö and Gothenburg, and the former 'bruks' and saw-mill communities which have developed into larger urban areas. Consequently, the lack of 'traditional' and occupationally homogeneous urban communities could be conducive to important

differences between Sweden and Britain in terms of life-styles and
socio-political attitudes; even between workers of similar occupational
groups.[20]

Despite that possibility, however, this review of patterns of industrialisation in Britain and Sweden suggests that their social structures
are characterised more by similarities than differences; especially in
terms of those factors which determine class inequalities. A number of
writers, for example, while recognising the importance of property
inheritance in capitalist societies, have stressed the significance of occupational roles for the determination of life chances, life-styles and the
general allocation of economic rewards. Thus Parkin has argued that:

> As far as advanced Western capitalist societies are concerned, we
> can represent the backbone of the reward system as a hierarchy of
> broad occupational categories. This runs from high to low as
> follows:
>     Professional, managerial and administrative
>     Semi-professional and lower administrative
>     Routine white collar
>     Skilled manual
>     Semi-skilled manual
>     Unskilled manual.[21]

This suggests, then, that for an analysis of class inequalities in Britain
and Sweden it is necessary to give prime emphasis to their occupational
profiles, and in view of the similarities in these, to predict that the two
countries will have highly comparable reward structures. But why
should this be the case? Sociologists have advanced two major explan-
ations.

First, it has been claimed that industrial societies are confronted
with particular 'needs' and that managerial and professional occupations
are 'functionally more important' for the fulfilment of these than
others. As a result such occupations are more highly rewarded in order
to motivate those with 'talent' to fulfil the 'functionally important'
tasks.[22] But, of course, such an assertion is highly questionable if only
because there are no 'objective' criteria for determining 'functional
importance' and such a claim can only, at best, be interpreted as an
ideological justification for existing inequalities rather than an explanation of them.[23] Secondly, it has been suggested that the major reason
why managerial, administrative and professional workers are more
highly rewarded than others is because of the greater power which they

are able to exercise in society.[24] Within labour markets they can create
a demand for their skills by adopting strategies of professionalism, controlling patterns of occupational recruitment, and stipulating lengthy
periods of training for entrants.[25] Indeed, high earnings are often
justified by managerial and professional groups on the grounds that
they constitute a form of compensation for the financial and psychological 'costs' incurred during training. Furthermore, managerial and
professional workers occupy dominant positions within employing
organisations so that they are able to protect and perpetuate their
privileges in relation to other occupational groups; a process which is
reinforced outside the workplace by political parties which represent
their wider economic and social interests. In these ways, therefore, the
overall pattern of rewards will reflect the power exercised by different
occupational groups in society. If these processes operate to the same
degree in both Sweden and Britain so that the two countries can be
regarded as having similar power structures, it could be expected that
they will have highly comparable profiles of class inequality. But if this
is not the case, it is possible that the reward structures of the two
countries will differ. In order to investigate this it is necessary to
summarise, if only briefly, political developments.

### (ii) Political developments

Britain and Sweden are capitalist countries in the sense that they are
market economies in which the means of production are predominantly
privately owned. In both countries there are shareholders, rentiers,
property-owners and wage labour. Thus they possess characteristics
common to all capitalist societies. At the same time they are similar in
that they are 'welfare states'; both of their governments finance a wide
range of social services. Since it would require a detailed study to
describe the differences and the similarities in the provision of these
services in the two countries, only two general points will be made.[26]
First, trends in the growth of the proportion of gross national product
devoted to social security spending have been fairly similar in both
countries. These are shown in Table 1.6, which compares developments
in Britain and Sweden between 1949 and 1966.

Secondly, social security provisions in Sweden and Britain are
financed from central government funds to a far greater extent than in
other Western countries. A United Nations Report, published in 1967,
claimed that in 1960 the central government provided 59 per cent of
the finance required for social security provision in Britain and 67 per
cent in Sweden. The comparable figures were 21 per cent for Austria,

Table 1.6: Expenditure on social security as a percentage of gross national product in Britain and Sweden

| Date | Percentage of GNP | |
|------|---------|--------|
|      | Britain | Sweden |
| 1949 | 10.6 | 9.1 |
| 1952 | 11.4 | 9.7 |
| 1955 | 10.9 | 11.6 |
| 1958 | 12.1 | 12.8 |
| 1961 | 12.6 | 12.9 |
| 1964 | 13.2 | 15.6 |
| 1966 | 14.4 | 17.5 |

Source: Extracted from H.L. Wilensky, *The Welfare State and Equality*, London, 1975, Table 2.

20 per cent for France, 26 per cent for West Germany, 23 per cent for Italy, 13 per cent for the Netherlands, and 27 per cent for Switzerland. Among the countries compared, only Norway with a government contribution of 40 per cent came within reach of the proportions in Sweden and Britain.[27] Thus, in view of such figures, it is possible to argue that Sweden and Britain can be regarded as capitalist societies with highly developed *state* welfare systems. But in spite of this, important differences remain between them in terms of their political traditions. One of the more important of these is the relative strength of their respective working-class movements; particularly as regards the development of (1) trade unions and (2) the Labour and Social Democratic parties.

*(1) Trade Unions*

Because of its late industrialisation, the origins of trade unionism in Sweden are fairly recent. It was not until the 1880s that they were first established, although workers' associations existed before that time; it is often claimed that the oldest dates from 1846, when the Union of Typographers was formed in Stockholm. But this was not a trade union in the contemporary sense; it was a 'club' which provided educational facilities for its members.[28] Similarly, during the 1860s and 1870s there were many comparable organisations but few of these provided the bases for 'genuine' trade unions, established to pursue the economic objectives of their members.[29] Trade unions only began to flourish during the 1880s among printers, machinists and other skilled craftsmen in the larger urban areas.[30] By contrast, the smaller industrial towns with traditions derived from the 'bruks' were of little consequence for the development of trade unionism because their 'paternalistic' social structures reduced the degree to which workers could organise themselves for the purposes of bargaining, and also because the strains of industrialisation were less severely experienced by these workers than by those who had migrated to the growing industrial communities. Consequently, it was among the craftsmen of the larger urban areas that the bases of Swedish trade unionism were established. Often these workers had travelled abroad, especially to England and Germany, in order to obtain craft skills and this had brought them into contact with trade union organisations.[31] This, coupled with the deprivations which they experienced in Swedish industrial communities, together with the absence of 'welfare benefits' available to workers in 'bruks', led to the rapid acceptance of trade union ideas. Thus, during the 1880s a number of local trade unions developed, particularly in Stockholm and the growing industrial communities in southern Sweden. But it was not until the end of the decade that national federations emerged; the first was established in 1886 and in the 1890s this became the dominant form of union structure among both unskilled and skilled workers.[32] At this time, however, Swedish trade unions were numerically weak. Bäckström claims that at the beginning of the 1880s there were only 9,000 members and by the end of the century this had only increased to 66,000; a figure equivalent to about 25 per cent of all industrial workers.[33]

In 1898 Swedish trade unions formed their own central organisation — the Confederation of Trade Unions (Landsorganisation, LO); until then, the activities of the national unions had been co-ordinated by the Social Democratic Party.[34] But in its early years LO had only limited influence and its major function was to provide advisory services and information to the various affiliated unions.[35] It was not until the formation of the Confederation of Swedish Employers (Svenska Arbetsgivareföreningen, SAF) in 1902 that LO began to operate as an effective centralised negotiating body for the trade union movement. As a result, collective agreements were negotiated between SAF and LO. The first of these was in 1905 and possibly because of this, there was an increase in union membership. by 1909 the number had reached 231,000 — equivalent to approximately two-thirds of the industrial labour force.[36] But then SAF organised a lockout; LO lost more than one-half of its membership and it was not until 1917 that the 1909 figures were again achieved.[37] From 1911, however, trade union membership continued to grow so that, despite temporary setbacks, it had reached a figure of more than 1,600,000 by 1967.[38] The growth of LO membership during the twentieth century is shown in Table 1.7.

Table 1.7: The growth of membership among trade unions affiliated
to LO

| Date | Nos. of Unions Affiliated to LO | Nos. of Members |
|------|---------------------------------|-----------------|
| 1899 | 16 | 37,523 |
| 1907 | 28 | 186,226 |
| 1911 | 26 | 79,926 |
| 1920 | 31 | 280,029 |
| 1929 | 36 | 508,107 |
| 1939 | 45 | 961,216 |
| 1949 | 44 | 1,255,987 |
| 1959 | 44 | 1,467,117 |
| 1967 | 37 | 1,607,077 |

*Source:* T. Karlbom, *Arbetarnas Fackföreningar (Workers' Trade Unions),* Helsinki,
       1969, p. 72.

During the 1920s the labour movement had several policies for changing
the structure of society and for improving the economic, political and
social conditions of workers, but little was achieved because of its weak
bargaining position. The decade was characterised by high unemployment, political instability and a labour movement divided by a wide
range of ideological issues.[39] Nevertheless, membership of LO continued to grow and this, coupled with an increase in the number of
working days lost through strikes, led to pressure from Conservative
groups for the government to introduce laws to 'regularise' the labour
market. Consequently, in 1928 laws were passed which made
strikes illegal while collective agreements between LO and SAF
were in force. Although the trade union movement protested, these
laws continue to constitute one of the bases for industrial relations in
present-day Sweden.[40]

   In the 1930s the position of trade unions in Sweden was fundamentally altered by the general election of 1932; this produced the first
Social Democratic government to have an effective majority in Parliament. It meant that trade unions were now in partnership with the
government rather than in opposition to it and for the first time LO
was actively involved in the formulation of economic and social
policies. This, of course, strengthened the position of trade unions in
Sweden, but it also led to the development of internal strains within the
labour movement, since Social Democratic governments formulated
policies in collaboration with LO which were often contrary to the
economic interests of specific affiliated unions. The priority given to
economic growth by LO and Social Democratic governments, for

example, led to attempts to develop a 'rational' economy and this often produced unemployment among workers of specific unions within particular industries. Since the 1940s, furthermore, LO's policy of 'wage solidarity', backed by government support, has meant that unions in powerful bargaining situations have often been forced to moderate their wage claims.[41]

The 1932 general election was not the only factor which strengthened the influence of trade unions in Sweden; an important event was the 1938 'Saltjöbaden Agreement' which reinforced the 'centralised' features of Swedish industrial relations which had existed since 1905. As a result of this agreement, LO and SAF established a code of practice for regulating industrial relations at the plant, company and industrial levels.[42] One of the major consequences of the agreement was that it confirmed the superordinate authority of LO over the member unions. Thus, power within the labour movement became more concentrated in the full-time officials of LO with the result that member unions became highly constrained in terms of the policies which they could independently pursue. Whether or not this has been to the advantage of rank-and-file members is problematic but because LO has been the central negotiating body for manual unions, it has been able to pursue egalitarian policies in two directions. The first, in attempting to narrow wage differentials between various groups of manual workers by its policy of 'wage solidarity', and the second in trying to reduce differences in the earnings and employment conditions of manual workers and other occupational groups in society.[43] It is possible that with a less centralised structure, Swedish trade unions would have been less concerned about narrowing such differentials and that various manual unions would have been in greater competition with each other over wage increases. Furthermore the centralised system of collective bargaining in Sweden has enabled LO, together with the Social Democratic Party, to present itself as the institutional representative of the organised working class. With a more fragmented union structure it is doubtful whether it could perform this function as effectively. Consequently, it can be argued that the highly centralised Swedish working-class movement has, potentially, been in a better position to impose 'constraints' upon the prerogatives of capitalism than labour organisations in other countries where they have been more divided and fragmented. But the strength of LO is not determined solely by its centralised structure; it is also a product of the high allegiance which it commands from industrial manual workers. This is shown in Table 1.8 which gives the percentage of workers who, in 1968, were members of

LO-affiliated Unions.

Table 1.8: Percentage of LO membership among manual workers different sectors of the Swedish economy in 1968

| Sector | Nos of Employees (OOO's) | % of Employees who are Members of LO-Affiliated Unions |
| --- | --- | --- |
| Wood and Paper Products | 103 | 88.8 |
| Fabricated Metal Goods, Machinery and Equipment | 340 | 87.9 |
| Building and Construction | 233 | 87.3 |
| Textile and Leather | 77 | 83.5 |
| Engineering Goods | 94 | 76.1 |
| Food, Beverages, Tobacco | 96 | 71.0 |
| Public Utilities | 414 | 67.5 |
| Transport and Services | 69 | 61.3 |
| Retail Trades | 217 | 54.3 |
| Forestry and Farming | 110 | 38.1 |
| Other Sectors | 154 | 50.8 |
| Unemployed | 104 | 43.3 |
| Total | 2,012 | 69.7 |

Source: C.V. Otter, 'Arbetarnas Fackliga Organisationsgrad' ('The Strength of Trade Unions'), *Arkiv för Studier i Arbetarrörelsens Historia (Journal for the Study of the History of Labour Movements)*, No. 4 (1973).

From Table 1.8 it is evident that the level of LO penetration among manual workers is very high; approximately 70 per cent. Indeed, among men it is as high as 80 per cent, while for women it is 52 per cent.[44] Clearly, LO is a very influential movement within the social structure of contemporary Sweden if only because it is the largest organisation of any kind as measured in terms of its membership.[45] It is, furthermore, together with the Social Democratic Party, the major institutional reflection of working-class interests in Sweden and its essentially working-class character is reinforced by the fact that most categories of non-manual employees belong to separate unions which, in turn, are linked to central confederations.

After LO, the largest union confederation is the Central Organisation of Salaried Employees (Tjänstemännens Centralorganisation – TCO).[46] Its origins are more recent than those of LO since there was little union activity among white-collar workers before the 1930s. White-collar unions in private industry formed their own confederation in 1931 – the Central Organisation for Employees (De Anställdas Centralorganis- ation – DACO) and this was followed by the formation in 1937 of the

Central Organisation of Salaried Employees (Tjänstemännens Centralorganisation – TCO). These organisations then amalgamated in 1944 to
form the present-day TCO. Since then, the growth of TCO has been
rapid and the size of its membership has more than trebled: from
204,650 in 1945[47] to 719,493 in 1970.[48] This has been reflected in a
high level of union 'density' among white-collar workers; Elvander calculates that in 1967 about 90 per cent of all white-collar workers in the
public sector and approximately 70 per cent of those employed in the
private sector were members of unions affiliated to TCO.[49] Within the
private sector there is a wide variation between banking and insurance
where the proportion reaches 90 per cent, manufacturing industry with
a figure of about 75 per cent and the service trades with a level of about
50 per cent.[50] Unlike LO, however, TCO performs few 'political'
functions; it is not directly linked to any of the major political parties
in the manner in which LO is associated with the Social Democratic
Party. This is probably because TCO's membership is more heterogeneous, consisting of both male and female white-collar workers with
a wide range of skills and technical qualifications undertaking a large
number of different tasks in a variety of work situations; from large-
scale public and private bureaucracies located in large urban areas to
small private businesses in rural communities. But a further reason why
it tends to be apolitical is because of the voting behaviour of its members. Whereas in the 1973 general election 71 per cent of all LO members voted for the Social Democratic Party, the votes of the TCO membership were more widely distributed between the political parties; 35
per cent went to the Social Democratic Party, 12 per cent to the Folk
(Liberal) Party, 14 per cent to the Moderata Samlingspartiet (Conservative) Party and 33 per cent to the Centre Party.[51] In fact, the distribution of voting preferences among lower-grade white-collar workers is
a clear indication of the non-political role of TCO and the degree to
which it devotes little attention to explicit political socialisation.

   In addition to TCO, there are two other white-collar trade union
confederations in Sweden. The oldest is the National Federation of
Civil Servants (Statsjänstemännens Riksförbund – SR), founded in
1917 and which represents the interests of higher civil servants and
military officers. It is the smallest of the confederations with a membership of only 19,279 in 1970.[52] One of the reasons for this is that a
number of SR-affiliated unions joined SACO in the 1950s. The Swedish
Confederation of Professional Associations (Sveriges Akademikers
Centralorganisation – SACO) has, after TCO, the largest number of
white-collar employees affiliated to it. It consists of a number of unions

representing the interests of such groups as doctors, teachers, dentists, lawyers and engineers, and the only common element which unites them is that their members all have academic qualifications from universities and other higher educational establishments. SACO, in terms of its present organisational structure, was founded in 1947 with a membership of approximately 15,000.[53] But changes in the occupational structure, the creation of professional skills, the growth of higher education and the resignation of a number of white-collar unions from SR in the 1950s have increased SACO's affiliated membership by more than seven times so that it had reached 114,991 by the end of 1970.[54] Elvander has estimated that 70 per cent of all those with university degrees and equivalent qualifications were affiliated members of SACO in 1967.[55]

This, then, concludes a very brief outline of the development of trade unionism in Sweden. Clearly, the overall density of unionism in Sweden is very high. But two further comments need to be made. First, the structure of trade unionism is highly centralised; it is the confederations which are important for the purposes of national wage negotiations, consultations with governments and as general pressure groups in society. But secondly, and perhaps more importantly, there is a direct relationship between divisions within the occupational structure and the composition of the separate confederations. SAF represents the interests of employers, SR those of higher civil servants, SACO those of professional and higher administrative workers, TCO those of lower-grade and non-professional white-collar employees, and LO those of manual workers. Admittedly the 'fit' is not quite so clear-cut as this because of the small proportion of lower-grade white-collar workers affiliated to LO, and the rather ambiguous division between 'professional' and 'non-professional' workers which constitutes the basis for some conflict between TCO and SACO about the eligibility of some occupational groups for membership. But despite this, the occupational structure is linked to the various trade union confederations in the following manner:

Table 1.9: The relationship between Occupational Categories and Trade Union Confederations

| Occupational Category | | Trade Union Confederation |
|---|---|---|
| Professional, managerial and administrative workers | ) ) | SACO and SR |
| Semi-professional, lower administrative and routine white-collar workers | ) ) | TCO |
| Skilled, semi-skilled, and unskilled manual workers | ) ) | LO |

A consequence of these interrelationships is that it is conducive to generating an awareness of the social and economic rewards of different occupational groups. When there are national wage negotiations it is evident that SACO, SR, TCO and LO are pursuing the interests of clearly delineated socio-economic groups. Fulcher, in fact, has argued that the structure of trade unionism in Sweden is such that it constitutes an institutionalised form of class conflict.[56] If this is so, it can be suggested that it is conducive to resentment among manual and lower-grade white-collar workers, if only because they are aware of the higher rewards accruing to other occupational groups. Indeed, such attitudes are likely to be more pronounced among manual workers in Sweden than among those in other countries where patterns of trade unionism are less consistent with occupational divisions. In such countries it might be expected that there will be less awareness of *class* inequalities and limited resentment over economic rewards.

If the structure of Swedish trade unionism is conducive to the expression of class interests, then LO is in a better position to do this than any of the other confederations. The high level of LO density among industrial manual workers strengthens its bargaining position but also, unlike the other confederations, it acts as a political pressure group. Whereas they explicitly stress their political non-allegiance, LO, at all organisational levels, is closely connected to the Social Democratic Party.[57] Consequently, it performs a number of 'political' functions in addition to those of an 'industrial' or 'economic' kind; taken with the fact that the Social Democratic Party has been in office since 1932, it means that the institutional basis for the expression of working-class interests is extensive. It certainly seems to be better established than in Britain where the development of trade unionism has been less impressive, both in terms of its 'penetration' among industrial workers and the degree to which it is conducive to the articulation of class-based interests. To quote a PEP enquiry, 'By the standards of Sweden (and Austria) . . . British trade unions have a long way to go.'[58]

It is difficult to give an accurate account of the size and structure of British trade unionism before the 1890s; 1892 is the first year for which there are satisfactory statistics. Clegg, Fox and Thompson have estimated that in 1888 about 5 per cent of the 'occupied population' and 10 per cent of all male manual workers were trade union members.[59] They claim that only rough estimates can be given for union 'density' because of difficulties in determining the number of workers in various industrial groups. But they do suggest that engineering, shipbuilding, mining and quarrying probably had 'densities' of 20 per cent, building and printing of 15 per cent, textiles and woodwork of 10 per cent and the transport industries of about 5 per cent.[60] In other sectors of industry, the proportions of trade unionists were negligible. However, even within the same industry there was often a wide variation in the degree of unionism among craftsmen and skilled workers on the one hand, and semi-skilled operatives and labourers on the other. At the same time the level of unionisation fluctuated according to the state of the economy; it increased during periods of prosperity and declined in times of depression.[61]

The first reliable statistics on British trade unionism were published in the Board of Trade's 6th *Report on Trade Unions* in 1894; this claimed that in 1892 union membership was only 1,576,000.[62] However, by 1911 there were more than three million members, and by 1920 this had increased to more than eight million. The numbers then declined so that by 1933 there were less than a half million members. But during the later years of the 1930s there was a large increase so that in 1938 there were again more than six million members and by 1948 this figure had increased to over nine million. But then the rapid growth of trade unionism came to an end and in 1965 only a further 800,000 workers had been enrolled to make a total membership of rather more than ten million. However, there was a further big increase when membership expanded by another 800,000 by 1970.[63]

According to Bain, the long-term growth of British trade unionism has been quite impressive; the overall 'density' among all employees increased from a little more than 10 per cent in 1892 to about 47 per cent in 1970.[64] The principal features in this development are shown in Table 1.10.

As in Sweden, there are wide variations between different industrial sectors in terms of the proportions of workers unionised. The figures, taken from Bain, are shown in Table 1.11.

Table 1.11 shows that in 1964 the highest levels of unionism were in the 'traditional' industries of coal-mining and the railways, and in national and local government. In 'metals and engineering', on the other hand, which in 1964 was the largest industry in the economy with 4,537,000 employees, the proportion of trade union members was only 54 per cent. Furthermore, the second largest industrial sector, 'distribution', had a percentage membership of not more than 15 per cent. Although the distributive trades may have a number of organisational features which create difficulties for union recruitment, the level of union 'density' among workers in this sector is still remarkably low by Swedish standards. Perhaps the most difficult category of employees to

Table 1.10: Total union membership in the United Kingdom 1892-1970

| Year | Labour Force (000's) | Total Union Membership (000's) | Density of Union Membership % |
|------|------|------|------|
| 1892 | 14,126 | 1,576 | 11.2 |
| 1901 | 16,101 | 2,025 | 12.6 |
| 1911 | 17,762 | 3,139 | 17.7 |
| 1920 | 18,469 | 8,348 | 45.2 |
| 1923 | 17,965 | 5,429 | 30.2 |
| 1933 | 19,422 | 4,392 | 22.6 |
| 1938 | 19,829 | 6,053 | 30.5 |
| 1945 | 20,400 | 7,875 | 38.6 |
| 1948 | 20,732 | 9,362 | 45.2 |
| 1950 | 21,055 | 9,289 | 44.1 |
| 1955 | 21,913 | 9,741 | 44.5 |
| 1960 | 22,817 | 9,835 | 43.1 |
| 1965 | 23,920 | 10,181 | 42.6 |
| 1970 | 23,446 | 11,000 | 46.9 |

*Source:* Extracted from G. Bain and R. Price, 'Union Growth and Employment Trends in the United Kingdom, 1964-1970', *British Journal of Industrial Relations,* Vol. 10 (1972), Table 8.

Table 1.11: The density of union membership by industry in the United Kingdom, 1964

| Industry | Employees (000's) | Density per cent |
|------|------|------|
| Education | 1,094 | 50 |
| Professional and business services | 1,268 | 24 |
| Insurance, banking and finance | 637 | 31 |
| Distribution | 3,026 | 15 |
| Paper, printing and publishing | 632 | 57 |
| Gas, electricity and water | 413 | 51 |
| Building | 1,708 | 37 |
| Metals and engineering | 4,537 | 54 |
| Chemicals and allied | 515 | 20 |
| Food, drink and tobacco | 842 | 11 |
| Transport and communications | 1,320 | 75 |
| Local government | 776 | 84 |
| Theatres, cinemas, sport, etc. | 251 | 39 |
| Furniture, timber, etc. | 296 | 37 |
| Footwear | 116 | 63 |
| Clothing | 452 | 30 |
| Textiles other than cotton | 613 | 21 |
| Cotton | 228 | 75 |
| National government | 550 | 83 |
| Coal-mining | 596 | 89 |
| Railways | 396 | 84 |
| Agriculture, forestry and fishing | 551 | 27 |

*Source:* Extracted from G. Bain, *The Growth of White-Collar Unionism,* London, 1972, Table 3.2.

unionise in Sweden is forestry and farm workers and yet despite their
relative geographical and social isolation, no less than 38 per cent were
union members in 1968.[65] Indeed, the lower level of unionism in
Britain applies to both manual and non-manual employees. Bain and
Price have calculated that in 1970 only 43 per cent of male white-collar
workers were unionised, compared with an overall figure of 61 per cent
for male manual workers.[66] As with total union membership, the proportion of white-collar unionists varies between industrial sectors; Bain
suggests that in 1960 the density of white-collar unionism was 84 per
cent in local government, 83 per cent in national government, 50 per
cent in the educational system, 31 per cent in insurance, banking and
finance, and only 12 per cent in manufacturing industry.[67] These
figures are much lower than those for white-collar works in comparable sectors of the Swedish economy. In 1967, according to Elvander,
approximately 90 per cent of all white-collar workers in the public
sector and in banking and insurance were unionised, compared with 75
per cent of those in manufacturing industry and 50 per cent of those in
service trades.[68]

However, the higher density of trade unionism among Swedish
manual and white-collar workers is not the only difference between the
two countries; there are also important contrasts in their patterns of
unionism. In the first place, British trade unionism is not characterised
by the same degree of centralisation as the Swedish movement. Although
the Trade Union Congress (TUC) often functions as a centralised
negotiating body for affiliated unions, it does not do so to the same
extent as LO and other union confederations in Sweden. The TUC may
negotiate with governments and the Confederation of British Industry
about levels of economic growth, income policies and wage increases,
but any agreements do not have the same binding consequences for the
behaviour of affiliated unions in the same manner as in Sweden; they
are, at best, only recommendations. Consequently, LO and the other
trade union confederations are vested with greater power in their bargaining encounters with governments and other pressure groups than
the TUC in Britain. In this sense, then, the more centralised structure
of Swedish trade unionism enables LO to appear as the major representative of working-class union interests.

Secondly, there is less of a consistency between the occupational
structure and the organisation of trade unionism in Britain. Generally
speaking, unions often have a varied membership which transcends
occupational and industrial divisions. At the same time, although there
are a number of unions which are purely 'white-collar' or 'manual' in

their social composition, there are also many which consist of a mixed membership of both types of workers. Consequently, manual/non-manual differences are less relevant in industrial relations and wage negotiations than in Sweden.[69] Furthermore, the 'mixed' occupational composition of British trade unions means that the TUC represents a membership of both manual and white-collar workers. Bain has calculated that approximately 20 per cent of the total TUC membership was made up of white-collar workers in 1964;[70] by contrast, less than 10 per cent of LO membership consisted of white-collar employees in 1967.[71] Consequently, the TUC is not a manual workers' confederation in the same manner as the Swedish LO with the result that it is less able to pursue policies intended to further the interests of manual workers *as a class* in society. Indeed, it can be argued that the fragmented structure of British trade unionism, which often transcends manual and non-manual divisions, generates less awareness of the economic rewards and privileges of different occupational groups; particularly as they exist between professional, white-collar and manual workers. Such differentials are not reflected in institutional structures comparable to the Swedish trade union confederations. There is, in fact, no genuine British equivalent to LO, which operates both as a political pressure group and as a trade union organisation, representing almost exclusively the interests of manual workers. The TUC lacks many of the manifest political functions of LO and it does not solely represent the interests of manual workers.[72] The absence of centralised trade union confederations in Britain, therefore, closely related to major divisions within the occupational structure, reduces the degree to which the political and economic interests of manual workers can be pursued; at least, to the extent they are in Sweden.

Furthermore, it can be argued that the structure of British trade unionism severely limits the degree to which it can adhere to long-term policies of the kind which have been pursued by LO since the early 1940s. First, it is extremely difficult for the TUC to implement a policy of 'wage solidarity', in the sense of attempting to narrow differentials in the economic rewards of various groups of manual workers. One of the major features of wage bargaining in Britain has been the efforts of specific unions to preserve, if not increase, differentials as they exist between themselves and others; different craft and trade unions have tended to compete with each other, thus emphasising the sectionalism and the divisions that exist within the British working-class movement. Although the TUC has often stressed the need to improve the relative economic position of lower-paid workers, it lacks the institutional means whereby it can exercise any influence upon the actions of affiliated unions.[73] In Sweden, by contrast, the more centralised structure of LO means that, potentially, it is in a far better position to enforce policies; central negotiations are conducted between LO and SAF which provide the frameworks for agreements between specific companies and unions. At these later discussions, representatives of LO and SAF act as arbitrators. If the equalisation of wages among different groups of manual workers is considered to be a desirable objective, then the structure of Swedish unionism is more conducive to its success. Secondly, because of its heterogeneous composition of manual and white-collar workers, the TUC is limited in the degree to which it can pursue egalitarian policies in relation to the social and economic rewards of manual and non-manual occupations; it is prevented from doing so for fear of 'alienating' its white-collar membership. In contrast, by operating as the institutional representatives of professional, white-collar and manual workers, the Swedish trade union confederations advertise the major social and economic divisions in society. LO is, therefore, in a better position to bargain for the narrowing of differentials between manual workers and other occupational groups than the TUC.[74] Policies formulated to reduce the economic deprivations of manual workers cannot be pursued by the TUC in the same explicit manner as in Sweden.[75]

These, then, are some of the major differences between the structure of British and Swedish trade unionism, having important consequences for the kinds of policies which can be pursued. At the same time, however, it appears that the legitimacy of the trade union movement is better established in Sweden than in Britain. This, of course, has had implications for the degree to which it has been able to command the support of rank-and-file members, to influence their attitudes, and to bargain with other groups in society. Thus, in a study of attitudes among Swedish manual and white-collar workers Dahlström asked, 'What factors, do you think, explain the increase in living standards over the last fifty years?' He found that only a small proportion — generally fewer than 10 per cent — of any occupational group claimed that any improvements had been the result of efforts by private enterprise. On the other hand, no less than one-half of all the manual respondents in his sample attributed improvements to the activities of labour unions.[76] Similarly, in a study of two industrial communities in Sweden, Segerstedt and Lundquist asked a number of open-ended questions among which were, 'In what ways do you think that the working conditions of workers have improved over the past 40 to 50

years?' and 'What is it that has brought about these improvements?'
Among all the respondents, 44 per cent said it was the activities of
labour unions, 23 per cent mentioned labour political movements, and
only 8 per cent claimed it was because of general technological progress.[77] The investigators found that there was no significant variation
in these responses among members of different occupational groups.
Dahlström also asked, 'Do you think that trade unions have too much
or too little power in this country?' He found that less than 5 per cent
of the manual workers in his sample stated that unions were too powerful.[78]

By contrast, the legitimacy of the British union movement appears
to be less established. Goldthorpe and Lockwood, for example, in their
study of workers in Luton asked, 'Some people say that trade unions
have too much power in the country: would you agree or disagree, on
the whole?' They found that as many as 41 per cent of their sample of
manual workers agreed with the statement.[79] McKenzie and Silver also
found in their investigation of political attitudes in Britain that a substantial proportion of manual workers felt that trade unions exercised
too much influence. They discovered that 55 per cent of Labour voters
agreed with the general statement that 'trade unions have too much
power in the country.'[80] In yet another enquiry into political opinions
in Britain, Butler and Stokes concluded:

> . . . the fact that attitudes towards the unions were, on balance,
> unfavourable in the period of our studies is none the less plain. When
> we asked our respondents whether their sympathies were generally
> for or against strikers, 61 per cent of respondents from non-union
> families, and even 45 per cent from union families, said 'against'.
> Nearly three-quarters of our respondents who were not union mem-
> bers said that unions have too much power; and very nearly half of
> the respondents from union households expressed the same view.[81]

In view of such findings, it is not surprising that the degree of trade
union 'density' is much lower in Britain than in Sweden. Obviously,
there are a number of factors which determine the development of
trade unionism — the attitudes of employers, the recruitment policies
of unions, and so on — but the legitimacy which they are able to
command is also important. Thus, it does appear that the Swedish
trade union movement has not only developed a more coherent class-
based structure but also that it exercises a greater degree of normative
influence than its British counterpart. As will be discussed later, this has

had a number of consequences for the formation of socio-political
attitudes among industrial manual workers. It is now necessary to compare the 'political wings' of the two labour movements, as reflected in
the development of the Labour and Social Democratic parties.

## (2) *The Development of the Labour and Social Democratic parties*

The Social Democratic Workers Party (Socialdemoratiska Arbetart-
partiet, SAP) was founded in 1889. Before the foundation of LO in
1898, it was the central organisation of the working class.[82] With the
formation of LO, strong links were established so that LO and the
Social Democratic Party became closely interrelated wings of the same
movement. As Branting, the first leader of the Social Democratic
Party, stated in 1898,

> the Labour movement is a single entity, working in a trade-union
> direction and in a political direction, neither stifling the other, but
> supporting each other and working hand in hand for social emanci-
> pation.[83]

Indeed, until the present the Social Democratic Party and LO have continued to be ideologically and organisationally connected.

The origins of the Social Democratic Party were among skilled
workers who had been introduced to socialist ideas in different
European countries: for example, in Germany, Denmark and, to a lesser
extent, Britain.[84] The ideological basis of the party was Marxist and
within the context of Swedish politics in the latter part of the nineteenth century, it emphasised the need for universal suffrage. During
the 1890s only one-quarter of men over the age of 21 were entitled to
vote. This meant that the two-chamber Parliament was dominated by
the land-owning class in the Upper House and by farmers and urban
traders in the Lower House; in the latter, farmers generally held a
majority. In 1890 a Universal Franchise Union was formed in order to
press for electoral reform. This consisted mainly of 'radical' intellectuals
and the more liberal representatives of the urban lower middle classes;
in 1902 they organised themselves into a national political group, the
Folk Party.[85] The Social Democratic Party, although committed to
universal suffrage, had no representatives in Parliament until 1897
when Branting was elected. Consequently, the Folk and the Social
Democratic parties co-operated against the vested interests of the
upper classes. In order to protect these interests, the Conservatives
organised themselves into a national party — the Högern Party — in

1904.

Universal suffrage was gradually introduced in 1907 but by then membership of the Social Democratic Party had grown rapidly. Tomasson has suggested that between 1895 and 1907 it had increased from 10,000 to 133,000.[86] In the elections which were held in 1911 — the first after the franchise reforms — the Social Democrats won 64 of the 230 seats in the Lower Chamber, with the Folk Party gaining 101 and the Högern Party, 65.[87] The franchise reforms, therefore, had increased Social Democratic representation in the Lower Chamber but the Upper Chamber continued to be dominated by wealthy businessmen and land-owners. This was because representatives to this chamber were elected by municipal and county councils. The electoral reforms had not been applied to municipal and county elections so that in the 150-seat Upper Chamber there were only 12 Social Democrats but as many as 87 representatives of the Högern Party.[88] However, after the 1917 elections a coalition government consisting of the Folk and Social Democratic parties was formed which introduced further electoral changes so that the domination of the Högern Party in the Upper Chamber was broken.

The coalition government, formed as a result of the 1917 elections, was the first to include representatives of the Social Democratic Party. But in 1920 the coalition collapsed and the Social Democrats continued in office as a minority government. This only lasted for six months but for this period it could regard itself as the first elected socialist government in the world. A major reason for the breakdown in co-operation between the Social Democratic and Folk parties was that their joint programme for constitutional reform had been completed by 1920 and there was little else to keep them together. They had very different socio-economic policies; whereas the Social Democrats were in favour of nationalisation and increased state intervention in the economy, the Folk Party only wanted to reform the existing system. Public ownership of the means of production became the major source of cleavage between the political parties with the Folk, Högern and the newly established Bonderförbundet (agrarian) parties opposed to further state intervention, and the Social Democratic and Communist parties in favour.[89]

The period 1920-1932 has often been called the era of 'minority parliamentarism'.[90] During the 1920s the electoral support of the Folk Party declined, the Bondeförbundet became an influential national political organisation and since 1917 the left wing of the Social Democratic Party had formed its own separate organisation, the Communist

Party. None of the political parties was able to establish majority governments and it was almost impossible to form coalitions; the Social Democrats failed to reach agreement with any of the 'non-socialist' parties and these, in turn, were unable to collaborate with each other. Consequently, there were frequent changes of administration but with the election of a Social Democratic government in 1932 political instability in Sweden came to an end. Since then, except for a brief period of three months in 1936, Sweden has been governed by either a majority Social Democratic government or by a coalition, with the Social Democratic Party as the dominant partner. The history of Swedish governments since 1905 is shown in Table 1.12:

Table 1.12: The composition of Swedish governments 1905-1975

| Dates | | | | Government |
|---|---|---|---|---|
| July | 1905 - | October | 1905 | National Coalition (no Social Democrats) |
| October | 1905 - | May | 1906 | Folk |
| May | 1906 - | October | 1911 | Högern* |
| October | 1911 - | February | 1914 | Folk |
| February | 1914 - | March | 1917 | Högern |
| March | 1917 - | October | 1917 | Högern (caretaker government) |
| October | 1917 - | March | 1920 | Folk/Social Democratic |
| March | 1920 - | Autumn | 1920 | Social Democratic |
| Autumn | 1920 - | Autumn | 1921 | Non-party government |
| Autumn | 1921 - | April | 1923 | Social Democratic |
| April | 1923 - | October | 1924 | Högern |
| October | 1924 - | June | 1926 | Social Democratic |
| June | 1926 - | October | 1928 | Folk |
| October | 1928 - | June | 1930 | Högern |
| June | 1930 - | September | 1932 | Folk |
| September | 1932 - | June | 1936 | Social Democratic |
| June | 1936 - | September | 1936 | Bondeförbundet* |
| September | 1936 - | December | 1939 | Social Democratic/Bondeförbundet |
| December | 1939 - | July | 1945 | Social Democratic/Folk/Högern/Bondeförbundet |
| July | 1945 - | October | 1951 | Social Democratic |
| October | 1951 - | October | 1957 | Social Democratic/Bondeförbundet |
| October | 1957 - | October | 1975 | Social Democratic |

*The 'Högern' Party is now known as the 'Moderata Samlingspartiet' (The Conservative Party) and the 'Bondeförbundet' as the 'Centerpartiet' (Centre Party).
Source: K. Samuelsson, From Great Power to Welfare State, London, 1968, Appendix 3.

It is clear from Table 1.12 that 1932 is an important watershed in Swedish politics; indeed, the dominance of the Social Democratic Party since then has led Tomasson to remark that 'probably no democratic party anywhere has been able to maintain for such a long period the overall legislative and popular support enjoyed by the Swedish Social Democrats . . . '[91] Thus, he claims that the Swedish Social Democrats are the pre-eminent example of Maurice Duverger's 'dominant party'. Similarly, in a speculative account of contemporary Sweden, Huntford has argued that the success of the Social Democratic Party has led to a 'new totalitarianism', characteristic of Aldous Huxley's *Brave New World*.[92] Clearly, the political ascendancy of the Swedish Social Democrats has been impressive, certainly by comparison with similar parties in other countries.[93]

Although the Social Democratic Party was in government for brief periods during the 1920s, they achieved little; there was no nationalisation of the economy and few other socialist measures were introduced. When they came to power in the 1930s, they pursued policies which established the basis for the welfare state and the 'mixed economy'. There were no attempts to transfer the means of production to state ownership since it was argued that socialist ideals could be attained by 'gradual' and 'indirect' means.[94] This, in fact, has been the major characteristic of successive Social Democratic policies; they have tended to concentrate upon measures intended to regulate the distribution of income and personal wealth *after* it has been created. But these policies have not, as yet, altered the essential generic features of any capitalist society; the means of production remain privately owned. This is justified by some sectors of the Social Democratic Party on the grounds that successive governments have been able to develop sufficient controls over economic production. There is no injustice in the private ownership of wealth, therefore, since economic rewards can be redistributed by government action. Consequently, it is claimed that it is unnecessary to *own* in order to *control* the means of production and that socialist ideals, particularly those relating to economic and social equality, can be as easily achieved in a society where property is privately owned as in one in which all the resources are owned by the state.[95] Although this view has been challenged by the Swedish 'New Left' in recent years, there is little doubt that the policies of the Social Democratic Party have enabled it to retain a high degree of electoral support among the more disadvantaged groups in society, particularly industrial manual workers. This is illustrated in Table 1.13, which shows the electoral support for the Social Democratic Party among voters of different occupational groups in general elections between 1956 and 1973.

Table 1.13: Electoral support for the Social Democratic Party among voters of different occupational groups, 1956-1973 (percentages)

| Occupational Group | Percentage supporting the Social Democratic Party in General Elections held in: | | | | | |
|---|---|---|---|---|---|---|
| | 1956 | 1960 | 1964 | 1968 | 1970 | 1973 |
| Employers, Company Directors, Managers and Professional Workers | 4 | 10 | 8 | 14 | 15 | 16 |
| Small Business Owners | 21 | 19 | 26 | 32 | 28 | 21 |
| Lower-grade White-Collar Workers | 37 | 42 | 46 | 47 | 41 | 37 |
| Shop Assistants and Service Workers | 72 | 68 | 64 | 67 | 60 | 61 |
| Industrial Manual Workers | 77 | 83 | 78 | 79 | 71 | 69 |
| Farmers | 14 | 7 | 7 | 6 | 5 | 9 |
| Agricultural Workers | 58 | 57 | 53 | 57 | 51 | 64 |

Source: O. Petersson and B. Särlvik, 'The 1973 Election', General Elections 1973, Vol. 3, Central Bureau of Statistics, Stockholm, 1975, pp. 88-9.

Table 1.13 suggests that since 1956 the Social Democratic Party has never failed to obtain at least 69 per cent of the votes of industrial manual workers. Indeed, in elections during the 1960s the level of support among this occupational group was around 80 per cent. At the same time, it has been able to command the voting allegiance of two-thirds of all shop assistants, service workers and agricultural employees, and about 40 per cent of the electoral support of lower-grade white-collar workers. It is, then, the dominant party in Swedish politics; it always gets a greater degree of electoral support than any of the other parties and, as a result, in 1975 it had been in government for 43 years. It is the party which is overwhelmingly supported by agricultural, industrial and service workers and, to a lesser extent, by lower-grade white-collar workers. In essence, it is a working-class party.[96]

Thus, in view of its long period in government, it can be argued that the interests of industrial workers in Sweden have been better represented in the formal political structure than in other capitalist countries where similar parties have commanded less electoral support. Without doubt, the Social Democratic Party has been more successful in obtaining the allegiance of manual workers than its British counterpart, the Labour Party.

In Britain, electoral reforms were carried out much earlier than in Sweden. There were a number of legislative changes, including the extension of the franchise in 1832, the Second Reform Bill of 1867 and the redistribution of parliamentary seats in 1885. But, as Moorhouse has argued, these reforms did not immediately increase the participation of the urban working class in politics.[97] Consequently, there was no rapid growth in the membership of the Labour Party. In 1890 the Labour Representation Committee was formed, providing the basis for the development of the Labour Party.[98] But in the 1900 elections only 2 of its 15 candidates were elected and it received less than 2 per cent of the total votes.[99] In the 1922 general election – the first in which the urban working class was fully enfranchised – the Labour Party gained 30 per cent of the total votes.[100] Although it then supplanted the Liberals as the major alternative to the Conservative Party, it never seriously challenged the Conservatives' political ascendancy until 1945. Until then it had only been in a position to form minority governments on two occasions – in 1924 and in 1929-31. After the Second World War, however, the electoral performance of the Labour Party improved. In the 1945 election it gained a large majority over the other parties but this was dramatically reduced in the following election of 1950. It then lost all subsequent elections until 1964, when it came into office for a period of six-and-a-half years. But in 1970 the Conservative Party regained power and held government for almost four years.

The Labour Party, then, has been far less successful than the Swedish Social Democrats. Unlike the Social Democratic Party, it has held office for only two substantial periods of time – 1945 to 1951 and 1964 to 1970 – and until 1975 it had been in office for a total period of only 14 years; an unimpressive record by comparison with the 43 years of Social Democratic ascendancy in Sweden. Indeed, as McKenzie and Silver have stated, 'since 1885, the [British] Conservatives have had a record of electoral success almost unrivalled among political parties in parliamentary systems.'[101] The inability of the Labour Party to form majority governments is shown in Table 1.14, which describes the outcome of general elections held in Britain since 1922.

One of the major reasons for the lack of electoral success by the Labour Party is that, by comparison with the Swedish Social Democrats, it has been unable to command a high degree of voting allegiance among industrial manual workers. Whereas an average of more than 75 per cent of all Swedish industrial manual worker voters supported the Social Democratic Party between 1956 and 1973, the proportion of

Table 1.14: Governments in Britain as a result of general elections held since 1922

| Year of Election | Government Elected |
|---|---|
| 1922 | Conservative |
| 1923 | Labour |
| 1924 | Conservative |
| 1929 | Labour |
| 1931 | National Coalition |
| 1935 | National Coalition |
| 1945 | Labour |
| 1950 | Labour |
| 1951 | Conservative |
| 1955 | Conservative |
| 1959 | Conservative |
| 1964 | Labour |
| 1966 | Labour |
| 1970 | Conservative |
| 1974 (Feb.) | Labour |
| 1974 (Oct.) | Labour |

Source: Extracted from D. Butler, *British Political Facts, 1900-1967* (2nd ed.), London, 1968.

such workers committed to the Labour Party is a good deal smaller. Leonard, for example, has pointed out that at most general elections since the war the Conservative Party has enjoyed the support of a substantial minority of working-class voters, seldom falling much below one-third.[102] The more limited appeal of the Labour Party among working-class voters in Britain, compared with the Social Democrats in Sweden, is confirmed by Table 1.15, which analyses National Opinion Poll figures of voting behaviour in elections held between 1964 and 1974; a period during which the Labour Party became electorally more successful.

A further reason for the Labour Party's lack of electoral success, compared, that is, to the Social Democratic Party, is that it has been unable to obtain a substantial degree of support from non-manual workers. Whereas generally more than 40 per cent of all lower-grade white-collar workers in Sweden vote for the Social Democratic Party, the proportion stating its allegiance to the Labour Party is lower. As Table 1.15 shows, only an average of 26 per cent of such workers supported the Labour Party in general elections held between 1964 and 1974. Although these figures are not directly comparable with the Swedish data in Table 1.13, they do suggest that the British Labour Party has a narrower electoral base than the Swedish Social Democrats.

Table 1.15: Electoral support for the Labour Party among voters of
different occupational groups, 1964-1974 (percentages)

| Occupational Group | NOP Classification | Percentage supporting the Labour Party in General Elections held in: | | | |
|---|---|---|---|---|---|
| | | 1964 | 1966 | 1970 | 1974 |
| Managerial, Admin-istrative and Professional Workers | AB | 9 | 15 | 10 | 10 |
| Lower-grade White-Collar Workers | C1 | 25 | 30 | 30 | 21 |
| Skilled Manual Workers | C2 | 54 | 58 | 55 | 47 |
| Semi-skilled and Unskilled Workers and Pensioners | DE | 59 | 65 | 57 | 54 |

*Sources:* Extracted from P. Pulzer, *Political Representation and Elections in Britain,* London, 1972, Figure IV.6; and D. Butler and D. Kavanagh, *The British Election of February 1974,* London, 1974, p. 263.

All this suggests, then, that the British Labour Party has been unable to command the level of electoral support among manual and lower-grade non-manual workers of the kind enjoyed by the Swedish Social Democrats. In fact, comparison can be made between the Social Democratic Party and the British Conservative Party: both have been able to obtain a high level of support among their 'natural' supporters — the working and middle classes respectively — while at the same time acquiring the votes of substantial proportions of other social classes in society. The British Labour Party, by contrast, has been unable to do this with a similar degree of success.

Consequently, it can be argued that there are important differences between Britain and Sweden in terms of their political histories during the twentieth century, and particularly since the early 1930s. Although the Labour Party and the trade union movement have obtained wide-spread support in Britain, they cannot be seen as having achieved the same level of commitment as the equivalent Swedish institutions. Indeed, of all capitalist countries, Sweden can be regarded as having one of the most well-developed working-class movements; measured, that is, in terms of the level of trade union membership among manual workers and the degree of support which the working class gives to the Social Democratic Party. This has been reinforced by the structure of Swedish trade unionism, which has enabled LO to operate as the institutional representative of manual workers' interests and by the election to office of Social Democratic governments over the past 43 years. But in addition to these factors, the normative impact of the Swedish working-class movement has been reaffirmed by the educative functions of LO.

The Workers' Educational Association (Arbetarnas Bildingsförbund, ABF) is an integral part of LO, dominating the provision of adult education in Sweden; in 1971/72, for example, there were 203,523 study groups and almost one-third of these — 68,742 — were organised by ABF. In that year there were no fewer than 650,000 students registered on ABF courses in a country with a total population of little more than eight million people.[103] Despite the fact that a number of these courses provided for interests in languages and the arts, almost one-third focused upon the social sciences; an appropriate basis for the discussion of labour movements. Although ABF is not explicitly committed to political socialisation, it tends to emphasise the achievements of Swedish labour organisations. Consequently, many of its activities contribute to heightening the generalised legitimacy of the working-class movement. In Britain, by contrast, the trade union movement devotes few of its resources to the education of its members and it does not contribute to the provision of adult education in the same manner as the ABF in Sweden.[104] As a result, an important mechanism whereby the achievements of trade unions and the wider working-class movement could be legitimated is absent. Indeed, the overall conclusion of this section must be that the working-class movement in Sweden, both in terms of its political and industrial branches, enjoys a greater degree of legitimacy and support than the equivalent institutions in Britain.[105]

Clearly, this discussion suggests that any comparison of class inequality in Britain and Sweden must take into account two important factors. First, both countries possess sufficient common features to be regarded as similar types of industrial society. Secondly, despite the fact that both are capitalist countries, they differ to the extent of the influence of their respective working-class movements. Consequently, it is pertinent to ask whether the institutions of industrial capitalism have generated similar profiles of class inequality in the two countries, or whether the Swedish working-class movement has created a more egalitarian society. This is the subject of the next chapter.

## Notes

1.   For discussions of the impact of industrialisation on class inequalities see, for example, M. Levy Jr., *Modernisation and the Structure of Societies,*

# The Social Structures of Britain and Sweden

49

Princeton, 1966; C. Kerr, J. Dunlop, F. Harbison and C. Myers, *Industrialism and Industrial Man*, Cambridge (Mass.), 1960; and W. Moore, *The Impact of Industry*, New Jersey, 1965. The consequences of political change are most explicitly discussed by J. Goldthorpe, 'Social Stratification in Industrial Society', *Sociological Review Monograph*, No. 8 (1964), and F. Parkin, *Class Inequality and Political Order*, London, 1971.

2. E. Heckscher, *An Economic History of Sweden*, Cambridge (Mass.), 1954, Table II.
3. The development of trade in Sweden during the seventeenth and eighteenth centuries is discussed by K. Samuelsson, *From Great Power to Welfare State*, London, 1968, Chs. 1 and 2.
4. P. Mathias, 'The Social Structure in the Eighteenth Century: A Calculation by Joseph Massie', *Economic History Review* (2nd Series), Vol. 10 (1957-8).
5. K. Samuelsson, op. cit., Ch. 1.
6. For a discussion of whether or not industrialisation raised the standard of living for the English working class see E. Hobsbawm, 'The British Standard of Living 1790-1850', *Economic History Review* (2nd Series), Vol. 10 (1957-8).
7. This table refers to the total Swedish population. Retired persons are categorised according to their former industry, domestic servants according to the industry of their employers, and other dependants according to the industry of their head of household.
8. Expressed as a percentage of the total gainfully occupied population.
9. K. Samuelsson, op. cit., Ch. 1.
10. B. Carlson, *Trade Unions in Sweden*, Stockholm, 1969.
11. For a concise account of early industrialisation in Sweden, see E. Heckscher, op. cit. Ch. 6.
12. Central Bureau of Statistics, *Historical Statistics of Sweden, Vol. 1*, Stockholm, 1955, Table A.12.
13. W. Rostow, *The Stages of Economic Growth*, Cambridge, 1961. However, it is important to emphasise that any effective outcome from 'take-off' was long delayed in Sweden. During the latter decades of the nineteenth century there was extreme pauperisation which contributed to heavy emigration.
14. W. Rostow, op. cit., Table 2.
15. Central Bureau of Statistics, *Statistical Abstract of Sweden*, Stockholm, 1971, Table 106; and Central Statistical Office, *Social Trends*, London, 1970, Vol. 1, Table 26.
16. Central Bureau of Statistics, *Historical Statistics for Sweden*, Vol. 1, Stockholm, 1955, Table A3.
17. C.-G Janson, 'Urbanisering och Flyttning' ('Urbanisation and Migration') in E. Dahlström (ed.), *Svensk Samhällsstruktur i Sociologisk Belysning (Sociological Perspectives on the Swedish Social Structure)*, Stockholm, 1969, Table 7.4; and Central Statistical Office, *Social Trends*, London, 1970, Table 20.
18. C.-G. Janson, op. cit., Table 7.4; and K. Davis, 'The Urbanisation of the Human Population' in *Scientific American*, Vol. 213 (1965), p. 44.
19. For a review of some of the studies which have been conducted in Britain, see J. Klein, *Samples From English Cultures*, Vol. I, London, 1965.
20. To give but one example, the life-styles of Swedish workers could be more 'privatised' and family-centred than those of their English counterparts living in 'traditional' urban working-class communities. Unfortunately, there have been few studies of working-class life-styles in urban commun-

50 The Social Structures of Britain and Sweden

ities in Sweden. For an interesting, if rare, attempt, see T. Segerstedt and A. Lundquist, *Människan i Industrisamhället (Man in Industrialised Society)*, Stockholm, 1955.

21. F. Parkin, op. cit., p. 19.
22. See, for example, the ideas expressed by K. Davis and W. Moore, 'Some Principles of Social Stratification', *American Sociological Review*, Vol. 10 (1945).
23. M. Tumin, 'Some Principles of Stratification: A Critical Analysis', *American Sociological Review*, Vol. 18 (1953).
24. See, for example, G. Lenski, *Power and Privilege*, New York, 1966; and F. Parkin, op. cit.
25. These points are discussed by N. and J. Parry, 'Collective Social Mobility and Social Closure', in R. Scase (ed.), *Industrial Society: Class, Cleavage and Control*, London, 1977.
26. A comparison of various welfare services in Britain and Sweden has been undertaken by H. Heclo, *Modern Social Politics in Britain and Sweden*, New Haven, 1974.
27. United Nations, *Incomes in Post-War Europe*, Geneva, 1967, Ch. 6.
28. T. Karlbom, *Arbetarnas Fackföreningar (Workers' Trade Unions)*, Helsinki, 1969, p. 12.
29. For discussions of the development of trade unionism in Sweden, see K. Bäckström, *Arbetarrörelsen i Sverige, Vols. I and II, (The Labour Movement in Sweden)*, Stockholm, 1971; B. Carlson, op. cit., Ch. 3; and T. Karlbom, op. cit., Ch. 1.
30. T. Karlbom, op. cit.
31. B. Carlson, op. cit.
32. B. Carlson, op. cit.
33. K. Bäckström, op. cit., Vol. I, p. 231.
34. D. Blake, 'Swedish Trade Unions and the Social Democratic Party; The Formative Years', *Scandinavian Economic History Review*, Vol. 8 (1960).
35. T. Lindbom, *Den Svenska Fackföreningsrörelsens Uppkomst och Tidigare Historia (The Growth and Early History of Swedish Trade Unions)*, Stockholm, 1938.
36. K. Samuelsson, op. cit. p. 208.
37. N. Elvander, *Intresseorganisationerna i Dagens Sverige (Interest Groups in Contemporary Sweden)*, Lund, 1969, p. 27.
38. T. Karlbom, op.cit., p. 72.
39. For a detailed discussion of economic and political developments in Sweden during this period, see H. Tingsten, *The Swedish Social Democrats*, New Jersey, 1973.
40. The development of industrial relations in Sweden has been described by T. Johnston, *Collective Bargaining in Sweden*, London, 1962.
41. For a discussion of these and other strains within the labour movement see J. Fulcher, 'Class Conflict in Sweden', *Sociology*, Vol. 7 (1973).
42. The details of this agreement are discussed by T. Johnston, op. cit.
43. LO's policy of wage solidarity has been evaluated by R. Meidner, 'Samordning och Solidarisk Lönepolitik under tre Decennier' ('Coordination and the Policy of Wage Solidarity'), in LO, *Tvärsnitt (Cross-Section)*, Stockholm, 1973. See also J. Ullenhag, *Den Solidariska Lönepolitiken i Sverige (The Policy of Wage Solidarity in Sweden)*, Stockholm, 1971.
44. C.V. Otter, op. cit., Table 2.
45. See N. Elvander, op. cit., Ch. 1.
46. For an account of the size and the development of TCO, see N. Elvander, op. cit. Ch. 1.

47. N. Elvander, op. cit., Table 1.
48. Central Bureau of Statistics, *Statistical Abstract of Sweden*, Stockholm, 1971, Table 243.
49. N. Elvander, op. cit., p. 48.
50. N. Elvander, op. cit., p. 48.
51. O. Petersson and B. Sarlvik, 'The 1973 Election', *General Elections 1973*, Vol. 3; Central Bureau of Statistics, Stockholm, 1975, p. 84.
52. Central Bureau of Statistics, *Statistical Abstract of Sweden*, Stockholm, 1971, Table 243.
53. N. Elvander, op. cit., p. 32.
54. Central Bureau of Statistics, op. cit., Table 243.
55. N. Elvander, op. cit., p. 48.
56. J. Fulcher, op. cit.
57. R. Tomasson, *Sweden: Prototype of Modern Society*, New York, 1970, Ch. 2.
58. PEP (Political and Economic Planning), *Trade Union Membership* (Planning 463), London, 1962, p. 154.
59. H. Clegg, A. Fox and A. Thompson, *A History of British Trade Unionism Since 1889*, Oxford, 1964, pp. 1-2.
60. H. Clegg *et al.*, op. cit., p. 2.
61. H. Clegg *et al.*, op. cit., Ch. 1.
62. This and the following figures are taken from G. Bain, *The Growth of White-Collar Unionism*, London, 1972, Table 3.1.
63. G. Bain and R. Price, 'Union Growth and Employment Trends in the United Kingdom, 1964-1970', *British Journal of Industrial Relations*, Vol. 10 (1972), Table 8.
64. G. Bain and R. Price, op. cit.
65. See Table 1.8 above.
66. G. Bain and R. Price, op. cit., Table 11.
67. G. Bain, op. cit., Table 3.5.
68. N. Elvander, op. cit., p. 48.
69. Indeed, one of the striking features of wage bargaining in Britain has been the concern by unions to preserve existing differentials, particularly between various manual trades.
70. G. Bain, op. cit., p. 25.
71. N. Elvander, op. cit., Ch. 2.
72. In the sense of actively urging the trade union membership to support a particular political party. However, over recent years, the TUC has tended to become more involved in political matters. After the 1970 general election, for example, it almost took over the functions of Opposition to the Conservative government. After the 1974 elections, with Labour in office, the TUC became more directly involved in the formulation of policies.
73. This point was particularly emphasised in 1974 in terms of the degree to which the TUC was able to enforce the requirements of a 'Social Contract' with a Labour government. In 1975, however, it was able to influence the attitudes of affiliated unions about 'acceptable' wage increases.
74. The 1975 voluntary incomes agreement in Britain, negotiated between a Labour government and the union movement, allowing for £6 a week wage increases for all occupational groups except for those earning more than £8,500 a year, was egalitarian in consequence. However, within six months union leaders were arguing that such a policy could only continue for a limited period and that over the long term, occupational and craft differentials must be respected.

75. Not only in terms of wages, but also with respect to working conditions and various fringe benefits.
76. E.Dahlström, *Tjänstemännen, Näringslivet och Samhället (Management, Unions and Society)*, Stockholm, 1954, pp. 97-9.
77. T.Segerstedt and A. Lundquist, op. cit., Pt. II, p. 335-6.
78. E. Dahlström, op. cit., p. 86-7.
79. J. Goldthorpe, D. Lockwood, F. Bechhofer, J. Platt, *The Affluent Worker: Industrial Attitudes*, Cambridge, 1968, p. 112-13.
80. R. McKenzie and A. Silver, *Angels in Marble*, London, 1968, p. 126-33.
81. D. Butler and D. Stokes, *Political Change in Britain*, Harmondsworth, 1971, p. 209-10.
82. For a detailed account of the development of the Social Democratic Party during the last decades of the nineteenth century, see H. Tingsten, op. cit.
83. Quoted by D. Blake, op. cit., p. 21.
84. This point is made by H. Tingsten, op. cit.
85. 'Folk Party' is often translated as 'Liberal Party'. It has traditionally represented the interests of the more 'progressive' sectors of the Swedish middle class.
86. R. Tomasson, op. cit., p. 30.
87. Central Bureau of Statistics, *Historical Statistics of Sweden, (Statistical Survey)*, Stockholm, 1960, Table 276.
88. Central Bureau of Statistics, *Historical Statistics*, op. cit., Table 274.
89. See H. Tingsten, op. cit.
90. For a detailed account of political developments during the 1920s, see H. Tingsten, op. cit.
91. R. Tomasson, 'The Extraordinary Success of the Swedish Social Democrats', *Journal of Politics*, Vol. 31 (1969), p. 772.
92. R. Huntford, *The New Totalitarians*, London, 1971.
93. For a comparative account of the development of Social Democratic parties in different European countries, see R. Tomasson, 'The Extraordinary Success of the Swedish Social Democrats', op. cit. For a very scholarly and detailed analysis of the same topic, see C. Landauer, *European Socialism*, Vols. I and II, Berkeley, 1959.
94. The central thesis of H. Tingsten, op. cit., is that the development of the Social Democratic Party, up until the late 1930s, was characterised by the increasing rejection of revolutionary ideals and the adoption of reform-welfare ideologies.
95. For such a view, see, for example, G. Adler-Karlsson, *Functional Socialism: A Swedish Theory for Democratic Socialisation*, Stockholm, 1967.
96. This is emphasised by M.D. Hancock, *Sweden: The Politics of Post-Industrial Change*, Hinsdale (Ill.), 1972.
97. H. Moorhouse, 'The Political Incorporation of the British Working Class: An Interpretation', *Sociology*, Vol. 7 (1973).
98. For an account of the early development of the Labour Party, see H. Pelling, *A Short History of the Labour Party*, London, 1961, Ch. 1.
99. D. Butler, *British Political Facts, 1900-1967* (2nd ed.), London, 1968, p. 141.
100. D. Butler, op. cit., p. 142.
101. R. McKenzie and A. Silver, *Angels in Marble*, London, 1968, p. 10.
102. R. Leonard, *Elections in Britain*, London, 1968, p. 140.
103. Central Bureau of Statistics, *Statistical Abstract of Sweden*, op. cit., 1973, Table 374.
104. The Workers' Educational Association in Britain has no formal links with

trade unions and it cannot be regarded as an integral component of a more broadly based working-class movement.

105. Indeed, this is symbolised in most Swedish communities by the *Folkets Hus (The People's House)* which usually provides facilities for a wide range of social, recreational and educational activities.

# 2 CLASS INEQUALITY IN BRITAIN AND SWEDEN

The study of class inequality has always been an area of interest to sociologists and yet it is fraught with many conceptual, methodological and practical problems. Among these are difficulties of definition, the specification of dimensions, and complexities related to the collection of data. For the purposes of the present analysis, class inequality in Britain and Sweden will be considered in terms of three components: (i) economic condition; (ii) opportunity; and (iii) power.

## (i) Inequalities of economic condition

Discussions of economic condition have often focused upon distributions of income and wealth using data collected by national tax authorities.[1] However, there are difficulties in making international comparisons since tax systems vary considerably from one country to the next so that the information upon which most calculations are based are not always directly comparable.[2] Sweden, for example, has wealth and gift taxes neither of which, as yet, exist in Britain. Furthermore, it is uncertain whether various forms of tax avoidance and evasion are practised to the same extent in both countries. Despite these limitations, however, it is feasible to summarise evidence which enables comparisons to be made, both within the two countries over a period of time and between them. More specifically, it is possible to comment about trends since the early 1930s, when the Social Democrats became the dominant party in Swedish politics.[3]

It appears that between 1935 and 1949 there was a greater shift towards economic equality in Sweden than in Britain; measured, that is, in terms of the distribution of both pre-tax and post-tax incomes. The figures, derived from a comparative study of incomes in different European countries, are shown in Table 2.1:

As Table 2.1 suggests, between 1935 and 1948 the share of pre-tax income accruing to the 'top' 10 per cent recipients in Sweden declined from 40 per cent to 30 per cent. In Britain, by contrast, the proportion of the total income taken by this group fell by only 5 per cent; from 38 per cent in 1938 to 33 per cent in 1949. Furthermore, the share received by the 'bottom' 60 per cent increased from 23 per cent to 29 per cent in Sweden while that of the comparable group in Britain remained more or less the same; 33 per cent in 1938 and 32 per cent in

Table 2.1: Percentage distribution of pre- and post-tax income received by decile groups in Britain and Sweden, 1935-49

| Decile Group | United Kingdom | | | | Sweden | | | |
|---|---|---|---|---|---|---|---|---|
| | 1938 | | 1949 | | 1935 | | 1948 | |
| | Before Tax | After Tax | Before Tax | After Tax | Before Tax | After Tax | Before Tax | After Tax |
| Top 10 per cent | 38.0 | 33.6 | 33.0 | 26.7 | 39.5 | 36.9 | 30.3 | 27.0 |
| 11-20 per cent | 12.0 | } 22.7 | 14.5 | } 14.0 | 16.6 | 17.2 | 16.3 | 16.1 |
| 21-30 per cent | 9.3 | | 10.8 | | 12.2 | 13.0 | 12.9 | 13.7 |
| 31-40 per cent | 7.5 | 8.0 | 9.7 | } 32.3 | 9.0 | 9.5 | 11.4 | 11.5 |
| 41-50 per cent | } | } | 8.0 | | 6.7 | 7.5 | 9.0 | 9.7 |
| 51-60 per cent | | | 7.0 | } 13.7 | } | } | 7.3 | 8.0 |
| 61-70 per cent | | | 5.5 | | | | 5.6 | 6.1 |
| 71-80 per cent | } 33.2 | } 35.7 | 4.3 | 5.0 | } 16.0 | } 15.9 | 4.0 | 4.4 |
| 81-90 per cent | | | } | } 8.3 | | | } | } |
| 91-100 per cent | 7.2 | | 7.2 | | | | 3.2 | 3.5 |
| Total | 100.0 | 100.0 | 100.0 | 100.0 | 100.0 | 100.0 | 100.0 | 100.0 |
| Maximum Equalisation Percentage | 30 | 27 | 28 | 24 | 38 | 37 | 31 | 28 |

Source: Extracted from United Nations, *Economic Survey of Europe*, Geneva, 1957, Ch. 9, Tables 3 and 12.

1949. Consequently, whereas Sweden had a more unequal distribution
of pre-tax income than Britain during the late 1930s, by the end of the
1940s the patterns for the two countries were similar. However, it is
important to take into account the role of taxation since this constitutes the major means whereby governments in capitalist countries
can modify patterns of rewards as they have been generated by the
occupational structure and the market system of production. From
Table 2.1 it seems that taxation had less of a redistributive effect in
Sweden than in Britain during the late 1930s, but much the same effect
in both countries by the end of the 1940s. This is shown by changes in
the *maximum equalisation percentage* which measures the share of total
income that must be transferred from groups above the mean to those
below in order to obtain complete equality. Despite the overall shift
towards equality during this period, however, Sweden remained a more
inegalitarian country than Britain, both in terms of the distribution of
pre- and post-tax incomes. Furthermore, the developments in Sweden
were more the consequence of structural changes such as the growth of
industrial occupations and the concomitant decline of agricultural
employment than of government fiscal policies.[4]

Between the late 1940s and the mid-1950s there was a continuation
in the shift towards greater equality in Sweden. Thus, the *maximum
equalisation percentage* for pre-tax income was reduced from 31 to 26.[5]
The trend, however, was not maintained and during the late 1950s and
early 1960s the share of the total income received by individuals in the
higher income groups increased while that of those in the lower groups
declined; the watershed, as shown in Table 2.2, seems to have fallen
between the fifth and sixth decile groups. In Britain there was a fall in
the income share of the top decile group as well as by the three lowest
groups; the net gainers appear to have been the middle decile groups.
Table 2.2 suggests that in both countries the gap between individuals in
the low income groups, in which non-earners such as pensioners are a
high proportion, and those in the middle groups increased between the
mid-1950s and the 1960s. Indeed, during the period, Sweden and
Britain seem to have had similar pre-tax income distributions.

Unfortunately, the comparative study from which the figures shown
in Table 2.2, are extracted did not investigate the distribution of post-
tax incomes. However, it did state that:

the Netherlands and the United Kingdom probably have the most
progressive system of income tax among Western European countries.
In Norway and Sweden, tax rates are not very different from those

in the United Kingdom or in the Netherlands, but the system is less progressive and the overall tax-rate is higher.[6]

Table 2.2: Percentage distribution of pre-tax income received by decile groups in Britain and Sweden, 1954-64

| Decile Group | United Kingdom | | Sweden | |
|---|---|---|---|---|
| | 1954 | 1964 | 1954 | 1963 |
| Top 10 per cent | 30.4 | 29.3 | 27.3 | 27.9 |
| 11- 20 per cent | 14.8 | 14.9 | 15.5 | 16.1 |
| 21- 30 per cent | 12.7 | 12.9 | 12.7 | 13.2 |
| 31- 40 per cent | 10.4 | 11.0 | 10.6 | 11.4 |
| 41- 50 per cent | 8.6 | 9.1 | 9.3 | 9.7 |
| 51- 60 per cent | 7.3 | 7.5 | 7.8 | 7.7 |
| 61- 70 per cent | 5.8 | 6.0 | 6.2 | 5.5 |
| 71- 80 per cent | 4.5 | 4.2 | 5.0 | 4.1 |
| 81- 90 per cent | } 5.5 | } 3.1 | 3.6 | 2.8 |
| 91-100 per cent | | | 2.0 | 1.6 |
| Total | 100.0 | 100.0 | 100.0 | 100.0 |
| Maximum Equalisation Percentage | 29 | 28 | 26 | 29 |

Source: Extracted from United Nations, *Incomes in Post War Europe*, Geneva, 1967, Table 6. 10.

Thus, it seems reasonable to conclude that the effects of the Swedish taxation system were such that during the 1950s and 1960s, the distribution of post-tax income was no more egalitarian in Sweden than in Britain. More recent developments are shown in Table 2.3, which compares the distribution of pre- and post-tax income in the two countries during the early 1970s.

The figures in Table 2.3 should not be compared with those in the previous tables; whereas the earlier statistics refer to *tax units,* information in this table is for *household* income. This is because the official published statistics on income provided by the Swedish and British tax authorities can no longer be compared since the former now provide statistics for *individuals* while the latter give information on *tax units,* with the income of husband and wife combined.[7] Thus, in order to compare the distribution of income in Britain and Sweden during the 1970s, it is necessary to refer to the income received by *households*. In both countries the government conducts surveys, providing comparable information on the combined earnings of all members of households. In

58 Class Inequality in Britain and Sweden

Table 2.3, the data for the United Kingdom is based on Family Expenditure Surveys in 1972 and 1973 and the Swedish statistics on a survey of households in 1972.[8]

Table 2.3: Percentage distribution of pre- and post-tax income received by decile groups of households in Britain and Sweden, 1971-73*

| Decile Group | United Kingdom (1971-73) | | Sweden (1972) | |
|---|---|---|---|---|
| | Pre-Tax | Post-Tax | Pre-Tax | Post-Tax |
| Top 10 per cent | 26.9 | 23.5 | 28.8 | 20.3 |
| 11- 20 per cent | 16.8 | 15.5 | 18.4 | 15.3 |
| 21- 30 per cent | 13.9 | 12.9 | 14.7 | 12.8 |
| 31- 40 per cent | 11.8 | 11.0 | 12.3 | 11.1 |
| 41- 50 per cent | 10.0 | 9.7 | 10.2 | 9.9 |
| 51- 60 per cent | 8.4 | 8.4 | 8.1 | 8.5 |
| 61- 70 per cent | 6.6 | 7.0 | 5.3 | 7.2 |
| 71- 80 per cent | 4.2 | 5.6 | 1.9 | 5.6 |
| 81- 90 per cent | 1.3 | 4.0 | 0.3 | 5.3 |
| 91-100 per cent | 0.1 | 2.6 | − 0.2** | 4.1 |
| Total | 100.0 | 100.0 | 100.0 | 100.0 |
| Maximum Equalisation Percentage | 29 | 23 | 34 | 20 |

Sources: Extracted from Royal Commission on the Distribution of Income and Wealth, *Report No. I,* London, 1975, Table 24; and Central Bureau of Statistics, *Swedish Survey on Relative Income Differences,* 1972, Stockholm, 1974, Table 2.8.

Notes: * Pre-tax income refers to income from earnings and the ownership of assets, before all taxes and cash payments. Post-tax income relates to income as defined above, plus all direct cash benefits and after the payment of direct taxes.
** There were approximately 360,000 households in this decile group. Of these almost one-half were either students (74,000) or self-employed and small business owners (80,000). The latter were often able to claim investment and tax deductions and to arrange their affairs so that they made an accounting loss in 1972.

As suggested in Table 2.3, in 1972 the 'top' 30 per cent of all households received 62 per cent of the pre-tax income in Sweden compared with 58 per cent in Britain. However, after cash payments and direct taxes are taken into account, these Swedish households received 48 per cent of the income compared with 52 per cent in Britain; in other words, the income of this group was reduced by 6 per cent in Britain but by as much as 14 per cent in Sweden. Indeed, it seems that the Swedish tax system was more redistributive, with the effect that the *maximum equalisation percentage* was lowered to a far greater extent than in Britain. This, however, compensated for a more inegalitarian distribution of pre-tax income. Consequently, it appears that in the 1970s both countries had comparable distributions of post-tax household income. Any variations that exist do not refute the overall similarities.

An alternative method of comparing economic inequality in the two countries is in terms of wage differentials as they exist between various occupational groups. Mouly found that in Sweden inequalities between male wage-earners and male salaried employees in manufacturing industry were virtually the same in 1963 as in the early 1950s,[9] a pattern which has been confirmed by Holmberg.[10] Indeed, Johansson found that by 1968 no fundamental changes had occurred.[11] From these studies it appears that during the 1950s and 1960s the average earnings of lower-grade white-collar men were approximately 40 per cent more than those of all industrial manual workers, while those of qualified male technical workers were as much as 70 per cent higher.[12] Similarly, in Britain the pattern of differentials seems to have undergone little alteration during the past thirty years. Routh, for example, has commented upon the overall consistency of wage differences.[13] In Britain, as in Sweden, any changes have tended to be restricted to the relative earnings of lower-grade non-manual workers. Thus, over the past three decades, male clerks have dropped from a position of parity with skilled manual workers to a point midway between the skilled and semi-skilled. Indeed, by the 1970s, the average earnings of male clerks in both countries were lower than those of semi-skilled workers in a large number of industries.[14] Despite such changes, however, there have been no trends in either country which have, in any fundamental manner, radically altered the overall pattern of economic rewards. Indeed, although it is difficult to make rigorous comparisons of wage differentials in Britain and Sweden because, among other things, of variations in systems of classification, it does seem that the two countries are rather alike. The most comparable information, collected in the 1960s, is reproduced in Table 2.4.

From Table 2.4 it appears that in both countries, professional and managerial workers, for example, have tended to receive at least three times the average earnings of unskilled manual employees. Indeed, in view of the data in Table 2.4, it seems reasonable to conclude that both countries have rather similar profiles of economic inequality as meas-

Table 2.4: Average earnings of occupational groups in Britain and
Sweden (expressed as multiples of average earnings for male unskilled
manual workers)

| Occupational Category | United Kingdom | Sweden |
|---|---|---|
| Higher Administrative and Professional Workers | 3.5 | 3.1 |
| Lower Administrative and Professional Workers | 1.6 | 1.8 |
| Clerks | 1.3 | 1.3 |
| Foremen | 1.9 | 1.4 |
| Skilled Manual Workers | 1.5 | — |
| Unskilled Manual Workers | 1.0 | 1.0 |

Source: Extracted from United Nations, Incomes in Post-War Europe, Geneva,
1967, Table 5.16.

ured not only by the distribution of income but also by differentials in
the earnings of various occupational groups. This is interesting in view
of the fact that the Swedish Confederation of Trade Unions (LO) has,
especially since the Second World War, pursued a policy of 'wage solidarity', attempting to reduce the range of inequalities between occupations.[15] But Ullenhag, in an appraisal of LO policy, has claimed that
this has had little effect on the pattern of differentials because it has
been almost completely nullified by market forces which have tended
to favour the skilled and the highly paid.[16] In fact, his conclusions are
similar to those of Mouly, who also found that LO's policy of 'wage
solidarity' has had little consequence for reducing inequalities.[17] Indeed,
they seem to be no less than in Britain, despite the absence of 'wage
solidarity' as a feature of trade union policy.

   An important dimension of class inequality is the distribution of
personal wealth. Unfortunately it is almost impossible to make any
comparative statements about the ownership of wealth in Britain and
Sweden because of severe limitation of the data. In the Swedish official
statistics, for example, assets are valued not according to market prices,
but in relation to their tax values. In addition, there is the complete
omission of individuals' holdings in life insurance companies and pension
funds, as well as their ownership of consumer durables. Thus, it is only
possible to make extremely crude comments about trends within the
two countries and any conclusions to be drawn from a comparison of
Tables 2.5 and 2.6 need to be treated with extreme caution. The data
for Britain and Sweden are presented separately in order to emphasise
this.

Table 2.5: The distribution of personal wealth in Sweden

| Year | Proportion of total wealth owned by the 'Top': | | |
| | 1% | 5% | 10% |
| --- | --- | --- | --- |
| 1945 | 15 | 33 | 44 |
| 1950 | 13 | 29 | 40 |
| 1964 | 16 | 30 | 39 |

Source: Extracted from Statens Offentliga Utredningar (SOU), *Ägande och Inflytande inom det Privata Näringslivet (Ownership and Influence in the Private Economy)*, Stockholm, 1968, Table 6.4

Table 2.5 suggests that since 1945 the distribution of personal wealth in Sweden has remained fairly stable with 10 per cent of the population owning roughly 40 per cent of the wealth. In Britain there appears to have been some shift towards equality since the 1930s, although the level of concentration has continued to remain much higher than in Sweden. Thus, as suggested in Table 2.6, 10 per cent of the population owned no less than 67 per cent of the wealth in 1973.

Table 2.6: The distribution of personal wealth in Britain*

| Year | Proportion of total wealth owned by the 'Top': | | |
| | 1% | 5% | 10% |
| --- | --- | --- | --- |
| 1936-38 | 56 | 79 | 88 |
| 1954 | 43 | 71 | 79 |
| 1960 | 42 | 75 | 83 |
| 1965 | 33 | 59 | 73 |
| 1973 | 28 | 51 | 67 |

Source: Extracted from Royal Commission on Income and Wealth, *Report No. 1*, London, 1975, Tables 41 and 45.

Note: * No direct comparisons can be made between the figures before and after 1960 because of reasons relating to the coverage of the data. For a discussion of these see the Royal Commission's *Report,* Chapter 5.

Britain and Sweden, then, seem to have rather similar patterns of income and wage differentials but different concentrations of personal wealth. Does this mean that the overall profiles of economic inequality in the two countries are similar? It is difficult to give a straight answer to this question but in view of the foregoing discussion it seems reasonable to suggest that industrial manual workers occupy highly comparable positions within the reward structures of the two countries; the lower concentration of personal wealth in Sweden probably benefits white-collar workers much more than it does industrial manual workers.[18] Consequently, the reward structures of Britain and Sweden, and particularly the relative position of industrial manual workers, seem to be characterised more by their similarities than their differences. It is now necessary to investigate whether the *opportunities* for acquiring high economic rewards are greater in one country than in the other. This requires the consideration of another component of class inequality; namely, patterns of social mobility.

## (ii) Inequalities of opportunity

Studies of opportunity usually investigate patterns of recruitment into prestigeful and highly paid occupational rules. The evidence for Britain and Sweden suggests that these have tended to be highly restricted in both countries. In the late 1940s and 1950s the rate of intergenerational mobility between manual and non-manual occupations was much the same in Sweden as in Britain and a number of other European countries. Miller, for example, in a re-analysis of mobility studies, claimed the sons of manual workers in Britain and Sweden had similar chances of becoming white-collar workers, and that they were equally deprived in comparison to the sons of non-manual workers.[19] Miller demonstrates this by an *index of inequality* which he uses to compare the life chances of manual and non-manual workers' sons.

Table 2.7: Inequality of opportunity in Britain and Sweden

|  | (1)<br>Non-Manual<br>into Non-Manual | (2)<br>Manual<br>into Non-Manual | (3)<br>Index of Inequality<br>(1)/(2) |
|---|---|---|---|
| United Kingdom | 57.9 | 24.8 | 234 |
| Sweden | 72.3 | 25.5 | 284 |

*Source:* Extracted from S. Miller, 'Comparative Social Mobility', *Current Sociology,* Vol. 9 (1960), Table 4a.

Table 2.7 suggests that, if anything, the British class structure was rather more open than the Swedish, but that in both countries the chances of the son of a manual worker becoming a white-collar worker were roughly the same. However, since the 1950s rates of upward mobility seem to have increased in Sweden but not in Britain.[20] But this has tended to be in terms of recruitment into the more routine, less qualified white-collar occupations; a feature borne out by Table 2.8 which is taken from a national study of social mobility in Sweden, conducted in 1968.[21]

Table 2.8: Social mobility among the Swedish adult population

| Father's Social Group* | Respondent's Social Group | | | Total | |
|---|---|---|---|---|---|
| | I | II | III | % | Nos. |
| I | 50 | 37 | 13 | 100 | 254 |
| II | 11 | 45 | 44 | 100 | 1,981 |
| III | 4 | 32 | 64 | 100 | 3,274 |
| Total | 8 | 37 | 55 | 100 | 5,509 |

Source:  R. Erikson, *Uppväxtförhallonden och Social Rörlighet (Childhood Living Conditions and Social Mobility)*, Stockholm, 1971, Table 6.31.

*In this and the following tables, 'Social Group I' refers to senior civil servants, owners of large business firms, professional people and senior managerial executives in private businesses; 'Social Group II' to lower-grade non-manual workers, owners of small businesses, independent artisans and foremen; and 'Social Group III' to manual workers.

From Table 2.8 it appears that 36 per cent of the sons of Swedish manual workers were in white-collar occupations in 1968; a noticeable increase compared with the findings reported by Carlsson in the 1950s.[22] In Britain, on the other hand, a review by Noble of studies conducted throughout the 1960s suggests that as recently as 1967, only 26 per cent of the sons of manual workers were employed in non-manual occupations;[23] an insignificant change compared with the Glass findings for 1949.[24]

However, it is arguable whether such indices of mobility adequately 'measure' the rigidity of class structures if only because, as Lipset and Bendix have suggested, the exchange of personnel between manual and non-manual occupations tends to be over a short range; that is, between skilled manual and 'routine' non-manual occupational roles.[25] Lipset and Bendix claim that mobility of this kind is related to changes in the occupational structure, generated by industrialisation. In view of this, rates of 'elite' mobility, that is movement into managerial and professional occupations, are probably better measures of class rigidity. If this is the case, then the data presented in Table 2.8 suggests that, although there may now be greater mobility within the Swedish class structure

than during the 1950s, it tends to be between lower-grade white-collar
and manual occupations rather than in terms of movement into professional, managerial and administrative roles. As Table 2.8 indicates,
only 4 per cent of the sons of manual workers were employed in occupations of this kind in 1968. More information on these patterns is
given in Table 2.9, which demonstrates the proportion of sons from
different occupational backgrounds in Sweden acquiring positions that
have been classified in Social Groups I and III.

Table 2.9: Proportion of sons in social groups I and III according to
fathers' occupation

| Fathers' Occupations | Sons' Social Group | |
|---|---|---|
| | I | III |
| Senior civil servants | 65.6 | 8.3 |
| Owners of large business concerns and professional people | 52.6 | 8.2 |
| Senior managerial and executive workers in private concerns | 50.7 | 18.5 |
| Lower-grade non-manual workers in private concerns | 33.7 | 27.8 |
| Lower-grade non-manual workers in public concerns | 24.4 | 32.0 |
| Owners of small business concerns and independent artisans | 15.8 | 39.8 |
| Foremen | 13.1 | 47.6 |
| Manual workers in public concerns | 8.5 | 58.0 |
| Farmers | 4.0 | 41.3 |
| Manual workers in private concerns | 5.2 | 61.3 |
| Small farmers, fishermen | 2.6 | 71.3 |
| Farm and forestry workers | 3.3 | 75.7 |

Source: Extracted from R. Erikson, *Uppväxtförhallonden och Social Rörlighet
(Childhood Living Conditions and Social Mobility)*, Stockholm, 1971,
Table 6.47.

The data in Table 2.9 confirm that the Swedish class structure was rigid
in 1968. The son of a senior civil servant, for example, appears to have
had about thirteen times the chances of obtaining a 'Social Group I'
occupation than the son of a manual worker in private industry. Even
the son of a lower-grade white-collar worker in private industry had
more than six times the chances of getting such a position than a
manual worker's son. In other words, recruitment into professional,
managerial and other highly rewarded occupations is highly restricted in
Sweden.

In the absence of comparable national surveys it is difficult to assess whether élite mobility is as equally limited in Britain as in Sweden. Miller's analysis suggested that 2.2 per cent of the sons of manual workers attained élite positions in Britain during the late 1940s, compared with 3.5 per cent in Sweden in the 1950s; figures which should be contrasted with the rate of 7.8 per cent for the United States.[26] Rates of élite mobility, therefore, would appear to have been relatively similar in both countries; indeed, investigations of recruitment into specific occupations confirm that both countries have very low rates of mobility of this kind.

In an analysis of 245 business leaders in Sweden, Malmström and Widenborg found, in the late 1950s, that 16 per cent were the sons of lower-grade white-collar workers and industrial manual workers, while at least 30 per cent were the sons of owners and managers of large businesses which employed at least two hundred people.[27] Studies conducted in Britain during the 1950s by such investigators as Clements[28] and Copeman[29] suggest a similar pattern. Copeman, whose analysis is probably the most comparable with the Swedish study, found that only 8 per cent of company directors were the sons of lower-grade white-collar workers and manual workers, while 51 per cent were the sons of directors, small businessmen and industrial managers.[30] Other investigations undertaken during the 1960s and early 1970s confirm that extremely few manual workers' children obtain élite positions in British industry and commerce; this has been shown by studies of managers by Clark[31] and Nichols,[32] of company chairmen by Stanworth and Giddens,[33] and of directors by Whitely.[34] Of course, it is difficult to compare trends in Britain and Sweden, but the findings of such studies do suggest that the chances of a son of a manual worker acquiring an élite position in industry are highly restricted in both countries.

A similar pattern is evident in the social origins of individuals occupying élite roles within the non-industrial sectors of the two countries. In an investigation into the social background of top Swedish civil servants, Landström found that there had been no overall change in patterns of recruitment between 1917 and 1947; only 7 per cent of these officials came from working-class homes in 1947 compared with 3 per cent in 1917.[35] Samuelsson has also suggested that in 1965, of 200 higher state adminstrators in Sweden, only 10 per cent were of working-class social origin.[36] Indeed, this pattern is confirmed by a comprehensive study of top Swedish state officials conducted in 1968.[37] The figures are reproduced in Table 2.10:

Class Inequality in Britain and Sweden

Table 2.10: The social origins of Swedish higher civil servants in 1968

| Department | Social Background | | | |
| | Social Group | | | Total |
| | I | II | III | |
| --- | --- | --- | --- | --- |
| Central Department | 54 | 37 | 9 | 100 |
| Central Administration, excluding State Industries | 32 | 50 | 18 | 100 |
| Central Administration of State Industries | 25 | 54 | 21 | 100 |
| County Administration | 45 | 43 | 12 | 100 |
| Regional and Local Administration, excluding State Industries | 18 | 66 | 16 | 100 |
| Local and Regional Administration of State Industries | 30 | 52 | 18 | 100 |
| All Departments | 32 | 52 | 16 | 100 |

*Source:* Extracted from U. Christoffersson, B. Molin, L. Månsson and
L. Strömberg, *Byråkrati och Politik (Bureaucracy and Politics)* Stockholm, 1972, Table 2.

Table 2.10 shows that only 9 per cent of top civil servants in the
Central Department came from working-class backgrounds compared
with 54 per cent recruited from Social Group I. Although a rather
higher proportion have working-class origins in other sectors of the
civil service — especially in the state industries — more than one-third
have been recruited from Social Group I and less than one-fifth from
Social Group III. If, then, there has been any 'democratisation' of
recruitment into the higher grades of the Swedish civil service, the process has been far from dramatic. In fact, the patterns are not unlike
those for Britain. Kelsall, for example, found that the proportions of
civil servants (above the rank of assistant secretary) recruited from
higher administrative, professional and managerial backgrounds were 39
per cent and 32 per cent in 1929 and 1950 respectively.[38] But, at the
same time, there was an increase in the percentage of those with fathers
who were manual workers; from 7 per cent in 1929 to 20 per cent in
1950. Since then, however, there appears to have been little change in
overall patterns of recruitment; particularly in terms of those recruited
from manual working-class homes. In a recent analysis Kelsall claims
that in 1967 the percentage of civil servants above the rank of assistant
secretary with manual working-class fathers was 17 per cent.[39] Table
2.11, extracted from Chapman, provides some recent data on the social

origins of entrants into the administrative class of the British civil
service.

Table 2.11: The social background of entrants into the administrative
class of the British civil service between 1948-56 and 1957-63

| Fathers' Occupational Groups | 1948-56 | | 1957-63 | |
|---|---|---|---|---|
| | Nos. | % | Nos. | % |
| Administrative, Professional and Managerial Workers | 202 | 38.3 | 212 | 45.8 |
| Lower-grade Professional, Managerial and Technical Workers | 205 | 38.9 | 176 | 38.0 |
| Highly Skilled Workers, Foremen, Supervisors and Clerks | 105 | 19.9 | 55 | 11.9 |
| Skilled and Semi-skilled Workers | 6 | 1.2 | 13 | 2.8 |
| Unskilled Workers | 7 | 1.3 | 2 | 0.4 |
| Unknown | 2 | 0.4 | 5 | 1.1 |
| Total | 527 | 100.0 | 463 | 100.0 |

Source: Calculated from R. Chapman, *The Higher Civil Service in Britain*, London,
1970, Table 14.

There are, of course, problems in any international comparison of élite
mobility. In the study of higher civil servants it is difficult to ascertain
whether comparisons are being made between occupations of similar
rank. In addition, the ratio of departmental heads to all other civil
service positions may vary between two countries so that competitition
for the 'top' appointments may be more intense in the one country than
in the other. Furthermore, there may be inter-societal variations in the
prestige of such positions in relation to other professional and managerial occupations. In view of these factors, any conclusions about
patterns of recruitment into elite occupations such as the higher civil
service must be treated with caution. However, the sons of manual
workers in Britain and Sweden do seem to be equally disadvantaged in
their chances of obtaining such positions; a conclusion which is confirmed by studies that have been conducted into a wide range of non-
industrial occupations. Petrén, for example, in a study of the social
origins of university professors at Lund and Uppsala universities, found
that between 1800 and 1950 there was no marked tendency towards
'broader' social recruitment; in 1950 only 8 per cent were from manual
working-class homes.[40] Similarly, Carlsson, in a discussion of the social
recruitment of military leaders, suggests that between 1900 and 1961

the proportion from manual working-class families remained very small.[41] In fact, such patterns seem to be much the same as for Britain; this is the inference to be drawn from Halsey and Trow's data on university teachers,[42] Guttsman's investigation of politicians,[43] Otley's study of the military[44] and Thompson's analysis of Anglican bishops.[45] Consequently, and despite the limitations of comparative analysis, the conclusion to be taken from investigations of social mobility in the two countries is that they are characterised by relatively common profiles; certainly, the position of manual workers is in no way fundamentally more advantageous in one society than in the other. Industrial manual workers appear to occupy similar positions within the class structures of the two societies.

### (iii) Inequalities of power

In the light of the analysis of economic inequalities and mobility chances, it is evident that in both countries the respective working-class movements have achieved little power; defined, that is, in terms of the degree to which they have been able to alter the principles upon which Swedish and British capitalism is established. Thus, capitalism, as a socio-economic system, determines the allocation of resources in both countries on the basis of the private ownership of the means of production and according to principles of profit, rent, wage labour and forces of supply and demand. Consequently, *power* for the purposes of the present discussion is considered solely in terms of the degree to which the working-class movements in the two countries have been able to *represent* the interests of industrial manual workers *within* the socio-economic parameters of contemporary capitalism. Since, then, this analysis focuses upon what may be termed *representative power,* it is necessary to investigate the role and the objectives of working-class movements *within* the two capitalist systems.

A government enquiry published in Sweden in 1968 concluded that in 1964, the fifty largest companies employed 21 per cent of all workers in private industry, and that in 1963, the one hundred largest companies accounted for 46 per cent of the total output of Swedish private industry.[46] Furthermore, in terms of the ownership of company shares, the enquiry suggested that 17 groups of shareholders had, in 1963, a majority or a substantial minority holding in companies accounting for 36 per cent of all industrial output. The investigators claimed that the concentration of stocks and shares in Swedish private industry was probably greater than in either the United States or Britain. An explanation for this, according to the authors, is that although Sweden is a small country, it requires large units of production in order to compete in international markets. Indeed, the concentration of economic power in Sweden has been encouraged by Social Democratic governments on precisely these grounds: that 'structural rationalisation' is necessary if Sweden is to increase exports and to enjoy high living standards.

Comparisons with Britain suggest that the concentration of industrial assets is probably less than in Sweden, although it has tended to increase since the Second World War. Barratt Brown, for example, claims that in 1953/54, the one hundred largest industrial companies in Britain accounted for 32 per cent of all net assets and 19 per cent of gross income.[47] By 1961/63, the proportion of net assets held by this group of companies had increased to 40 per cent and the share of gross income to 23 per cent. Within manufacturing industry, the degree of concentration was even greater: in 1953/54 the 'top' 100 companies owned 50 per cent of the net assets and accounted for 35 per cent of gross income, and by 1961/63 the proportions had increased to 60 per cent and 50 per cent respectively. These figures are, of course, in no way comparable with those mentioned for Sweden, but they do indicate a high concentration of economic power in Britain. To what extent, then, is this economic power in the two countries 'checked' or 'restrained' by other social forces?

It is in relation to this issue that further consideration needs to be given to the British and Swedish labour movements and the degree to which they represent the interests of industrial manual workers. It has already been suggested in Chapter 1 that levels of trade union membership and union legitimacy are much higher in Sweden than in Britain. As a result, it can be suggested that the Swedish trade union movement is more able to operate as a 'check' to the economic power of companies than its British counterpart. However, a number of Swedish observers, particularly the 'New Left', have claimed that the labour movement in Sweden has become bureaucratised and that it no longer represents workers' interests.[48] Although bureaucracy and centralisation of decision-making have generated tensions within the movement, it can be argued that this has enabled the labour movement to compete more effectively with other power groups in society. Furthermore, the concern by the Swedish labour movement to increase equality, particularly in terms of the earnings and working conditions of manual and white-collar workers, suggests that national union negotiators have not completely neglected the interests of rank-and-file members.[49]

In view of the lack of comparative evidence, it is uncertain whether Swedish labour unions have been more effective in representing the interests of their members than their British counterparts. Certainly, in terms of income distribution and wage differentials, little appears to have been achieved by LO. But it does seem to have been able to impose greater constraints upon the prerogatives of management. For example, as a result of recent legislation, the boards of companies with more than 100 employees must include trade union representatives. Similarly, there have been attempts to 'democratise' private companies by increasing the level of trade union participation in company planning and policy formulation.[50] By contrast, British Labour governments and trade unions have made few attempts to bring about similar reforms, and thereby increase the influence of workers within the formal structures of industrial companies; at least to a level enjoyed by their Swedish counterparts. Indeed, a comparative analysis of a Swedish and English factory, undertaken in 1970, suggested that trade unions imposed far greater 'constraints' upon managerial prerogatives in the former than in the latter.[51] When, for example, management in the Swedish factory wanted to discipline a worker for failing to adhere to collectively agreed rules and procedures, it had first to notify union officials before the worker could be warned. If, after this, management considered that the behaviour had continued and it wanted to dismiss the employee, the reasons had to be explained to union officials. If there was agreement with these officials, the worker could then be dismissed with three weeks' notice, but if not, negotiations proceeded to higher level. In the English factory, by contrast, there was far less consultation between management and union officials. Procedures were less clearly defined and at best the worker could only appeal through a union official after he had already been given notice of dismissal.

This is but one example and it is based on a comparison of only two workplaces, yet it is indicative of wider patterns in both countries. Thus, in day-to-day activities and in negotiations with employees, Swedish management is more 'constrained' by rules and procedures which have been established in agreement with trade unions than its British counterpart.[52] This is reinforced by the fact that union membership in most sectors of Swedish manufacturing industry is very high and that it commands considerable support from rank-and-file members.[53] Consequently, although industrial power is overwhelmingly concentrated in the hands of shareholders and managers in both countries, an influential working-class movement represents the interests of employees to a far greater degree in Sweden than in Britain.[54] A similar statement can be made about the exercise of power in the non-industrial sectors of the two countries.

It has already been noted in Chapter 1 that the first Social Democratic government in Europe was elected to office in Sweden in 1920
and since 1932 it has either been in office as a majority government or
as the dominant partner in a  government coalition. By contrast, the
British Labour Party, up until 1975, has been in government for only
two significant periods of time.[55] However, the influence of the
Swedish working-class movement in Sweden is not only reflected in
terms of electoral support for the Social Democratic Party; it is also
represented by the existence of a set of organisations and norms which,
according to Anderson, significantly penetrates the life-styles of
manual and lower-grade white-collar workers.[56] These play a significant
role in such areas as vocational training, adult education, sport, leisure
and various political and social activities. As a result, members of
Swedish society, particularly manual and routine white-collar workers,
are drawn into a complex of voluntary associations, a large number of
which are closely related to, or affiliated with, the working-class
movement.[57] In fact, the extent to which such organisations exercise an
organisational and normative influence has been demonstrated by
Anderson in a study of perceived 'influentials' in four Swedish
communities.[58] Although each of the communities represented different political, economic and social structures, he found that 95 per
cent of all 'influentials' mentioned by respondents were union officials.
Furthermore, in an enquiry into voting behaviour and its relationship to
patterns of social mobility, he found that upwardly mobile sons from
working-class homes were more likely to retain their voting allegiance
to the Social Democratic Party than were upwardly mobiles in the
United States who tended to shift their political allegiance from the
Democratic to the Republican Party.[59] Anderson argues that this is a
result of the greater significance of Swedish working-class institutions
in the life-styles of manual workers. These, he suggests, are so salient in
the political socialisation of working-class youth that they are retained
after the mobility experience.

Similarly, Seeman found in a study of Swedish manual workers that
the experience of alienation at work was not generalised to non-work
situations.[60] He found that these workers were not less knowledgeable
about, or less engaged in, political matters; indeed, they demonstrated
a degree of political and social awareness which he had not found in
similar studies conducted in the United States. He suggests in his study
of Swedish workers that,

It is entirely possible that the effects of work alienation are tempered

by the surrounding social system – in the present case, by the highly
organised, relatively stable, fundamentally democratic and economically advanced order that modern Sweden represents. It is
possible that alienated work, especially at the lower income level, is
something else again in the United States.[61]

Seeman's description of Sweden may be somewhat exaggerated but it
does lend support to the claim that working-class norms and institutions
are highly signficant within the social structure of that country.

By contrast, Britain lacks a similar set of social institutions that have
developed out of the working-class movement and which are salient for
the *non-work* life-styles of manual workers;[62] it appears to be only in
'traditional' working-class communities that such institutions as trade
unions and the Labour Party exercise an organisational and normative
influence of the kind found in Sweden.[63] Indeed, Parkin has argued
that these communities in Britain constitute 'deviant' cases in that they
are characterised by norms and institutions which lead to high levels of
voting for the Labour Party.[64]

In view of such factors, the interests of manual workers tend to be
better represented within the Swedish capitalist system than they are in
Britain; this is certainly the case if the large number of Swedish voluntary associations, pressure groups and co-operatives which represent the
interests of consumers, housing tenants, pensioners, students, the ill and
the handicapped are taken into account.[65] Britain, of course, has
similar organisations but, with a few exceptions, they operate less
effectively as pressure groups, particularly in terms of representing the
interests of various subordinate groups. There is no British equivalent to
the Swedish State Pension Fund which, by 1978, will be the biggest
source of finance in the country; it will have assets greater than those of
all the Swedish banks and credit institutions cominbed. The Fund is
being used to finance the construction of new state factories and to buy
stocks and shares in private industry; an activity which, if continued in
the future, could give the State a controlling interest in many of the
largest Swedish companies.[66] The Commission which oversees invest-
ments made by the Fund consists of eleven members; five from trade
unions, two from private companies, two from local authorities and a
chairman and vice-chairman appointed by the government.

Sweden and Britain, then, are both capitalist countries in which
wealth and income are disproportionately concentrated within restricted groups of individuals. Accordingly, there is a temptation to argue
that the power structures of both countries are similar. But to do so

would be to ignore the differential degree to which the interests of
manual workers are represented in each of the two countries. At the
very least, voluntary associations, labour unions and a succession of
Social Democratic governments have, combined, provided some kind of
'check' and 'balance' to the concentration of private power and wealth
in Sweden; certainly, to a far greater degree than in Britain. However,
some observers of Swedish society have argued that the leadership of
the Social Democratic Party has become 'removed' from the mass
membership and that it no longer represents its interests. They often
claim that the leaders of the party, together with 'Big Business', constitute a national élite.[67]

Certainly, the leadership of the Social Democratic Party consists of
professional, middle-class individuals, but the 'middle-class' character of
the parliamentary Social Democratic Party is probably less than that of
the Labour Party in Britain. In 1937, 53 per cent of Social Democratic
members of Parliament were from manual working-class homes and
although this figure had declined to 47 per cent during the 1960s, the
proportion was higher than among British Labour MPs.[68] For the latter,
36 per cent came from working-class backgrounds in the 1960s and
after the 1970 general election the figure had fallen to 27 per cent.[69]
When Labour and Social Democratic MPs are classified according to
their own occupations, then 28 per cent of both parties consisted of
former industrial manual workers after the 1973 Swedish and the
February 1974 British general elections.[70] Even if the leaders of the
Social Democratic Party are members of a Swedish national élite — and
this has yet to be empirically demonstrated — it can still be argued that
they have pursued at least *some* of the objectives of rank-and-file
members; they certainly have not been the legislative spokesmen of big
business. In fact, over the years, Social Democratic governments have
passed legislation which has been contrary to the financial self-interest
of private business; for example, the creation of the State Pension
Fund[71] and legislation within the areas of consumer protection, price
control, conditions of work and employment, fiscal policies, and so on.
More recently, too, there have been explicit policies to equalise the conditions of service and employment of different categories of manual and
non-manual employees; a commitment which, if implemented, would
substantially increase labour costs in private industry.[72]

If Britain is also characterised by the existence of a power élite —
and this, too, has yet to be proved — it has not generally included
leaders that have been prepared to represent the interests of manual
workers when they have been contrary to the financial objectives of

private business. Except for two periods of any length of time, Britain
has had, up until the mid-1970s, Conservative governments, none of
which have given priority to improving the quality of working life for
industrial workers, the protection of consumers' interests, the streng-
thening of trade unionism and the legislative control of large, privately
owned financial interests. Furthermore, they have made fewer attempts
than the Social Democratic Party to restrict the transmission of
financial privileges from one generation to the next.[73] The extent to
which Conservative governments are reluctant to pass legislation of this
kind can be inferred from an analysis of the business interests of Conservative members of Parliament. Roth, for example, has suggested that
in 1966 among the 253 Conservative members of Parliament, there were
290 company chairmen, 601 company directors, 64 executives and
only two manual workers.[74] Similarly, Spiegelberg found in 1970 that

> just after the election, Members of Parliament with readily identi-
> fiable business interests numbered 218, or just over one-third of the
> House of Commons. Not surprisingly, an overwhelming number were
> Conservative M.P.'s — a mere 27 were Labour.[75]

Thus, it would appear that even if there is a power élite in each of the
two countries, the social composition of these differs to the extent that
the interests of manual workers are better represented in Sweden than
in Britain. This would seem to be the case in view of legislative histories
of the two countries over the past forty years and the degree to which
working-class institutions have acted as 'checks' to the institutional
power of private wealth and property. But having said this, it is clear
that the influence of the Swedish working-class movement has been
directed more to representing the interests of industrial manual workers
*within* a capitalist framework than to changing its structure. The tendency, with some exceptions, has been to pursue reformist welfare
policies rather than to bring about large-scale structural changes. As
Tingsten has argued, the development of the Social Democratic Party
from the late nineteenth century until the 1930s was characterised by a
process of ideological change whereby it became increasingly accepted
by party leaders that economic and social equality could be achieved
within the framework of capitalist society rather than by replacing it
with an alternative economic system.[76] Thus, they have pursued few
policies which can be interpreted as 'anti-capitalist' in the sense of
destroying the predominant role of private property and market forces
in determining the distribution of economic and social resources. How-

ever, although by comparison with socialist countries the power structures of Britain and Sweden may be similar, within the context of capitalist societies the exercise of power in Sweden incorporates the interests of subordinate groups to a greater extent than in Britain where the industrial and political 'wings' of the working-class movement have been less effective in representing the interests of industrial manual workers against the economic and political ambitions of big business.

This chapter has suggested that patterns of economic inequality are similar in Britain and Sweden despite differences in the distribution of wealth. Thus, manual workers in both societies appear to be equally deprived in terms of their share of economic rewards compared to those of other occupational groups.[77] At the same time, the chances for manual workers' sons to be upwardly mobile do not seem to be fundamentally different in the two countries. Furthermore, they seem to have comparable power structures except that in Sweden the interests of subordinate groups are better represented. The reasons for this have already been discussed: namely, the differential normative and institutional effects of working-class movements within each of the two countries. But in view of this, why are there no fundamental differences in patterns of class inequality between Britain and Sweden?

In terms of income distribution and rates of social mobility, it appears that working-class institutions have had little effect in Sweden. In Britain and Sweden distributions of *pre-tax* incomes have remained similar because in both countries income and wage differentials are primarily shaped by market forces. But why do these similarities persist in structures of *post-tax* income? One possible reason is that put forward by a United Nations enquiry on income distribution in different European countries.[78] It states:

Structural changes – such as the falling share of agriculture in manpower distribution and the reduction of self-employment generally – have probably had a more significant influence in dispersion of final household incomes than government policies.[79]

This statement seems as relevant for Sweden as for Britain and other capitalist countries in Europe, despite the fact that the Swedish tax system in the 1970s seems to be more redistributive, and that the Social Democratic Party and LO have pursued policies for greater equality. Until there is greater direct government intervention in the economy, market forces would seem to be more significant than those of Social Democracy in determining income and wage differentials. It is now

Social Democratic policy to participate directly in the decision-making processes of business concerns; the major banks already have government directors on their boards and it is the intention that this should occur in large manufacturing companies. Similarly, the resources of the State Pension Fund have been utilised in order to increase the level of state intervention within the economy. Furthermore, LO has adopted as policy that trade unions should acquire shares in Swedish companies so that in the 1980s they will have majority holdings. If this occurs, it will constitute a fundamental transformation in the nature of Swedish capitalism.[80] Thus, in these ways the Social Democratic Party and LO hope to increase the influence of employees within the economic structure of society and to create a greater degree of economic equality. It is only if such developments continue that the forces of Swedish capitalism will be subject to some kind of challenge by the working-class movement so that income and wage differentials are reduced.

The effects of Social Democracy in increasing rates of social mobility also seems to have been limited. Although the rate of intergenerational mobility between manual and non-manual occupations has increased to a greater extent in Sweden than in Britain since the 1950s this is probably a consequence of changes in the occupational structure; Lipset and Bendix suggest in their comparative study that social mobility of this kind is related to economic change.[81] But it is interesting that both countries should have similar rates of élite mobility, if only because Social Democratic governments have emphasised the need to improve opportunities in society, particularly for those of children from manual working-class homes. Thus, successive governments have completely reorganised the Swedish school system.[82]

Until the early 1950s, Sweden had a highly selective system of education. All children attended elementary schools and either after the fourth or sixth grades the more 'able' were given the opportunity to transfer to secondary schools where they pursued an 'academic' curriculum before going to 'gymnasium' and, often, to university. The rest — those not chosen for secondary education — continued their studies at elementary school before direct entry into the labour market, although some would also attend technical colleges. A consequence of this system, as in many other countries, was that the children from upper- and middle-class homes were more likely to attend the 'gymnasium' than those from working-class backgrounds. For example, in a study of males born in 1934, Härnqvist found that only 35 per cent of pupils with the highest academic grades and from working-class homes transferred to the 'gymnasium', compared with 85 per cent of upper-class children attaining the same level of academic competence.[83] Similarly, in terms of the social origins of university students, only 8 per cent of newly registered students came from working-class homes in 1947.[84]

Since the 1950s there has been a gradual introduction of non-streamed comprehensive schools so that by the late 1970s Sweden will be the only country in non-socialist Europe with a completely non-selective educational system. Furthermore, there is little doubt that these reforms have improved the educational opportunities for working-class children; Reuterberg found that 87 per cent of working-class males born in 1948 and with the highest academic grades transferred from secondary schools to the 'gymnasium' — almost three times as many as those born in 1934.[85] At the same time, there has been a rapid increase in the population of university students from working-class homes; in the academic year 1962/63 working-class entrants accounted for 16 per cent of all places and by 1969 this figure had increased to 20 per cent.[86] In Britain, by contrast, the proportion has remained at about 25 per cent since the pre-war years.[87] Indeed there has been the introduction of a number of measures in Sweden designed to broaden the bases for recruitment into institutions of higher education; student loans and grants have been made more readily available and greater financial assistance has been offered to give individuals 'a second chance', particularly manual workers who have been employed for several years. Thus there are a number of university disciplines which admit students without the formal entrance qualifications provided they are at least 25 years old and have had no less than five years of vocational experience.

Although reforms in the educational system have improved the opportunities for working-class children, there remain important differences in the proportions of children from different social backgrounds that acquire higher educational qualifications. In 1968, a national survey found that even among the youngest age cohort (20-29) the percentage of individuals with fathers in Social Group I and with at least the 'studentexamen' (taken at the termination of studies in the 'gymnasium' and, earlier, a necessary qualification for entry into institutions of higher education) was more than six times greater than for those individuals from Social Group III homes.[88] The figures are shown in Table 2.12.

Reforms have improved the educational opportunities of Swedish working-class children but this does not necessarily mean that their mobility chances have improved within the occupational structure. Within the context of a Swedish economy which is overwhelmingly

Table 2.12: Percentage of individuals in Sweden with the 'student-examen' or other higher educational qualification, according to age and socio-economic background

| Fathers' Social Group | Age of Respondents | | |
|---|---|---|---|
| | 20-29 | 30-54 | 55-75 |
| I | 45 | 42 | 31 |
| II | 12 | 7 | 3 |
| III | 7 | 2 | 1 |
| Total | 12 | 6 | 3 |

Source: L. Johansson, Utbildning — Empirisk Del (Education — Some Empirical Data), Stockholm, 1971, Table 7.46.

privately owned, it is difficult to envisage how recruitment into the more highly rewarded occupations can be 'democratised' without an increase in government intervention. Otherwise, whether or not recruitment into these positions will change must depend upon the personal aptitude of managers and the controllers of private industry who may be far from committed to the Social Democratic goal of greater social equality. As Carlsson has suggested in a discussion of the relationship between education and social mobility, there can be at least two consequences stemming from a broadening of educational opportunity.[89] First, he says,

It is quite conceivable that the very relationship between educational and occupational status may change as a result of the extension of educational services to larger segments of the population. Figuratively speaking, because education is more widespread it might take more education to 'buy' a given type of occupation than was formerly the case.[90]

Secondly, he suggests, 'It might . . . be argued that the more general prevalence of higher education will make . . . employers more prone to take other things into consideration.'[91] Here, presumably, Carlsson is referring to such 'intangible' factors as 'character', 'breadth of vision', 'qualities of leadership' and so on; factors which may lead to discrimination — implicitly if not explicitly — against the selection of applicants from manual working-class homes. In view of this, it is problematic whether Social Democratic governments can broaden the structure of opportunity within society by reforms solely of the educational system and without influencing patterns of recruitment and selection within the occupational structure. In fact, this touches upon one of the major dilemmas confronting any Social Democratic government in a capitalist country; it may be committted to 'meritocratic' and even 'egalitarian' aims, and to promoting the social and economic interests of its working-class supporters but it does so within the context of constraints imposed by the forces of a market economy.[92] Consequently, it is questionable whether such objectives can be achieved without greater state control over these forces.

Thus it seems that similarities between Britain and Sweden in terms of these dimensions of class inequality − mobility rates as well as economic differentials − are largely the outcome of forces operating in any capitalist country. Why, then, has the working-class movement in Sweden accepted the institution of private property when this imposes severe constraints upon ideological commitments? In short, has the Swedish Democratic Party become deradicalised in terms of its objectives, particularly as stated since the turn of the century?[93]

It would be difficult to empirically prove the point, since an analysis of the declared objectives of labour unions and of the Social Democratic Party suggest that these are much the same today as they have always been. What seems to have changed are the tactics which Social Democratic and union leaders regard as legitimate for attaining these objectives; there appears to have been a deradicalisation of *means* rather than of *ends*. Thus, since its inception, the Social Democratic Party has emphasised the desirability of creating a more egalitarian society, in the sense that the distribution of economic and social resources should be allocated according to need rather than on the basis of property relationship and the capitalist mode of production.[94] In the latter part of the nineteenth and during the first two decades of the twentieth century, the Party emphasised the necessity of dismantling capitalism as a *means* whereby egalitarian *ends* could be attained.[95] However, from the 1920s onwards, Party leaders have stressed that egalitarian goals can be achieved by the adoption of welfare-reformist policies within the context of capitalism as a socio-economic system.[96] Thus, it has claimed that by the introduction of progressive taxation and other fiscal measures, inequalities of economic rewards can be reduced while inequalities of opportunity can be abolished by reforms of the educational system. In these ways the leadership of the Social Democratic Party has always been committed to egalitarian goals, although the *means* whereby these can be attained have been subject to revision. Thus, a deradicalisation of *means* has meant that the leaders of

the Social Democratic Party and the trade union movement have
stressed the desirability of 'functional socialism', the ideas of which are
appropriately reflected in a quotation taken from a Social Democratic
thinker, G. Adler-Karlsson:

> Let us look upon our capitalists in the same way as we have looked
> upon our kings in Scandinavia. A hundred years ago a Scandinavian
> king carried a lot of power. Fifty years ago he still had considerable
> power. According to our constitution the king still has equally as
> much formal power as a hundred years ago, but in reality we have
> undressed him of all his power functions so that today he is in fact
> powerless. We have done this without dangerous or disruptive in-
> ternal fights. Let us in the same manner avoid the even more dan-
> gerous contests which are unavoidable if we enter the road of
> formal socialisation. Let us instead strip and divest our present
> capitalists of one after another of their ownership functions. Let us
> even give them a new dress, but one similar to that of the famous
> emperor in H.C. Andersen's tale. After a few decades they will then
> remain, perhaps formally as kings but in reality as naked symbols of
> a passed and inferior stage of development.[97]

If these are the objectives of working-class leaders in Sweden, then it
could be that class inequalities, both in terms of economic rewards and
life chances will, in the long run, be shaped less by the forces of modern
capitalism and more by the political influences of 'functional socialism'.
Certainly, by virtue of enjoying a greater degree of representation both
at the workplace and in society the Swedish working-class movement
might seem to be in a better position to reduce class inequalities than
its counterpart in Britain. Indeed, an increase in the representative
power of the working-class movement is consistent with the ideas of
'functional socialism' and can be regarded as a means for attaining, over
time, this end.

If, in Sweden, there is a strong Social Democratic ideology of egalitarianism within the context of a society characterised by marked
social and economic inequalities, has this created socio-political
tensions, particularly among industrial manual workers? More specifically, do Swedish manual workers — whose interests the Social Democratic Party and LO claim to represent — perceive the class structure
differently to workers in Britain where ideological egalitarianism has
been less pronounced? As Parkin has suggested,

although there is a factual and material basis to class inequality, there is more than one way in which it can be interpreted. Facts alone do not provide meanings and the way a person makes sense of his social world will be influenced by the nature of the *meaning systems* he draws upon.[98]

How, then, has Social Democracy affected Swedish workers' interpretations of the class structure? In order to answer this question it is necessary to refer to the findings of a social survey conducted among two samples of English and Swedish industrial manual workers.

## Notes

1. It should be emphasised that these are only two, although the major, aspects of economic condition. In addition, there are, for example, the effects of social welfare provisions. In both Britain and Sweden social scientists have documented patterns of government expenditure and tried to calculate the redistributive effects of these for different income groups. But the conclusions of these enquiries have been so tentative that little can be said with confidence of whether social policies are more redistributive in one country than in the other. For a recent attempt at comparing a large number of countries see H. Wilensky, *The Welfare State and Equality*, London, 1975. For a detailed account of the development of the welfare state in Britain and Sweden, see H. Heclo, *Modern Social Policies in Britain and Sweden*, New Haven, 1974. Unfortunately Heclo does not discuss the possible redistributive effects of social welfare in the two countries.
2. For a discussion of the many problems relating to the comparative study of income distributions, see United Nations, *Incomes in Post-War Europe*, Geneva, 1967, Ch. 6.
3. Only the more important developments will be described. For a detailed account of trends in Britain see The Royal Commission on Income and Wealth *Report No. 1*, London, 1975; and for Sweden, R. Spånt, *Den Svenska Inkomstfördelningens Utveckling (The Development of the Distribution of Income in Sweden)*, Uppsala, 1976.
4. Bentzel claims that about 25 per cent of the process towards greater income equalisation between the mid-1930s and late 1940s can be regarded as a consequence of 'fiscal' forces and the remaining 75 per cent to various structural changes in the economy. See R. Bentzel, *Inkomstfördelningen i Sverige (The Distribution of Income in Sweden)*, Stockholm, 1952.
5. See Table 2.2 below.
6. United Nations, 1967, op. cit., Ch. 6, p. 24.
7. Reforms in the Swedish tax system were introduced in 1971.
8. For a discussion of the advantages of estimating the distribution of income on the basis of Family Expenditure Surveys compared with Inland Revenue statistics on tax units, see the Royal Commission, op. cit., Ch. 4.
9. J. Mouly, 'Wages Policy in Sweden', *International Labour Review*, Vol. 95 (1967).

10.  P. Holmberg, *Arbete och Löner i Sverige (Work and Wages in Sweden)*, Solna, 1963.
11.  S. Johansson, *Inkomstutvecklingen, 1966-1969 (The Development of Incomes, 1966-1969)*, mimeo., 1972.
12.  Holmberg claims that with the average earnings of all industrial manual workers indexed at 100, lower-grade white-collar workers earned 138 in 1950 and 141 in 1960. In 1968, according to Johansson, the figure was 143. See, Holmberg, op. cit., and Johansson, op. cit.
13.  G. Routh, *Occupation and Pay in Great Britain*, Cambridge, 1965.
14.  For a thorough statistical confirmation of these trends see, for Britain, J. Westergaard and H. Resler, *Class in a Capitalist Society*, London, 1975, Part Two; and, for Sweden, R. Spånt, op. cit.
15.  LO wage policies are discussed by R. Meidner, 'Samordning och Solidarisk Lönepolitik under Tre Decennier', ('Coordination and Policy of Wage Solidarity'), in LO, *Tvärsnitt (Cross-Section)*, Stockholm, 1973.
16.  J. Ullenhag, *Den Solidariska Lönepolitiken i Sverige (The Policy of Wage Solidarity in Sweden)*, Stockholm, 1971.
17.  J. Mouly, op. cit.
18.  In 1964, for example, the 'top' 50 per cent owned 75 per cent of the wealth. See Statens Offentliga Utredningar (SOU), *Ägande och Inflytande inom det Privata Näringslivet (Ownership and Influence in the Private Economy)*, Stockholm, 1968, Table 6.4. A possible explanation for the more equal distribution of wealth in Sweden could be the widespread ownership of second homes in the form of summer houses. However, these tend to be owned more by white-collar workers than by manual workers.
19.  S. Miller, 'Comparative Social Mobility', *Current Sociology*, Vol. 9 (1960).
20.  This statement is made in the absence of recent data for Britain. However, research into national mobility trends which is currently being undertaken by J.H. Goldthorpe and his associates at Nuffield College, Oxford, may show that the rate of mobility has also increased in Britain.
21.  R. Erikson, *Uppväxtförhallånden och Social Rörlighet (Childhood Living Conditions and Social Mobility)*, Stockholm, 1971.
22.  G. Carlsson, *Social Mobility and Class Structure*, Lund, 1958.
23.  T. Noble, 'Social Mobility and Class Relations in Britain', *British Journal of Sociology*, Vol. 23 (1972). It is important to stress, however, that Noble's review does not give a comprehensive picture.
24.  D. Glass, *Social Mobility in Britain*, London, 1967.
25.  S. Lipset and R. Bendix, *Social Mobility in Industrial Society*, California, 1959.
26.  S. Miller, op. cit., Table 7.
27.  G. Malmeström and B. Widenborg, '245 Svenska Företagsledare' ('245 Swedish Business Leaders'), *Studier och Debatt* (1958), Diagram 1.
28.  R. Clements, *Managers: A Study of their Careers in Industry*, London, 1958.
29.  G. Copeman, *Leaders of British Industry*, London, 1955.
30.  G. Copeman, op. cit., Table 14.2.
31.  D. Clark, *The Industrial Manager: His Background and Career Pattern*, London, 1966.
32.  T. Nichols, *Ownership, Control and Ideology*, London, 1969.
33.  P. Stanworth and A. Giddens, 'An Economic Elite: A Demographic Profile of Company Chairmen', in P. Stanworth and A. Giddens (eds.), *Elites and Power in British Society*, London, 1974.
34.  R. Whitely, 'The City and Industry: The Directors of Large Companies, their Characteristics and Connections', in P. Stanworth and A. Giddens

Class Inequality in Britain and Sweden 83

(eds.), op. cit.
35. S. Landström, 'Svenska Ämbetsmäns Sociala Ursprung' ('The Social
    Background of Higher Civil Servants in Sweden'), *Statsvetenskapliga
    Föreningen i Uppsala*, Vol. 34 (1954).
36. K. Samuelsson, *From Great Power to Welfare State*, London, 1968, p. 285.
37. U. Christoffersson, B. Molin, L. Månsson and L. Strömberg, *Byråkrati och
    Politik (Bureaucracy and Politics)*, Stockholm, 1972.
38. R. Kelsall, *Higher Civil Servants in Britain*, London, 1955, Table 26.
39. R. Kelsall, 'Recruitment to the Higher Civil Service: How has the Pattern
    Changed?', in P. Stanworth and A. Giddens (eds.), *op. cit.*, p. 174.
40. G. Petrén, *Några Uppgifter om Proffessorskåren i Uppsala och Lund under
    1800 Talet och Första Halften av 1900 Talet (Some Information on
    Professors at Uppsala and Lund during the Nineteenth and the First Half of
    the Twentieth Centuries)*, Lund, 1952.
41. S. Carlsson, *Bonde-Präst-Ämbetsman (Farmer, Priest and Official)*, Stock-
    holm, 1962.
42. A. Halsey and M. Trow, *The British Academics*, London, 1971.
43. W. Guttsman, 'The British Political Elite and the Class Structure' in
    P. Stanworth and A. Giddens (eds.), op. cit.
44. C. Otley, 'The Public Schools and the Army' in J. Urry and J. Wakeford
    (eds.), *Power in Britain*, London, 1973.
45. K. Thompson, 'Church of England Bishops as an Elite', in P. Stanworth
    and A. Giddens (eds.), op. cit.
46. Statens Offentliga Utredningar (SOU), op. cit. Ch. 1.
47. M. Barratt Brown, 'The Controllers of British Industry' in J. Urry and
    J. Wakeford, op. cit., Table 7.3.
48. This view was widely expressed in Sweden during the winter of 1969 when
    an unofficial strike was called by workers in the state-owned iron-ore
    mines of the north of Sweden. In the initial stages this was a conflict be-
    tween a 'coalition' of union leaders, management and the Social Demo-
    cratic government against rank-and-file workers.
49. LO's policy of 'wage solidarity', together with the desire to reduce wage
    differentials within the economy, has been the basis for friction among
    labour unions. One of the factors contributing to the strike by workers in
    the iron-ore mines in the winter of 1969 was LO's proposal that lower per-
    centage wage increases should be negotiated for miners than for lower-
    paid occupations.
50. LO's policies for the 'democratisation' of companies are summarised by
    B. Schiller, 'LO Paragraph 32 och Företagsdemokratin' ('LO, Paragraph 32
    and Company Democracy'), in *Tvärsnitt (Cross-Section)*, op. cit.; and in
    LO, *Demokrati i Företagen (Democracy in Companies)*, Stockholm, 1971.
51. For a more detailed discussion of the two factories, see Chapter 3.
52. Of course, even in the English factory manual workers were able to impose
    constraints upon management, especially on the shop floor. But these were,
    on the whole, less institutionalised and less effective in protecting the
    interests of individual employees; particularly in relation to such matters
    as dismissal procedures.
53. For the relevant statistical data on union membership in Sweden, see
    Chapter One.
54. For example, before the 1970 Swedish General Election, LO distributed
    literature and financed a large publicity campaign stating, 'De Sociala
    Orättvisorna i Jobbet ska Bort! Med en Social Demokratisk Regering kan
    vi Klara Det' ('Social Injustices at Work Must be Removed! This can be
    done with a Social Democratic government').

55. Between 1945 and 1951 and then from 1964 until 1970.
56. B. Anderson, 'Some Problems of Change in the Swedish Electorate', *Acta Sociologica*, Vol. 6 (1962).
57. See B. Anderson, op. cit.
58. B. Anderson, 'Opinion Influentials and Political Opinion Formation in Four Swedish Communities', *International Social Science Journal*, Vol. 14 (1962).
59. B. Anderson, 'Some Problems of Change', op. cit.
60. M. Seeman, 'On the Personal Consequences of Alienation in Work', *American Sociological Review*, Vol. 32 (1967).
61. M. Seeman, op. cit., p. 284.
62. 'Nationalised' industries can therefore be discounted for the purposes of the present discussion. In any case, they can hardly be regarded as a source of working-class norms.
63. It is only in these communities that working-class institutions, particularly trade unions and the Labour Party, play any significant role in the life-styles of manual workers.
64. F. Parkin, 'Working Class Conservatives: A Theory of Political Deviance', *British Journal of Sociology*, Vol. 18 (1967).
65. The role of voluntary associations in Sweden is documented by N. Elvander, *Intresseorganisationerna i Dagens Sverige (Interest Groups in Contemporary Sweden)*, Lund, 1966.
66. By July 1974, the Fund had bought shares in several large Swedish companies including Aga, Asea, Atlas Copco, LM Ericsson, SAAB-Scania, Volvo, Sandviken Steel and Perstop. Altogether it had acquired shares in twenty-three large companies. See *Dagens Nyheter*, 3 July 1974.
67. The strike in the state-owned mines during the winter of 1969 is frequently used as an example of this. See footnote 48 above.
68. L. Sköld and A. Halvarson, 'Riksdagens Sociala Sammansättning under Hundra År', ('The Social Composition of Parliament during 100 years'), in *Samhället och Riksdag, Del. I. (Society and Parliament, Part I)*, Stockholm, 1966.
69. W. Guttsman, op. cit., Table 6.
70. Calculated from D. Butler and D. Kavanagh, *The British Election of February 1974*, London, 1974, p. 214; and O. Petersson and B. Särlvik, 'The 1973 Election', *General Elections 1973, Vol. 3*, Central Bureau of Statistics, Stockholm, 1975, Table 1.4.
71. It is the intention of the Social Democratic Party and LO that the resources of the State Pension Fund should be used to inject financial resources into private industry so that these will provide a means whereby it will be possible to 'democratise' the authority relations of companies in the interests of their employees.
72. In the 1970 General Election, the Social Democratic Party adopted for its campaign the phrase 'Ökad Jämlikhet – för ett Rättvisare Samhälle' 'Increased Equality – for a More Just Society'. Since this election, issues of equality have continued to be at the centre of political debate in Sweden. They have also been widely discussed in all sectors of society, particularly in the press and on television.
73. For example, the British Conservative Party has never argued for the introduction of wealth and gift taxes.
74. A. Roth, *The Business Background of MPs*, London, 1972, p. 24.
75. R. Spiegelberg, 'Parliamentary Business', *The Times*, 3 July 1970.
76. H. Tingsten, *The Swedish Social Democrats*, New Jersey, 1973.
77. This is stated with the qualification that this analysis has made no attempt

to assess the redistributive effects of the British and the Swedish welfare systems. See note 1 above.

78. United Nations, 1967, op. cit.
79. United Nations, 1967, op. cit., Ch. 6, p. 41.
80. Landsorganisation (LO), *Kollektiv Kapital Bildning Genom Löntagarfonder (Capital Formation Through the Wage Earners' Fund)*, Lund, 1976.
81. S. Lipset and R. Bendix, op. cit.
82. For a concise discussion of reforms in the Swedish educational system, see R. Tomasson, *Sweden: Prototype of Modern Society*, New York, 1970, Chs. 4 and 5.
83. K. Härnqvist, *Reserverna För Högre Utbildning (Reserves of Talent for Higher Education)*, Stockholm, 1958.
84. J. Israel, 'Uppforstran och Utbildning' ('Socialisation and Education'), in E. Dahlström (ed.), *Svensk Samhällsstruktur i Sociologisk Belysning (Sociological Perspectives in the Swedish Social Structure)*, Stockholm, 1969, Table 13.9.
85. S.-E. Reuterberg, *Val av Teoretisk Utbildning i Relation till Sociala och Regionala Bakgrundsfaktorer (Choice of 'Academic' Education in Relation to Social and Regional Background)*, mimeo, Gothenburg, 1968.
86. Statens Offentliga Utredningar (SOU), *Val Av Utbildning och Yrke (Choice of Education and Work)*, Stockholm, 1971.
87. Committee on Higher Education (The Robbins Report), *Higher Education*, London, 1963, Appendix 2. However, it appears that in 1969, 30 per cent of British university undergraduates came from manual working-class homes. See H. Glennerster, 'Education and Inequality', in P. Townsend and N. Bosanquet, *Labour and Inequality*, London, 1972, p. 90.
88. L. Johansson, *Utbildning – Empirisk Del (Education – Some Empirical Data)*, Stockholm, 1971.
89. G. Carlsson, op. cit.
90. G. Carlsson, op. cit., p. 122-3.
91. G. Carlsson, op. cit., p. 126.
92. Of course, meritocratic selection is quite compatible with capitalism and should not be regarded exclusively as a 'socialist' doctrine. However, in capitalist societies meritocratic criteria are often applied to individuals who are the 'products' of educational and parental privileges. One of the policies of the Swedish Social Democratic Party has been the attempt to remove the influence of such privileges. See A. Myrdal, *Towards Equality*, Stockholm, 1971.
93. Michels has argued that as socialist movements develop and become successful, their political objectives become deradicalised. See R. Michels, *Political Parties*, New York, 1962.
94. See H. Tingsten, op. cit.; A. Myrdal, op. cit.; *Tvarsnitt (Cross-Section)*, op. cit.
95. H. Tingsten, op. cit.
96. H. Tingsten, op. cit.
97. G. Adler-Karlsson, *Functional Socialism*, Stockholm, 1967, pp. 101-2.
98. F. Parkin, *Class Inequality and Political Order*, London, 1971, p. 81.

# 3  THE SOCIAL SURVEY: A STUDY OF ATTITUDES AMONG TWO SAMPLES OF WORKERS

In order to investigate conceptions of class inequality in the two countries, it would be desirable to conduct a social survey of attitudes among representative samples of the populations. However, such an exercise would be costly, both in time and finance. Consequently, consideration was given to the possibility of conducting a modest investigation which, although unable to produce results generalisable to the total populations, would be *indicative* of patterns within the two countries. Two alternatives were considered as feasible; either to undertake a comparative study of random samples chosen from two communities — one in Sweden and the other in Britain — or to compare samples taken from similar occupational groups. The first was rejected on the grounds that the problems of matching 'like' with 'like' would be too great. It was found to be almost impossible to identify two English and Swedish communities that could be 'matched' according to size, industrial structure, political institutions, ecological arrangement and so on. In view of this, it was decided to compare matched samples of manual workers in the two countries. The major reason for this was that it would enable comparisons to be made of individuals occupying fairly similar positions within the two social structures. As Chapter 1 has shown, Britain and Sweden — despite their differences — have similar occupational structures. Chapter 2 has also suggested that the position of manual workers within the two class structures is highly comparable. Therefore, it was considered that by studying matched samples of workers it would be possible to determine the degree to which they held common conceptions of the respective class structures. More specifically, it would enable an assessment of whether similarities in the structural location of these workers were conducive to the development of similar attitudes and conceptions, or whether the ideological influences of the Swedish labour movement had affected interpretations. In order to investigate this, the two samples were chosen so that they had a number of common characteristics, both in relation to their occupational roles and their personal attributes.

The samples were chosen from two factories; one in each country. It is not possible to name these since management in both places co-operated on the condition that there was complete anonymity. However, the two factories can be described – if only in fairly rudimentary terms – in order to show that they did share a number of common characteristics. In the first place, they manufactured similar products; in each, a wide range of engineering components was produced. These varied from the construction of heavy equipment to the production of small, complex pieces of machinery. In addition, both factories had departments that were primarily concerned with servicing and repairing equipment owned by each of the two parent organisations.[1] Secondly, the two factories had similar technologies. In both places, the productive process enabled employees to communicate with each other while they were working, and for a large number of the tasks to be undertaken by work teams. The division of labour, although complex in the two workplaces, was less developed than that normally associated with assembly-line technology. Although tasks were broken into a number of specialised activities, they were less standardised than those found in, for example, the automobile industry.[2] Both factories had a number of workshops so that, depending on the tasks undertaken, there were variations in the size of work groups, the routinisation of work, and the degree to which operatives could regulate their output. Perhaps the major difference between the two factories was that the Swedish work-place was more highly capitalised than the English; a large number of tasks undertaken by machinery in the former were performed by manual labour in the latter.[3] There are a number of reasons for this, which include the more recent origins of the Swedish factory, its higher level of capital investment, and the greater pressure by trade unions on management to improve the quality of working life.[4] Nevertheless, despite this difference, the similar technologies of the two factories imposed common constraints upon work tasks; the activities of workers in both places were characterised more by similarities than contrasts. Thirdly, both factories were owned by organisations operating in 'static' or even contracting markets; neither had experienced growth over recent years and there was little expectation among managers and workers that this was likely to occur within the foreseeable future. However, at the time of the investigation, neither factory was confronted with the likelihood of redundancies and there was a general assumption among both work-forces that employment was secure. Finally, both factories were located in communities of the same size; the Swedish in a town of 25,000 and the English in one of 28,000 inhabitants.

Although the factories were similar in their products, technologies, market situations and community settings, they differed in two important respects. First, work and employment conditions by any *absolute* standard of comparison were much better in the Swedish factory. This was evident in the quality of heating, lighting and ventilation, in the provision of social and recreational amenities and in the general regulations controlling industrial safety and the use of machinery.[5] To some extent this was a reflection of the more recent origins of the Swedish factory, but it was also a consequence of the activities of the union movement. Swedish trade unions have given a high priority to the need for improvements in the working conditions of their members and also, particularly over recent years, for an erosion in differentials in the employment conditions of white-collar and manual workers.[6] Consequently, an important contrast between the two factories was that for many aspects of the employment relationship, manual and white-collar workers were treated more equally in the Swedish factory than in the English.[7] In the former, for example, both categories of workers were paid on a monthly basis although manual workers could, if they wish, receive their earnings at the end of every two weeks.[8] By contrast, manual workers in the English factory were paid weekly and white-collar workers monthly. In the case of dismissal procedures, as mentioned in Chapter 2, there were greater formal provisions for trade union representation in the Swedish than in the English factory. At the same time, in the event of a dismissal, Swedish manual workers were given three weeks' notice compared to one month for white-collar workers. In the English factory, by comparison, manual workers were given only one weeks' notice compared with the one month given to office workers. A further example of reduced differentials in the treatment of manual and white-collar workers in the Swedish factory was that manual workers were allowed to take fifteen days off work each year for personal reasons and for these they were paid 70 per cent of their average earnings. White-collar workers were also entitled to the same benefit, but no deduction was taken from their pay. In the English factory, on the other hand, manual workers were given no days off with pay for personal reasons — except to attend the funeral of a relative — and yet white-collar workers were granted days off for personal reasons without the loss of earnings.

   Although the working conditions of the Swedish sample were better than those of their English counterparts according to any absolute measure so, too, they were in a relative sense; that is, by comparison to those of white-collar workers. In terms of quality of lighting, ventilation, sanitation and heating, differences in provisions for manual and white-collar workers were less in the Swedish factory than in the English workplace.[9] This cannot be explained solely by reference to the more recent origin of the Swedish factory; consideration must also be given to the aims of Swedish trade unions and the legislative effects of successive Social Democratic governments.[10]

The second major difference between the two factories was that the Swedish workplace was smaller than the English; in spring 1970 there were 298 manual workers employed in the former compared with 972 in the latter. This difference could have had important consequences for industrial behaviour, particularly manager-worker relationships, and the frequency of industrial disputes.[11] But this does not seem to have been the case; strikes were virtually unknown in both factories and by comparison with other industries in the two countries there had been little industrial unrest.[12] Whether differences in size affected the samples' conceptions of inequality is difficult to ascertain since this was not investigated by the enquiry. But various studies have suggested that small workplaces are conducive to face-to-face contacts between managers and workers and that deferential attitudes are likely to develop.[13] If this is the case, then it could be expected that the Swedish workers would be more deferential than the English. However, it is reasonable to assume that the size of the Swedish factory did not have this consequence; although it was smaller than the English workplace, it was still too large to encourage close face-to-face relationships between managers and workers. Indeed, many studies of the connection between deference and organisational size have tended to refer to smaller workplaces. In fact, even if the appropriate conditions had existed within the Swedish factory, it is unlikely that deferential attitudes would have emerged if only because, as suggested in Chapters 1 and 2, of the normative influence exercised by the Social Democratic Party and the labour unions. Ideally it would have been desirable to have chosen samples employed in factories of a similar size but it was impossible to find workplaces of this kind.[14]

As far as wage differentials are concerned, it is difficult to make accurate calculations because earnings in both factories, particularly those of non-manual workers, varied according to age and length of service. Moreover, management, especially in the English factory, were reluctant to give detailed information about the structure of wages and salaries although they were prepared to give 'approximate' earnings. This information suggested that for the English factory in 1970 the highest-paid manual workers (skilled) could earn approximately £30 a week, or £1,560 a year, 'senior clerical officers' up to £2,000 a year and 'senior management' up to £4,500. In the Swedish factory during the same year, the highest-paid manual workers (skilled) could earn about

3,000 kr. a month, white-collar employees about 4,000 kr. and senior managers up to 6,750 kr. Thus, in terms of the remuneration of the more highly paid manual workers and senior management, there was less inequality within the Swedish workplace than in the English; the earnings of the Swedish senior managers were approximately two-and-a-quarter times more than those of highly paid manual workers, while those of their English counterparts could be as much as three times greater. However, differences in the earnings of these 'affluent' manual workers and white-collar employees were about the same in both work-places; 'higher' white-collar workers could be earning something like one-third more by the time they were forty years old. At the younger age levels, particularly among employees in their late teens and early twenties, there was often an overlap between the earnings of these two groups. But it must be emphasised that the above differentials refer to those that exist between the *highest-paid* manual workers and other occupational groups. It would, of course, have been useful to have had information on the earnings of all occupational and age categories but the reluctance of management, particularly in the English factory, pre-vented this. Data of this kind, disclosing the earnings of such low-paid groups as teenage clerks and young manual workers, would almost certainly have shown that wage differentials *within* the two factories were greater than those described above. In the absence of this infor-mation it was considered appropriate to describe differences by reference to the *highest* earnings that members of each occupational category coul1 hope to acquire; an analysis which does suggest that the position of manual workers within the reward structures of the two factories was more or less the same.

The two samples were chosen from manual workers between the ages of 25 and 54. This was in order to hold constant — as far as possible — stage in the family cycle and work career. Younger workers were excluded on the grounds that occupational preferences may not be firmly fixed and that attachment to present employment would be less than well established. It was also considered that a high proportion of workers under 25 years old would be either single or only recently married. These workers, then, were excluded on the grounds that factors of this kind could have implications for their conceptions of inequality.[15] Consequently, the samples were drawn from workers whose positions within the reward structures of the two countries were well established; they would be unlikely to change jobs with any degree of frequency and their attitudes would be *indicative* of opinions held among middle-aged, industrial manual workers. It was also for these

reasons that workers over the age of 54 were excluded; they would be
approaching retirement and their family responsibilities would be less
than those of younger workers.

In order to select the samples, management in the two factories gave
information listing the names, addresses and ages of all manual employees. Whereas the Swedish management was obliged to consult trade
union officials before deciding whether or not the research could be
undertaken, their English colleagues considered themselves to be under
no such obligation.[16] Furthermore, once this approval had been given,
the Swedish management was positively interested in the project and
not suspicious of its objectives in the same manner as its English
counterpart. Indeed, the sole involvement of the latter was to provide
the names, addresses and ages of employees, and to give the approximate earnings of different occupational groups. Other than this, it was
reluctant to be involved in the study.[17] Consequently, one of the major
limitations of the enquiry is that there is insufficient detail about
earnings and wage differentials among employees in the two factories
from which the samples were chosen.

Of the 298 Swedish manual workers, 141 were between the ages of
25 and 54. Every attempt was made to obtain the co-operation of each
of these and by the end of the study, 122 had participated. Of the 19
non-respondents, 13 refused to take part and 6 persistently postponed
an arranged appointment with the research worker. Consequently, there
was an overall response rate of 87 per cent for this group of workers.

In the English factory there were 528 manual workers between 25
and 54 years old. Because of financial constraints, it was impossible to
interview more than one in three of these. Consequently, 176 workers
were asked to take part in the enquiry but with 39 refusals and 9 others
who continually postponed appointments, 128 finally co-operated with
the study, providing a response rate of 73 per cent. There was no
attempt to investigate the characteristics of these non-respondents
except that among the 39 English 'refusals', 62 per cent (24) were
within the oldest age group; that is, between 45 and 54 years of age.
The characteristics of the two samples in terms of age distribution and
marital status are shown in Tables 3.1 and 3.2.

Table 3.1 shows that the only difference between the samples
was the slightly higher proportion of younger workers among the
English respondents.

The proportion of married respondents within the samples was much
the same; over 85 per cent in each case. The only major difference was
the higher representation of single men among the Swedish workers. On

the other hand, only one of the Swedish respondents was widowed
compared with five of the English workers.

Table 3.1: The age distributions of the two samples

| Age | Swedish Workers | | English Workers | |
|---|---|---|---|---|
| | Nos. | % | Nos. | % |
| 25 - 34 | 17 | 13.9 | 22 | 17.2 |
| 35 - 44 | 31 | 25.4 | 32 | 25.0 |
| 45 - 54 | 74 | 60.7 | 74 | 57.8 |
| Total | 122 | 100.0 | 128 | 100.0 |

Table 3.2: Marital status among the two samples

| Marital status | Swedish Workers | | English Workers | |
|---|---|---|---|---|
| | Nos. | % | Nos. | % |
| Married | 104 | 85.3 | 111 | 86.7 |
| Single | 16 | 13.1 | 11 | 8.6 |
| Widowed | 1 | 0.8 | 5 | 3.9 |
| Divorced | 1 | 0.8 | 1 | 0.8 |
| Total | 122 | 100.0 | 128 | 100.0 |

The two samples, then, shared a number of common characteristics;
their occupational roles and their work environments displayed a number of similarities, and as married men, they represented a comparable
range of ages. Consequently, these groups of workers may be regarded
as occupying similar positions within the two social structures.
Obviously they were not identical; it would be extremely difficult to
find groups which were exactly comparable according to *all* characteristics. Indeed, it would be strange if there were no differences both
within and between the samples in relation to life-style, work experience,
geographical and social mobility, family background and place of resi-
dence. All these factors could, conceivably, affect respondents' conceptions of social and economic inequality. But if an attempt was made
to obtain groups of workers in the two countries which could be
matched according to such factors, then the chances of obtaining a
sufficient number of cases for the purposes of comparative analysis
would be extremely limited. Thus, the two samples were only comparable at an unsophisticated level. But in spite of this, they shared

sufficient characteristics to be seen as similar 'types' of industrial worker in the two countries. But can they be regarded as representative of the two populations?

Because they were chosen from particular industrial and work environments, their representativeness is limited; their attitudes cannot be interpreted as typical of opinions within the two countries. They were chosen from workplaces which, like all industrial environments, have their own specific characteristics. Every industry has a tradition of technological change, industrial conflict, labour-management relations, and so on. The industries from which the samples were chosen were very alike in these respects. In both, labour relations were considered to be good and there had been very little industrial conflict.[18] The two employers had reputations for offering secure work and there had rarely been redundancies. Furthermore, neither industry was renowned for its technological innovation; within the respective countries, they had reputations for being 'conservative' and 'traditional'. Such characteristics mean that the respondents cannot be seen as typical of *all* industrial workers in the two countries. Thus, it is important to stress the dangers of generalising from the conclusions of this study and to bear in mind that the groups of workers were in no way statistically representative of the British and Swedish populations.

Despite this, however, it is still possible to make statements about attitudes in the two countries, even if they must be treated with caution. Although the samples were chosen from particular industries, they were also selected from two social structures, each of which consisted of norms, values, ideologies and institutions. Consequently, although industrial and occupational roles may shape workers' attitudes and experiences, these are also determined by 'wider' normative and institutional influences. Therefore, the two groups of workers may have articulated certain occupational ideologies but, at the same time, they reflected more widely held beliefs within the two countries. If, then, the opinions of the samples cannot be regarded as representative of those of the more general populations they can, at least, be seen as *indicative* of them. But the present enquiry is only exploratory; large-scale social surveys will be needed to substantiate whether or not the attitudes of the two samples are more widely shared in the two countries.

The data were collected from interviews with the respondents in the spring of 1970. A number of alternatives were considered before the final procedure was adopted. At first it was thought appropriate to conduct in-depth and relatively unstructured 'conversations' on the grounds that the subject matter of the enquiry prevented the fruitful use of questionnaires. Many investigators, for example, have argued that interview schedules are inappropriate for obtaining information about conceptions of inequality since they often include terms which are subject to wide and varied interpretation.[19] Therefore, an attempt was made to avoid the use of poll-type questions in the present enquiry. Twelve pilot interviews were conducted with manual workers in the two countries, each of which lasted approximately three hours. These were recorded on tapes and then transcribed. However, it soon became evident, despite the fact that the collection of data in this way could provide useful insights into attitudes, that little more could be achieved. Consequently, a more quantitative approach was adopted using the fairly structured questionnaire schedule. Although this procedure posed many of the problems relating to the use of poll-type questionnaires, it was considered that many of these could be avoided if great care was taken to ensure that respondents understood and defined the meaning of words such as, for example 'inequality', 'social class', 'power', and so on. This approach did not completely solve the difficulties relating to respondents' interpretations of questions or to the investigator's interpretations of responses, but it would be a mistake to assume that the interviews revealed *nothing* about the two groups' conceptions of society.[20] However, because the research was cross-national there were difficulties in ensuring that the questions would stimulate similar meanings among the two samples. In an attempt to deal with this, the following procedure was adopted.

On the basis of an analysis of the twelve pilot interviews, a draft questionnaire was produced in English. This was then tested with twelve workers and as a result of these interviews, the schedule was reformulated and used for the social survey. At the same time, the schedule was translated into Swedish and discussed with Swedish sociologists who compared it with the original English schedule.[21] They suggested a number of alterations which, in their view, would generate similar meanings for Swedish workers as the original version was supposed to do for the English sample. The schedule was then tested with six Swedish workers, reformulated and tested with a further six workers. A final questionnaire was then produced. Thus, there was every effort to ensure that the schedule was as similar as possible for both groups of workers; not in a 'literal' but in a 'sociological' sense.[22]

All of the Swedish and most of the English interviews were conducted by a research worker who was fluent in both languages.[23] She was Swedish by birth and had lived in both countries. While conducting the interviews she gave no indication to the respondents that they were taking part in a cross-national study. It was felt that an awareness of this may affect their attitudes towards inequality; notions of nationalism could conceal other consistently held beliefs.

The next three chapters present the results of the interview survey. Chapter 4 discusses the samples' conceptions of the respective class structures, together with their opinions about the opportunities for mobility within them. This is followed, in Chapter 5, by a discussion of their attitudes towards the distribution of economic rewards. Finally, in Chapter 6, there is an analysis of their beliefs about the distribution of power in society. In other words, whereas Chapter 2 described patterns of social, economic and political inequalities, the next three investigate workers' conceptions of them. Although the respondents' attitudes cannot be regarded as representative of more widely held beliefs in Britain and Sweden they are, more likely than not, *indicative* of them.[24]

## Notes

1. Both factories were owned by large national corporations.
2. For a discussion of the relationship between work tasks and assembly-line technology, see J. Goldthorpe, D. Lockwood, F. Bechhofer and J. Platt, *The Affluent Worker: Industrial Attitudes and Behaviour*, Cambridge, 1968; and H. Beynon, *Working for Ford*, Harmondsworth, 1973.
3. This was particularly evident in the movement of materials, components and equipment between workshops and from one area of the shop floor to another.
4. Swedish trade unions more than English unions have, since the 1930s, argued with governments and employers for the need to improve the quality of the working environment for their members. This has been related to LO's concern with the physical and psychological health of rank-and-file members and the frequency of industrial accidents. For a statement of LO's policy, together with data on working conditions as experienced by a sample of workers, see E. Bolinder, E. Magnusson and L. Nyren, Risker i Jobbet *(Risk at Work)*, Stockholm, 1970.
5. These comments are based on personal observations of conditions in the two factories.
6. As mentioned in Chapter 2, in the 1970 General Election, for example, LO financed a large publicity campaign, stating 'De Sociala Orättvisorna i Jobbet ska Bort! Med en Social Demokratisk Regering kan vi Klara Det.' ('Social Injustice at Work must be Removed! This can be done with a Social Democratic Government.') One of the major injustices which LO has stressed is the difference in the employment conditions of manual and non-manual workers in many Swedish factories; particularly in terms of hours of work, sickness and pension schemes and various fringe benefits.
7. For a comparison of differences in conditions of employment for various occupational groups in Britain, see D. Wedderburn and C. Craig, 'Relative

Deprivation in Work' in D. Wedderburn (ed.), *Poverty, Inequality and Class Structure,* London, 1974; for differences in Sweden, see H. Hart and C. V.-Otter, 'The Determination of Wages in Swedish Industry', in R. Scase (ed.), *Readings in the Swedish Class Structure,* Oxford, 1976.

8. This and the following information about conditions of employment was obtained from interviews with management and trade union officials in the two factories.

9. This is based on personal observation of conditions in the factories.

10. See note 4 above.

11. For a discussion of the relationship between organisational size and workers' attitudes, see G. Ingham, *Size of Industrial Organisation and Worker Behaviour,* Cambridge, 1970; and H. Newby, 'Paternalism and Capitalism' in R. Scase (ed.), *Industrial Society: Class, Cleavage and Control,* London, 1977.

12. According to information provided by management and union officials in the two workplaces.

13. See, for example, the discussion by H. Newby, op. cit.; and various contributions in M. Bulmer (ed.), *Working-Class Images of Society,* London, 1975.

14. And, at the same time, have a large number of other highly comparable characteristics.

15. For a discussion of the relationship between age, stage in the family cycle and work satisfaction, see H. Wilensky, 'Work as a Social Problem', in H. Becker (ed.), *Social Problems: A Modern Approach,* London, 1966.

16. This is a clear indication of the degree to which management in the Swedish workplace felt more constrained by union influence.

17. One of the major reasons was that senior management in the English factory identified sociology with 'left-wing' political activism. The research was conducted in a year (1970) when there was considerable and highly publicised student protest in English universities.

18. This and the following comments are based on interviews with management and union officials in the two factories.

19. Such an opinion has been expressed by J. Goldthorpe and D. Lockwood, 'Affluence and the British Class Structure', *Sociological Review,* Vol. II (1963); and J. Goldthorpe, D. Lockwood, F. Bechhofer and J. Platt, *The Affluent Worker in the Class Structure,* Cambridge, 1969, Ch. 5. However, for a discussion of the sociological relevance of structured interview schedules for the study of attitudes towards inequality, see W.G. Runciman, *Relative Deprivation and Social Justice,* London, 1966, pp. 152-4.

20. Runciman also makes this point. See W.G. Runciman, op. cit.

21. I am particularly grateful to Sten Johansson, Olavi Junus, Ann Lundén and Anita Ehn-Scase for their kind assistance.

22. The English and Swedish interview schedules have been omitted from the book because of the publisher's concern with length. These, together with the coding frames, are reproduced in the original Ph.D. thesis, available from the Library of the University of Kent at Canterbury. However, all the questions which were used for the present analysis are reproduced in full in the text.

23. I thank Anita Ehn-Scase for her help.

24. In this study there are no statistical tests of significance. This may seem strange in view of the large number of quantitative comparisons that are made. There are two major reasons for this. First, the present enquiry is exploratory in its objectives. Most tests of significance have been designed for data which are intended to test hypotheses that have been derived from the findings of earlier investigations. Secondly, the populations to which the theoretical discussion refers are not the same as those from which the

two groups of workers were chosen. Thus to replicate this study with other samples would seem to offer a more fruitful guarantee of the general validity of the findings of this analysis for an understanding of attitudes in Britain and Sweden *in general* than tests of significance. For a detailed comment about the advantages and limitations of statistical tests of significance in exploratory social surveys, see S. Lipset, M. Trow and J. Coleman, *Union Democracy*, Illinois, 1956, Appendix 1. See also R. Henkel and D. Morrison (eds.), *The Significance Test Controversy*, London, 1970.

# 4 CONCEPTIONS OF THE CLASS STRUCTURE: (1) INEQUALITIES OF OPPORTUNITY

Did the two samples of workers, occupying comparable positions within the social structures of Britain and Sweden, have similar conceptions of the respective class structures or were there differences which could be seen to be a consequence of the differential impact of working-class norms and institutions? In the study of class imagery investigators have emphasised the need to analyse actors' immediate social relationships. Lockwood, for example, has stated that:

> for the most part men visualise the class structure of their society from the vantage points of their own particular *milieux* and their perceptions of the larger society will vary according to their experiences of social inequality in the smaller societies in which they live out their daily lives.[1]

He goes on to suggest that:

> the industrial and community *milieux* of manual workers exhibit a very considerable diversity and it would be strange if there were no correspondingly marked variations in the images of society held by different sections of the working class.[2]

Similarly, Inkeles, in a comparative study of attitudes in different industrial societies, has argued that:

> people have experiences, develop attitudes and form values in response to the forces or pressures which their environment creates. By 'environment' we mean, particularly, networks of inter-personal relations and the patterns of reward and punishment one normally experiences in them.[3]

He suggests that:

> within broad limits, the same situational pressures, the same framework for living, will be experienced as similar and will generate the same or similar response by people from different countries.[4]

However, the processes whereby these social relationships are conducive to particular types of subjective responses are unclear. It has been suggested, for example, that roles which bring employees into close personal contact with their employers will lead workers to adopt deferential attitudes.[5] But it could also be argued that these relationships are conducive not to deference but to workers making comparisons with their employers so that they feel relatively deprived, resentful and adopt radical attitudes. If this is a possiblity, why has deference rather than radicalism been seen to be the more likely outcome? Of course, there is empirical evidence, although of a limited kind, to indicate that these patterns of relationships do lead to deferential attitudes,[6] while there is little to indicate that they are conducive to radicalism.[7] But is this a function of specific social relationships as such, or is it more a consequence of the procedures whereby these relationships have become *defined* and attributed with social meanings?

The point can be further clarified by reference to Lockwood's typification of the 'proletarian traditonalist'. He states that:

the dominant model of society held by the proletarian traditionalist is most likely to be a dichotomous or two-valued power model. Thinking in terms of two classes standing in a relationship of opposition is a *natural consequence* of being a member of a closely integrated industrial community with well-defined boundaries and a distinctive style of life (my italics).[8]

But why should such an image of society be regarded as an inevitable outcome of social environments of this kind? In fact Moore, in a study of mining communities in county Durham, found that there was little evidence of a heightened awareness of class consciousness among miners.[9] He states,

It is clear that the miners have developed a strong sense of occupational community (unlike the traditional deferential worker), but this does not mean that class consciousness emerged from this.[10]

He goes on, 'Lockwood does not consider the possibility that men have to be *converted* to a traditional proletarian outlook in certain situations.'[11] Consequently, he argues that in order to find out whether miners will adhere to a 'traditional-proletarian' image of society it is necessary to consider the role of ideologies as they shape actors' definitions of social reality; in the case of the Durham miners, the relative influences of Methodism, trade unionism and the Labour Party. Indeed, Moore's argument lends weight to Parkin's claim, already quoted in Chapter 2, that structural inequalities do not in themselves provide meanings, and the way a person interprets them will be influenced by the nature of the *meaning systems* he draws upon. These meaning systems, according to Parkin, are a function of the influence exercised by different groups in society.[12]

Arguments such as these do not, of course, refute the significance of social relationships in shaping individuals' images of society. But they do suggest that a consideration of only these factors is insufficient, and that it is also necessary to investigate the processes whereby such relationships become defined by the actors involved. Such arguments would further suggest that this is particularly important in the comparative study of attitudes in different industrial countries, if only because there has been a tendency for writers to imply that the institutions of advanced industrial capitalism are conducive to similar patterns of attitudes among workers in different societies which override variations generated by national, cultural and political factors.[13] Thus, if the two samples of workers had similar interpretations of their respective class structures, it would indicate that institutional environments do have major consequences for shaping individuals' conceptions of social reality. If, on the other hand, this is not the case, it would suggest the importance of other factors of the kind emphasised by Parkin and others.[14] More specifically, for the Swedish workers, it would indicate the impact of Social Democratic ideology.

In order to investigate this, both samples were asked, 'Some people say that there are no longer social classes in this country. Others say there are. What do you think?' An overwhelming majority of both groups stated that there were: 97 per cent (N = 118) of the Swedish and 93 per cent (N = 119) of the English workers.[15] These respondents were then asked the open-ended question, 'Why do you think this is the case?' The coded responses are shown in Table 4.1.

Any similarity between the two samples in terms of their recognition of social classes evaporated when they were asked to describe their reasons for the existence of these classes. As Table 4.1 shows, one-half of the Swedish respondents referred to economic and 20 per cent to educational factors. At the same time, only 2 per cent considered 'birth' and family background to be important.[16] By contrast, although one-third of the English workers mentioned economic factors, only 3 per cent referred to education, but more than 10 per cent to 'birth' and family background. At the same time, as many as 25 per cent con-

sidered social classes to be an inevitable feature of life; they made such
statements as 'you will always have leaders and followers', 'some people
are bound to be better than others', 'breeding makes social classes inevitable'.

Table 4.1: 'Why do you think this is the case?' (that there are social
classes)

| Because of: | Swedish Workers (N=118) | | English Workers (N=119) | |
|---|---|---|---|---|
| | Nos. | % | Nos. | % |
| 'Birth' and family background | 2 | 1.7 | 13 | 10.9 |
| 'Money', 'wealth' and various economic factors | 65 | 55.1 | 44 | 37.1 |
| Status and 'snobbery' | 7 | 5.9 | 15 | 12.6 |
| Educational qualifications and experience | 24 | 20.3 | 3 | 2.5 |
| 'An inevitable feature of life' | 1 | 0.9 | 30 | 25.2 |
| Occupation | 2 | 1.7 | 3 | 2.5 |
| Don't know | 3 | 2.5 | 3 | 2.5 |
| Other and non-classifiable responses | 14 | 11.9 | 8 | 6.7 |
| Totals | 118 | 100.0 | 119 | 100.0 |

A further question asked, 'What is the major factor, do you think, which
determines the class a person belongs to?' Whereas the previous question
tried to find out why the respondents thought there were social classes,
this attempted to identify the criteria which they used in allocating
individuals to class positions.

Table 4.2 shows that the Swedish workers considered an individual's
class position to be determined primarily by his economic circumstances and his level of education while other factors, such as his 'birth'
and family background, were regarded to be of limited importance.
Among the English workers, on the other hand, there was also a recognition of the importance of economic factors but they were much more
likely to emphasise the significance of 'birth' and family background
and to give little consideration to the role of education. Therefore, the
responses indicated that although both samples stressed the importance
of economic factors for determining the class position of individuals,
the Swedish workers were more likely to refer to 'meritocratic' factors
than the English. Indeed, this pattern was confirmed by their descriptions of different social classes.

Table 4.2: 'What is the major factor, do you think, which determines the class a person belongs to?'*

| Factors Mentioned | Swedish Workers | | English Workers | |
|---|---|---|---|---|
| | Nos. (118) | % | Nos. (119) | % |
| 'Birth' and family background | 12 | 10.2 | 45 | 37.8 |
| Educational qualifications and experience | 45 | 38.1 | 16 | 13.5 |
| 'Money', 'wealth' and economic factors | 81 | 68.6 | 69 | 58.0 |
| Occupation | 7 | 5.9 | 13 | 10.9 |
| Attitudes and appearances | 4 | 3.4 | 6 | 5.0 |
| Patterns of social interaction | – | – | 4 | 3.4 |
| Other and non-classifiable responses | 11 | 9.3 | 13 | 10.9 |

*Most respondents mentioned more than one factor and so the figures add to more than 100 per cent.

The workers that recognised the existence of social classes were asked, 'Which are the major classes in this country today?' In reply to this question all respondents mentioned more than one class: 28 per cent of the Swedish and 29 per cent of the English workers conceived of a two-class model of society; 66 per cent and 60 per cent, a three-class model and a further 5 per cent and 11 per cent, a class model consisting of four or more categories. In other words, somewhat less than one-third of both groups of workers mentioned two, and a further two-thirds three, major social classes. In terms of their own class positions, all those respondents of both samples who considered there were only two social classes placed themselves in the 'bottom' category. But among those who conceived of their society in terms of a three-class 'model', there was an important difference between the two groups. Whereas 47 per cent of the Swedish respondents adhering to this 'model' allocated themselves to the 'intermediate' category, this was done by only 21 per cent of the English; indeed, as many as 79 per cent placed themselves in the 'bottom' category.

The replies to the question, 'Which are the major classes in this country today?' were coded, as far as possible, according to the actual phrases used by respondents. The results are shown in Table 4.3.

Both samples were then asked, 'Which of these classes would you say that you belong to?', the replies to which are shown in Table 4.4.

In view of the fact that replies to these questions were coded according to the actual 'labels' used by respondents, it is interesting that they

used relatively few categories; both in terms of their descriptions of the
class structure and of their own class positions. This would suggest that
in their replies to these deliberately vague and ambiguous questions respondents did not consciously work out their own conceptions of the
class structure but instead 'gave back' a received cultural, ideological
interpretation of it.

Table 4.3: 'Which are the major classes in this country today?'

| | 'Labels' Mentioned | Swedish Workers (N = 118) | | English Workers (N = 119) | |
|---|---|---|---|---|---|
| | | Nos. | % | Nos. | % |
| 1. | 'Upper', 'top', 'higher classes' | 24 | 20.3 | 89 | 74.8 |
| 2. | 'The wealthy', 'rich', 'those with plenty of money' | 14 | 11.9 | 19 | 16.0 |
| 3. | 'Social Group I' | 57 | 48.3 | – | – |
| 4. | 'Middle class' | 19 | 16.1 | 90 | 75.6 |
| 5. | 'White-collar people' | 20 | 17.0 | 1 | 0.9 |
| 6. | 'Educated people' | 5 | 4.2 | 1 | 0.9 |
| 7. | 'Social Group II' | 56 | 47.5 | – | – |
| 8. | 'Social Group III' | 47 | 39.8 | – | – |
| 9. | 'Working class' | 46 | 39.0 | 89 | 74.8 |
| 10. | 'Ordinary people', 'average people' | 2 | 1.7 | 2 | 1.7 |
| 11. | 'Lower class' | 2 | 1.7 | 21 | 17.7 |
| 12. | 'The poor', 'the lower paid' etc. | 7 | 5.9 | 8 | 6.7 |
| 13. | Negative evaluation ('Those who don't want to work', etc.) | 10 | 8.5 | 1 | 0.9 |
| 14. | Other and non-classifiable responses | 15 | 12.7 | 13 | 10.9 |

Table 4.4: 'Which of these classes would you say that you belong to?'

| 'Labels' mentioned | Swedish Workers (N = 118) | | English Workers (N = 119) | |
|---|---|---|---|---|
| | Nos. | % | Nos. | % |
| 'Middle class' | 11 | 9.3 | 23 | 19.3 |
| 'Social Group II' | 30 | 25.4 | – | – |
| 'Social Group III' | 25 | 21.2 | – | – |
| 'Average people', 'ordinary people' | 2 | 1.7 | 2 | 1.7 |
| 'Working class' | 46 | 39.0 | 83 | 69.8 |
| 'Lower class' | 2 | 1.7 | 6 | 5.0 |
| 'The poor' | – | – | 4 | 3.4 |
| Other and non-classifiable responses | 2 | 1.7 | 1 | 0.8 |
| Total | 118 | 100.0 | 119 | 100.0 |

However, it is also clear that the two samples had rather different reasons in order to explain their own positions within the respective class structures. This is borne out by Table 4.5, which correlates respondents' self-assigned class with the factors regarded to be important in determining an individual's class position.

Table 4.5: Respondents' self-assigned social class related to the factors they considered important in determining an individual's position in the class structure (percentages)*

| Factors mentioned as Important | Respondents' Self-assigned Social Class | | | | |
| --- | --- | --- | --- | --- | --- |
| | Swedish Workers | | | English Workers | |
| | 'Social Group II' (N = 30) | 'Social Group III' (N = 25) | 'Working Class' (N = 46) | 'Middle Class' (N = 23) | 'Working Class' (N = 83) |
| 'Birth' and family background | 6.7 | 12.0 | 15.2 | 21.7 | 42.2 |
| Educational qualifications and experience | 40.0 | 40.0 | 41.3 | 17.4 | 12.1 |
| 'Money,' 'wealth' and economic factors | 86.7 | 72.0 | 58.7 | 56.5 | 57.8 |
| Occupation | 3.3 | 4.0 | 8.7 | 4.4 | 14.5 |
| Attitudes and appearances | − | − | 2.2 | 13.0 | 2.4 |
| Patterns of social interaction | − | − | − | 4.4 | 3.6 |
| Other and non-classifiable responses | 13.3 | 8.0 | 8.7 | 17.4 | 8.4 |

*Most respondents mentioned more than one factor and so the figures add to more than 100 per cent. Only those class 'labels' used by a substantial number of respondents have been used in this cross-tabulation (see Table 4.4).

Table 4.5 shows that both samples, irrespective of the specific terms which they used in order to describe their own class positions, considered economic factors to be the major determinants for an individual's placement within the class structure. But it is also clear that the Swedish workers persistently stressed the role of education to a degree unreflected in the English responses. In addition, although the number of Swedish workers that emphasised the importance of 'birth' and family background was greater among those considering themselves to be 'working class', this did not equal the high frequency of this response found among the English 'working-class' respondents. Indeed, 'birth' and family background were emphasised among these English workers to about the same degree as 'education' was among the Swedish respondents regarding themselves as 'working class'. In other words, Table 4.5

suggests that while the Swedish respondents perceived their own positions within the class structure to be largely determined by economic and educational factors, the English sample, although recognising the primary importance of economic criteria, was more likely to emphasise the role of 'birth' and family background. In fact it is only among the English respondents describing themselves as 'middle class' that education is given as much importance as 'birth' and family background.

Similar patterns emerged in respondents' descriptions of the 'top' social classes. These, together with their descriptions of all other social classes (as listed in Table 4.3), are presented in Table 4.6.

In their models of the class structure there were no respondents who placed themselves in the 'top' category. But it is useful to study their descriptions of the social classes which they included within this category. This can be done by comparing the Swedish workers' descriptions of the 'upper class', 'the wealthy', and 'Social Group I' with the English respondents' accounts of the 'upper class' and 'the wealthy'. More specifically, it is helpful to compare the samples' descriptions of the two groups which were most frequently mentioned in this category; for the Swedish workers, 'Social Group I', and for the English, 'upper class'. 'Labels', that is, which were mentioned by 49 per cent (N = 57) and 75 per cent (N = 89) of the Swedish and the English samples respectively.

In view of this, Table 4.6 suggests that both samples emphasised the importance of economic factors in their descriptions of these particular social classes. But at the same time, the Swedish workers mentioned a number of occupations which require individuals to undergo relatively long periods of formal education and, often, specialist training. Therefore, various professional occupations, 'engineers', 'higher white-collar workers', and 'educated people' were frequently mentioned, while 'lords and ladies', 'the aristocracy' and other descriptions that would indicate respondents perceived of the class structure in 'traditional' and 'ascriptive' terms were absent. Among the English sample, by contrast, 'traditional' attitudes of this kind were frequently expressed; these were mentioned by no less than 42 per cent of those who referred to the 'upper class' in their descriptions of the class structure.

Clearly, the foregoing analysis suggests that the two samples, despite the similarity in the emphasis which they gave to economic factors, had rather different conceptions of the respective class structures. From this it seems as though the Swedish workers would be more likely to conceive of the class structure as 'open' and as one in which there were considerable opportunities for individual upward mobility. Among the

Table 4.6: Respondents' description of the membership of different social classes*

SWEDISH WORKERS

SOCIAL CLASS

| Respondents' Descriptions | (1) 'Upper', 'top', etc. (N = 24) % | (2) 'The wealthy' etc. (N = 14) % | (3) 'Social Group I' (N = 57) % | (4) 'Middle class' (N = 19) % | (5) 'White-collar people' (N = 20) % | (6) 'Educated people' (N = 5) % | (7) 'Social Group II' (N = 56) % | (8) 'Social Group III' (N = 47) % | (9) 'Working class' (N = 46) % | (10) 'Ordinary people' etc. (N = 2) % | (11) 'Lower class' (N = 2) % | (12) 'The poor' etc. (N = 7) % | (13) Negative Evaluation (N = 10) % |
|---|---|---|---|---|---|---|---|---|---|---|---|---|---|
| 'Lords and ladies', 'people with titles', 'the aristocracy' | 4.2 | – | 1.8 | – | – | – | – | – | – | – | – | – | – |
| Economic factors ('the rich', 'the wealthy', etc.) | 29.2 | 35.7 | 31.6 | 5.3 | 5.0 | 20.0 | 17.9 | – | – | – | – | – | – |
| Big businessmen', 'directors' | 50.0 | 78.6 | 52.6 | 5.3 | 5.0 | – | 5.4 | – | – | – | – | – | – |
| 'Professionals' (or specific occupational title mentioned) | 33.3 | 42.9 | 56.1 | 26.3 | 20.0 | 100.0 | 10.7 | – | – | – | – | – | – |
| 'Higher white-collar workers' | 37.5 | 21.4 | 28.1 | 15.8 | 15.0 | 60.0 | 14.2 | – | 4.3 | – | – | – | – |
| 'Educated people' | 4.2 | 7.1 | 26.3 | 5.3 | 15.0 | 20.0 | 1.8 | – | – | – | – | – | – |
| 'Engineers' | 16.7 | 14.3 | 12.3 | 10.5 | 25.0 | – | 12.5 | – | – | – | – | – | – |
| 'Managers' | 25.0 | 21.4 | 26.3 | 15.8 | 10.0 | – | 1.8 | – | 2.2 | – | – | – | – |
| 'Small shopkeepers' | – | – | – | 5.3 | – | – | – | – | – | – | – | – | – |
| 'Lower white-collar workers' | – | – | – | 21.1 | 15.0 | – | 26.8 | 21.3 | 34.8 | 100.0 | – | – | – |
| 'Average people', 'ordinary people' | – | – | – | 15.8 | – | – | 7.1 | 6.4 | 8.7 | – | – | – | – |
| Specific non-manual occupation mentioned | – | – | – | 42.1 | 55.0 | – | 42.9 | – | 8.7 | – | 100.0 | – | – |
| 'Manual', 'factory workers' or specific occupational title | – | – | – | 52.6 | 5.0 | – | 55.4 | 70.2 | 100.0 | – | 100.0 | – | – |
| 'Those who don't work' | – | – | 1.8 | – | – | – | – | – | – | 100.0 | – | 100.0 | – |
| Positive evaluation | 4.2 | 7.1 | 1.8 | – | 15.0 | – | 8.9 | – | – | – | – | – | – |
| Negative evaluation | – | – | 3.5 | 5.3 | – | – | 1.8 | 25.5 | 2.2 | – | – | 14.3 | 90.0 |
| 'The poor', low incomes | – | 14.3 | – | – | – | – | – | 27.7 | – | – | – | 71.4 | 20.0 |
| Other and non-classifiable responses | 8.3 | 42.9 | 12.3 | 5.3 | 5.0 | – | 7.1 | 6.4 | 6.5 | – | – | – | 20.0 |

ENGLISH WORKERS

SOCIAL CLASS

| Respondents' Descriptions | (1) 'Upper' 'top' etc. (N = 89) % | (2) 'The wealthy' etc. (N = 19) % | (3) 'Social Group I' % | (4) 'Middle class' (N = 90) % | (5) 'White-collar people' (N = 1) % | (6) 'Educated people' (N = 1) % | (7) 'Social Group II' % | (8) 'Social Group III' % | (9) 'Working class' (N = 89) % | (10) 'Ordinary people' etc. (N = 2) % | (11) 'Lower class' (N = 21) % | (12) 'The poor' etc. (N = 8) % | (13) Negative evaluation (N = 1) % |
|---|---|---|---|---|---|---|---|---|---|---|---|---|---|
| 'Lords and ladies', 'people with titles', 'the aristocracy' | 41.6 | 26.3 | — | — | — | — | — | — | — | — | — | — | — |
| Economic factors ('the rich', 'the wealthy', etc.) | 20.2 | 31.6 | — | 5.6 | — | — | — | — | — | — | — | — | — |
| Big businessmen', 'directors' | 53.9 | 73.7 | — | 14.4 | — | — | — | — | — | — | — | — | — |
| 'Professionals' (or specific occupational title mentioned) | 14.6 | 5.3 | — | 17.8 | — | 100.0 | — | — | 1.1 | — | — | — | — |
| 'Higher white-collar workers' | 1.1 | — | — | 4.5 | — | — | — | — | — | 50.0 | — | — | — |
| 'Educated people' | 4.5 | — | — | — | — | — | — | — | — | — | — | — | — |
| 'Engineers' | — | — | — | 1.1 | — | — | — | — | 1.1 | — | — | — | — |
| 'Managers' | 27.0 | 21.1 | — | 18.9 | — | — | — | — | 1.1 | — | — | — | — |
| 'Small shopkeepers' | — | — | — | 25.6 | — | — | — | — | — | — | — | — | — |
| 'Lower white-collar workers' | — | — | — | 7.8 | — | — | — | — | 11.2 | 50.0 | — | — | — |
| 'Average people', ordinary people' | — | — | — | 7.8 | — | — | — | — | 24.7 | 50.0 | — | — | — |
| Specific non-manual occupation mentioned | — | — | — | 40.0 | — | — | — | — | 13.5 | — | — | — | — |
| 'Manual', 'Factory workers' or specific occupational title | — | — | — | 17.8 | — | — | — | — | 86.5 | 100.0 | 47.6 | 75.0 | — |
| 'Those who don't work' | 9.0 | 5.3 | — | — | — | — | — | — | 4.5 | — | — | — | — |
| Positive evaluation | 1.1 | — | — | 5.6 | 100.0 | — | — | — | 4.5 | — | 57.1 | 12.5 | 100.0 |
| Negative evaluation | 2.2 | 21.1 | — | 2.2 | — | — | — | — | 11.2 | — | 9.5 | 50.0 | 100.0 |
| 'The poor', low incomes | — | — | — | — | — | — | — | — | — | — | — | — | — |
| Other and non-classifiable responses | 18.0 | 31.6 | — | 13.3 | 100.0 | — | — | — | 6.7 | — | 19.0 | 50.0 | 100.0 |

*The results for the two samples are presented separately in order to assist interpretation of the data; only the percentages are given for the same reason. These should be treated with extreme caution in many of the columns because of the very small numbers which they represent. Since most respondents mentioned more than one factor in their descriptions of specific classes, the figures add to more than 100 per cent.

English respondents, on the other hand, it would appear that their conceptions of the class structure would lead them to have a limited belief in the possibilities for upward mobility, partly the result, as shown in Tables 4.5 and 4.6, of the importance which they gave to ascriptive and traditional factors in determining individuals' class membership.

In order to test whether this was the case, those workers recognising the existence of social classes were asked, 'Do you think that many people move from one class to another these days?' Among the Swedish workers, 70 per cent (N = 82) said 'yes' compared with 42 per cent (N = 50) of the English respondents: more than two-thirds compared with less than one-half. These workers were then asked, 'What are the reasons for this?' The coded responses are shown in Table 4.7:

Table 4.7: 'What are the reasons for this?' ('that many people move from one class to another these days')

| Because of: | Swedish Workers | | English Workers | |
|---|---|---|---|---|
| | Nos. | % | Nos. | % |
| Opportunities to improve personal economic circumstances | 27 | 33.0 | 19 | 38.0 |
| Possibilities for promotion at work | 5 | 6.1 | 8 | 16.0 |
| Possibilities for obtaining educational qualifications | 46 | 56.1 | 6 | 12.0 |
| 'Personal contacts' | — | — | 3 | 6.0 |
| 'Equal opportunity for everyone' | 2 | 2.4 | 2 | 4.0 |
| Individual effort and enterprise, etc. | — | — | 6 | 12.0 |
| Other and non-classifiable responses | 2 | 2.4 | 6 | 12.0 |
| Totals | 82 | 100.0 | 50 | 100.0 |

Similar proportions of both samples felt that people could now move from one class to another because of greater opportunities to improve their economic circumstances. But the factor mentioned most frequently by the Swedish respondents was that there were now better possibilities for obtaining formal educational qualifications; this was mentioned by only a few of the English workers. Instead, the latter were more likely to cite the need for 'personal contacts' and for individuals to exercise 'initiative', 'enterprise' and so on.

These results were further substantiated by the responses to a more specific question: 'How likely is the son of a factory worker to move from one class to another? Would you say that he was 'very likely', 'likely', 'unlikely', or 'very unlikely'? No less than 98 per cent of the

Swedish workers considered that he was either 'very likely' or 'likely' compared with 70 per cent of the English; indeed, 48 per cent of the Swedish respondents claimed that he was 'very likely' but this view was held by only 6 per cent of the English sample. Obviously both samples were optimistic about the mobility chances of the son of a factory worker, but this attitude was held to a far greater degree among the Swedish respondents. Whereas there was almost complete acceptance of this opinion among the Swedish workers, a substantial minority of the English respondents — 20 per cent — felt that it was either 'unlikely' or 'very unlikely'. Both samples were then asked, 'What would he have to do in order to move from one class to another?'

Table 4.8: 'What would he (the son of a factory worker) have to do in order to move from one class to another?'

|  | Swedish Workers | | English Workers | |
|---|---|---|---|---|
|  | Nos. | % | Nos. | % |
| Improve his personal economic circumstances | – | – | 3 | 2.5 |
| Obtain promotion at work, or get a 'better' job | – | – | 15 | 12.6 |
| Obtain some educational qualifications | 113 | 95.6 | 61 | 51.3 |
| Make use of, or establish 'personal contacts' | 1 | 0.9 | 2 | 1.7 |
| Exercise some 'individual effort', 'initiative', etc. | 1 | 0.9 | 7 | 5.9 |
| Don't know | 1 | 0.9 | 6 | 5.0 |
| Other and non-classifiable responses | 2 | 1.7 | 25 | 21.0 |
| Totals | 118 | 100.0 | 119 | 100.0 |

The results in Table 4.8 show that the Swedish sample regarded the ac-quisition of educational qualifications as almost the sole means by which individuals could be upwardly mobile within the class structure. Although this opinion was shared by one-half of the English workers, it is evident that educational qualifications were considered to be of far less importance. Indeed, of the 25 English respondents giving 'other and non-classifiable' answers, no less than 40 per cent (N = 10) mentioned 'ascriptive' factors such as 'he would need to be born into the right family' and 'make certain that he had a wealthy father'. Among the remainder, considerable importance was given to 'luck' and 'chance'; they suggested the need to 'win the pools', 'have a good bet', 'be left a fortune' and so on. But did the Swedish respondents consider that children from all social backgrounds enjoyed the same degree of 'participation' within the educational system? To investigate this, both samples were asked, 'A lot of children stay on at school and go to university these days. Do you think that the sons of some people are more likely to stay on than others?'[17] Similar proportions of both samples — 60 per cent (N = 73) of the Swedish and 61 per cent (N = 78) of the English — agreed that the sons of some people were more likely to stay on than others. These respondents were then asked, 'What sort of people are more likely to have their sons at university?'

Table 4.9: 'What sort of people are more likely to have their sons at university?*

|  | Swedish Workers (N = 122) | | English Workers (N = 128) | |
|---|---|---|---|---|
|  | Nos. | % | Nos. | % |
| 'Educated people' | 34 | 46.6 | 2 | 2.6 |
| 'The rich', 'the wealthy' | 14 | 19.2 | 32 | 41.0 |
| 'Professionals' (or specific occupation mentioned) | 65 | 89.0 | 24 | 30.8 |
| Big businessmen, 'directors' | 14 | 19.2 | 42 | 53.9 |
| Other non-manual (or specific occupation mentioned) | 8 | 11.0 | 15 | 19.2 |
| 'The aristocracy', 'lords and ladies' | — | — | 2 | 2.6 |
| 'Depends on parents' | 3 | 4.1 | 2 | 2.6 |
| 'Manual workers' (or specific occupation mentioned) | — | — | 2 | 2.6 |
| Other and non-classifiable responses | 1 | 1.4 | 11 | 14.1 |

*A number of respondents mentioned more than one 'sort of people' and so the figures add to more than 100 per cent.

Table 4.9 shows that both samples were aware of inequalities within the respective educational systems. But it is also clear that the Swedish workers perceived of these in terms of advantages accruing to the sons of 'educated' and other qualified, professional workers. By comparison, the English respondents rarely mentioned 'educated people' and they were less likely to refer to various categories of professional workers. Instead, they mentioned 'the rich', 'the wealthy' and 'businessmen'.

The results of the interview survey suggest, then, that there were important differences between the two samples in terms of their conceptions of the class structure and of social mobility within it. Although both groups gave primary emphasis to economic factors in their descriptions, the Swedish workers attached greater importance to education, while the English workers were more likely to stress the significance of 'ascriptive' and 'traditional' characteristics. Furthermore, the Swedish workers were more likely to express a belief in the possibilities for individual upward mobility and for this to occur, they emphasised the need to obtain formal educational qualifications. When privileges within the educational system were recognised to exist, these were seen to be enjoyed by the sons of 'educated' and other qualified people. For the English workers, on the other hand, possibilities for individual upward mobility were considered to be less likely and when this was seen as possible, fewer respondents mentioned the importance of education. In short, the Swedish workers were more likely than the English to conceive of the class structure as 'open' and meritocratic. Why was this?

It would be surprising if the attitudes were not shaped, at least to some extent, by a whole range of historical processes as well as by a large number of individual and group experiences.[18] Of these, an obvious factor to consider is the samples' experience of mobility at work, since it could be argued that their conceptions of the possibilities for individual mobility were a consequence of these. However, the evidence does not support this. Asked about the possibilities for promotion, both samples were invited to name an occupation which they would be most likely to get if they were given promotion.[19] For both groups 'foremen' and various supervisory manual occupations such as 'inspector' and 'charge-hand' were most frequently mentioned by well over 85 per cent of both the Swedish and the English workers. In other words, promotion was perceived in terms of movement within manual jobs, rather than into white-collar occupations. Indeed, these were 'realistic' assessments, since in neither factory was there an effective scheme that would enable manual workers to have become office employees. But the similarity in the samples' responses did not persist when they were asked, 'How likely is a factory worker to get promotion at work? Would you say that it was 'very likely', 'likely', 'unlikely', or 'very unlikely'?' Almost twice as many (73 per cent) of the English workers thought it either 'likely' or 'very likely' compared with the Swedish workers (39 per cent).

Clearly, the Swedish respondents' optimistic assumptions about mobility within the class structure were not a function of their assessments of the possibilities for promotion at work. Indeed, the discrepancy between their conceptions of promotion in the factory and of mobility in society indicated that they adopted very different frames of reference in their consideration of these issues. It suggests that they made a clear distinction between 'industry' and 'society' as institutional and normative systems. At the same time, they seemed to differentiate between the opportunities available to their children through the educational system and their own chances within the occupational structure. Consequently, it appears that their descriptions of the class structure were a function of factors other than those relating to immediate work experiences. Indeed, this claim can be supported by a consideration of the mobility patterns of the workers' sons. Those respondents with sons at work (there were 45 and 52 such sons among the Swedish and the English samples respectively) were asked to name and describe their sons' occupations. The results are shown in Table 4.10.

Table 4.10: Occupations of respondents' sons

|  | Swedish Workers | | English Workers | |
|---|---|---|---|---|
|  | Nos. | % | Nos. | % |
| Manual | 36 | 80.0 | 38 | 73.1 |
| Non-manual | 7 | 15.6 | 6 | 11.5 |
| Self-employed (not farmer) | 1 | 2.2 | — | — |
| Farmer | — | — | — | — |
| Farm worker | — | — | — | — |
| Military (conscription and regular) | 1 | 2.2 | 8 | 15.4 |
| Totals | 45 | 100.0 | 52 | 100.0 |

Table 4.10 indicates that there was little variation in patterns of occupational mobility among the sons of workers in the two samples; only 16 per cent of those of the Swedish workers were in non-manual occupations compared with 12 per cent of the English. Consequently, the difference is too small to explain the contrasts in the two samples' conceptions of mobility in society. Here, then, is an interesting paradox; the Swedish workers were optimistic about the general possiblities for mobility in society and yet they, themselves, had limited expectations about their own chances at work. Furthermore, their sons were also non-mobile in the sense that they were mainly employed in manual occupations. Again, this suggests the need to consider influences other than those relating directly to the respondents' own personal social experiences. An important factor to take into account is the rate of individual upward mobility in each of the two countries, since if this was higher in Sweden it could be reflected in the attitudes of the

Swedish workers. However, the evidence in Chapter 2 suggested that patterns of recruitment, especially into the more prestigeful and highly paid occupations, were highly restricted in Sweden and certainly to a greater extent than the beliefs of the Swedish sample would suggest.

Clearly, then, variations in the two samples' conceptions of their respective class structures cannot be seen as a consequence of different mobility patterns, either in terms of immediate social experiences or within the respective countries. As Chapter 2 suggested, the chances of the son of a manual worker becoming a lower-grade white-collar employee are probably greater in Sweden than they are in Britain, but differences between the two countries in terms of overall patterns of social mobility are insufficient to account for the considerable variation in the attitudes of the two samples. How, then, are the contrasts to be explained? Since they do not seem to be a function of 'structural' differences it is pertinent to suggest that they may be a consequence — if only partly — of certain normative influences: to follow Parkin, of a political character.[20]

Although Social Democratic governments, despite successive electoral appeals, have achieved little in reducing patterns of inequality in terms of recruitment into the more prestigeful and highly rewarded occupations, they have emphasised the desirability of establishing Sweden as a meritocratic society. A society, that is, in which all individuals will be able to acquire occupational roles compatible with their personal 'talents' and 'skills' and in which recruitment to occupations will be determined more by 'competence' and 'ability' than by social background.[21] This was particularly evident during the 1950s and the early 1960s, when the Social Democratic Party considered that equality in society could be achieved as much by improving educational opportunities as by creating a more equal distribution of economic rewards.[22] Thus, it has often been claimed that differences in the rewards accruing to occupations are acceptable provided that all children, irrespective of social background, are given the same chances of acquiring them. This ideological position of the Social Democratic Party has been reflected in large-scale reforms of the educational system of the kind described in Chapter 2.

Changes in the educational system seem to have generated a set of beliefs that has emphasised the openness of the class structure and the possibilities for upward mobility within it: provided, that is, individuals take advantage of the opportunities for obtaining the necessary qualifications in the much-praised 'democratised' and 'egalitarian' educational system. Furthermore, the Swedish mass media has emphasised the opportunities available for obtaining educational qualifications which can be used for career advancement. In addition to providing a large number of educational courses, the radio and television services of the Swedish Broadcasting Corporation devote 'peak' time to publicising the various part-time vocational and academic courses that are available throughout the country. LO is also very active in this work: the Workers' Education Association, for example, provides a large number of courses many of which award 'credits' that can be taken into account for the purposes of obtaining university degrees. During the 1970s LO has been negotiating with employers and the government so that workers should have time from employment in order to study and obtain higher educational qualifications. Furthermore, the government has, over recent years, conducted a large advertising campaign in news-papers explaining the 'new' opportunities that have become available by reforms of the educational system.[23]

With government policies of this kind, however, it could be that aspirations for individual upward mobility will become heightened but so, too, will feelings of frustration, failure and resentment when these expectations are not fulfilled. Therefore, although workers are led to believe there are widespread opportunities in society, they find they are employed in the lesser esteemed and more low-paid occupations. Indeed, such attitudes are likely to develop in a country like Sweden where there are highly restricted patterns of recruitment into the more highly rewarded occupations. Until now the ideological commitment of the Social Democratic Party to meritocratic goals has led to educational reforms and to the development of a widespread belief in the 'open-ness' of the class structure. Policies such as these have, so far, retained the allegiance of rank-and-file supporters but they could generate feelings of resentment, particularly if the class structure remains as rigid as it is at present.[24] Unfortunately, the interview sur-vey did not enquire into the Swedish respondents' personal reactions to the discrepancy between their beliefs in individual upward mobility and their own and their children's non-mobility. It could be that they explained the difference in terms of personal 'failure' and particular psychological and domestic attributes rather than according to charac-teristics of the social structure. In this way, the ideology of equal and widespread opportunities would remain unchallenged. Alternatively, it could be that the interview survey did not capture the respondents' own *personal* evaluations of opportunities in society, but rather what they considered to be the general factual state of affairs as defined for them by various ideological influences. In this sense, then, the discrepancy between their stated beliefs and their own personal experiences could be explained by the fact that they referred to these broadly based influences when they answered the interview questions. Indeed, the foregoing analysis suggests that this was the case.

In Britain, by contrast, meritocratic ideas have been less emphasised by the labour movement. Consequently, the class structure is still seen to be shaped by a number of 'traditional' factors and, by comparison with Sweden, there is less of a belief in the possibilities for upward mobility. As a result, it can be argued that manual workers will have more limited aspirations for the occupational advancement of themselves and their children. Indeed, feelings of failure are likely to be less pronounced among these workers and they are more likely than Swedish workers to regard their own positions within the class structure as inevitable.[25] However, should Britain have prolonged periods of Labour governments, it could be that meritocratic norms would become as widely accepted as they appear to be in Sweden.Certainly, with Labour governments there have been attempts to 'equalise' opportunities by introducing changes within the educational system. But most of the schemes relating to the introduction of comprehensive education which were approved between 1964 and 1970, and since 1974 by the Labour government have included selective elements and, on the whole, they have been less egalitarian in their objectives than the Swedish educational reforms.[26]

In conclusion, the evidence suggests that although the two samples occupied similar structural positions within the two countries, they differed in many of their conceptions of the respective class structures.[27] Whereas in Sweden the respondents determined the allocation of individuals to social positions according to meritocratic, achievement-orientated criteria, in Britain they were more likely to stress the importance of traditional and 'ascriptive' factors. This in turn affected the two samples' beliefs in the possibilities for individual upward mobility. The data indicate, then, that the two samples' conceptions were shaped not only by patterns of structural relationships, but also by their exposure to rather different political ideologies. Hence, the evidence suggests that the Swedish workers' attitudes were influenced, if only partly, by the meritocratic ideology of the Social Democratic Party. Consequently, the inference to be drawn from the interview survey is that although Social Democratic governments have, as yet, failed to alter the opportunity structure of Swedish society to the extent that is in any fundamental sense more egalitarian than in Britain, there has been the development of a belief system among industrial workers which emphasises the chances available for upward mobility in society. This, to some degree, legitimates the allocation of individuals to positions in the class structure. However, this does not take into account the extent to which the economic rewards that are attached to these positions are regarded as acceptable by workers. This is discussed in the next chapter.

## Notes

1. D. Lockwood, 'Sources of Variation in Working Class Images of Society', *Sociological Review*, Vol. 14 (1966), p. 249. This article is reprinted in M. Bulmer (ed.), *Working-Class Images of Society*, London, 1975.
2. D. Lockwood, op. cit., p. 250.
3. A. Inkeles, 'Industrial Man: The Relation of Status to Experience, Perception and Values', *American Journal of Sociology*, Vol. 66 (1960-1), p. 2.
4. A. Inkeles, op. cit., p. 2.
5. This claim has been discussed by H. Newby, 'Paternalism and Capitalism', in R. Scase (ed.), *Industrial Society: Class, Cleavage and Control*, London, 1977.
6. This evidence is reviewed by H. Newby, op. cit.
7. However, Bell and Newby have suggested that in some work and community situations, agricultural workers, although generally in close personal contact with their employers, will adopt 'radical' attitudes. See C. Bell and H. Newby, 'The Source of Variation in Agricultural Workers' Images of Society', *Sociological Review*, Vol. 21 (1973). Reprinted in M. Bulmer (ed.), op. cit.
8. D. Lockwood, op. cit., p. 251.
9. R. Moore, 'Religion as a Source of Variation in Working Class Images of Society', in M. Bulmer (ed.), op. cit.
10. R. Moore, op. cit., p. 53.
11. R. Moore, op. cit., p. 54.
12. F. Parkin, *Class Inequality and Political Order*, London, 1971, p. 81.
13. See, for example. N. Birnbaum, *The Crisis of Industrial Society*, London, 1969; and R. Miliband, *The State in Capitalist Society*, London, 1969.
14. F. Parkin, op. cit.
15. Unless otherwise stated, the questions that follow were put only to these respondents.
16. Only rounded-up percentages are given in the text.
17. This question was put to all respondents and not merely to those who recognised the existence of social classes.
18. Industrialisation and urbanisation, for example, have been much more recent in Sweden (see Chapter 1). This, of course, has affected the structure of communities and the development (or lack of) occupational subcultures.
19. This question was put after respondents had defined exactly what they meant by 'promotion'.
20. F. Parkin, op. cit.
21. This has been a feature of Social Democratic objectives since the 1880s. See G. Richardson, *Kulturkamp och Klasskamp: Ideologiska och Sociala Motsättningar i Svensk Skol – och Kulturpolitik under 1880 – Talet*

*(Cultural Struggle and Class Conflict: Ideological and Social Disputes in Swedish School and Cultural Politics During the 1880s)*, Gothenburg, 1963.

22.   See A. Myrdal, *Towards Equality*, Stockholm, 1971; and R. Tomasson, *Sweden: Prototype of Modern Society*, New York, 1970. Ch. 4.

23.   It is interesting to speculate about the proportion of English manual workers aware of the educational opportunities provided by, say, the Open University. It is probably small; not surprisingly in view of the very limited publicity it has received from those sectors of the mass media with which most manual workers have direct contact.

24.   If these attitudes were to develop, then the allegiance of rank-and-file supporters to the Social Democratic Party could become extremely tenuous, particularly since it has always presented itself as the party of reform, social justice and equality. It is in terms of these factors that it has asked to be judged at general elections.

25.   A selective educational system is likely to enforce these attitudes. One of the major socialising effects of the English school system is that it lowers the ambitions of working-class pupils so that they accord with opportunities available in the labour market. Conversely, a non-streamed, non-selective educational system of the Swedish type is unlikely to lower the occupational expectations of working-class youth.

26.   For example, a number of the comprehensive schemes introduced during these periods included academic 'streaming' either within or between schools.

27.   Despite the importance which both groups gave to economic factors.

# 5 CONCEPTIONS OF THE CLASS STRUCTURE: (2) INEQUALITIES OF ECONOMIC CONDITION

In Chapter 2 it was suggested that in Sweden there has been the development of a Social Democratic ideology of egalitarianism despite the existence of persisting inequalities in the economic condition of different occupational groups. If this is so, could it be that the Labour movement has led industrial workers to believe that incomes have become 'equalised'? Should this be the case, the awareness of economic inequalities among Swedish manual workers would be limited.

In Britain, Runciman found, for example, that only a small majority of manual workers considered that there were other occupational groups which were financially better off than themselves.[1] Furthermore, they generally made limited comparisons; they tended to mention either other groups of manual workers or individuals who could be compared with a specific aspect of their own personal situation. Hence, respondents referred to 'people with no children', 'people on night work', 'people with good health' and so on; comments which suggested that British manual workers did not perceive of inequality as a structural feature of society, but rather as a consequence of personal effort and circumstance.[2] Similarly, Goldthorpe and his colleagues found that 54 per cent of a sample of manual workers conceived of the class structure in terms of a 'money' model, in which there was a large central class consisting of most manual and white-collar workers, and one or more residual or 'elite' classes, differentiated in terms of wealth, income and material living standards.[3] As a result, Goldthorpe and his associates suggest that these workers' perceptions of their position in the class structure were inconsistent with their roles in the productive process; roles characterised by deprivation in the spheres of decision-making, working conditions, fringe benefits and status differentials. They argue that these attitudes were derived from social positions outside the workplace and that there was little awareness of inequality as a structural and socially organised feature of society.

In view of such findings, it seems likely that the two samples of workers, occupying comparable positions within the social structures of the two countries, would have fairly similar notions about economic differentials. If they do, the evidence would lend weight to the claims of some writers who argue that the institutions of different industrial capitalist societies have similar effects upon the cultural and political socialisation of manual workers, so that their attitudes are characterised by a 'false consciousness' and a restricted awareness of their *real* position in society.[4] Furthermore, and in view of the ideological egalitarianism of the Swedish labour movement, it could be that the Swedish respondents would not only be less knowledgeable but even less resentful of existing economic differentials than their English counterparts.

In his enquiry, Runciman asked respondents, 'Do you think there are any sorts of people doing noticeably better at the moment than you and your family?' He found that 25 per cent of all respondents and 27 per cent of manual workers stated that they could think of no other sorts of people.[5] A similar question was used in the present enquiry: 'Are there any people you can think of who are better off than workers like yourself?' Whereas only 8 per cent of the Swedish sample claimed that they could think of no other people, this opinion was held by 22 per cent of the English workers.[6] The figures are shown in Table 5.1:

Table 5.1: 'Are there any people you can think of who are better off than workers like yourself?'

|  | Swedish Workers | | English Workers | |
|---|---|---|---|---|
|  | Nos. | % | Nos. | % |
| Yes | 98 | 80.3 | 91 | 71.1 |
| No | 10 | 8.2 | 28 | 21.9 |
| Don't know | 14 | 11.5 | 9 | 7.0 |
| Total | 122 | 100.0 | 128 | 100.0 |

In view of the fact that patterns of wage differentials in the two countries are very similar,[7] the opinions expressed by the two samples would suggest that the awareness of economic inequality was greater among the Swedish respondents than among the English. All those workers who held that there were others better off than themselves were then asked: 'What sort of people?' Whenever possible, the responses were coded according to the actual terms used by workers.

Table 5.2 shows that the Swedish workers were more likely to mention non-manual occupations than were the English sample. Indeed various non-manual occupational titles, together with 'educated people' and 'the rich' were mentioned by 53 per cent of the Swedish workers compared with only 21 per cent of the workers in the English sample. On the other hand, 76 per cent of the English respondents mentioned

various manual occupations compared with only 44 per cent of the
Swedish workers; a difference between the two samples of 32 per cent.
In these responses, both samples stressed similar occupations – those in
the car, steel and dock industries. The only major difference between
the two groups was that the Swedish respondents gave greater emphasis
to the earnings of building construction workers. Indeed, the earnings
of Swedish workers employed in the building construction industry,
relative to other groups of workers, are high compared with the relative
earnings of English construction workers.[8]

Table 5.2: 'What sort of people?' ('are better off than workers like
yourself')

|  | Swedish Workers | | English Workers | |
| --- | --- | --- | --- | --- |
|  | Nos. | % | Nos. | % |
| 'Businessmen', 'directors' | 15 | 15.3 | 4 | 4.4 |
| 'Managers' | 2 | 2.0 | 6 | 6.6 |
| 'Professionals', 'professional people' | 7 | 7.1 | 5 | 5.5 |
| 'Higher white-collar workers' | 5 | 5.1 | – | – |
| 'White-collar workers' or specific non-manual occupation mentioned | 15 | 15.3 | 3 | 3.3 |
| 'Educated people' | 7 | 7.2 | – | – |
| 'The rich' | 1 | 1.0 | 1 | 1.1 |
| Specific manual occupation mentioned | 43 | 43.9 | 69 | 75.8 |
| Other and non-classifiable responses | 3 | 3.1 | 3 | 3.3 |
| Don't know | – | – | – | – |
| Total | 98 | 100.0 | 91 | 100.0 |

Clearly, the evidence indicates that the awareness of inequality was not
the same for both groups of workers; in fact, the responses of the
English workers were fairly consistent with those obtained by Runciman
in his analysis. He found that only 19 per cent of his samples of manual
workers who claimed that there were other people better off than themselves mentioned non-manual workers.[9] The present enquiry confirms
Runciman's contention that English manual workers make highly restricted comparisons when they assess their own economic position in
society. The Swedish workers, on the other hand, articulated a greater
frequency of relative deprivation and this seems to have been a consequence of their adoption of more broadly based reference groups, incorporating both non-manual and manual occupations. The differences
in the two groups of respondents were particularly striking in view of
the fact that wage differentials, both within the factories and the two

countries, were highly comparable.[10] Furthermore, the attitudes of the Swedish workers were such that they refuted any claims that a Social Democratic ideology of egalitarianism 'concealed', at least for them, 'objective' patterns of economic inequality.

The greater awareness of inequality among the Swedish workers was substantiated by their responses to questions which invited them to make comparisons between specific aspects of their own work roles with those of white-collar workers employed in the same factory. For the purposes of these comparisons, 'white-collar worker' was defined so that respondents understood the kind of occupation about which they were being asked to comment. It was emphasised that the term not only referred to office workers, but also to management and other higher officials. The samples were then asked to express their opinions about earnings, possibilities for promotion and conditions of work.

Respondents were asked: 'What do you think of the money you earn compared with that of white-collar workers? Would you say that it was 'much better', 'better', 'about the same', 'worse' or 'much worse'?' Among the Swedish workers, 63 per cent claimed that it was 'worse' or 'much worse', while only 4 per cent stated that it was 'better' or 'much better'. A further 30 per cent suggested it was 'about the same' for both manual and white-collar workers. By contrast, 44 per cent of the English sample said their earnings were 'better' or 'much better' and only 23 per cent thought that they were 'worse' or 'much worse'. There were 25 per cent who claimed they were 'about the same'. Clearly, the Swedish workers felt more deprived about their earnings, compared with those of white-collar workers, than the English respondents.

When they were asked about the possibilities for promotion, the Swedish workers were far less optimistic about their chances than their English counterparts.[11] Furthermore, when they were invited to compare these chances with those of white-collar employees, 80 per cent claimed that they were either 'worse' or 'much worse' and only 3 per cent said they were 'better' or 'much better'. By contrast, the English workers held a more favourable view of their promotion prospects compared with those of white-collar workers, with only 33 per cent stating these were either 'worse' or 'much worse', and 29 per cent suggesting they were 'better' or 'much better'. A further 31 per cent of the English sample perceived their chances to be 'about the same', compared with only 12 per cent of the Swedish workers.

The two groups of workers were then asked the open-ended question: 'Why is this?'; the responses to which were cross-tabulated with their opinions about opportunities for promotion compared with those available for white-collar workers. Of the 98 Swedish workers who claimed that their chances were 'worse' or 'much worse', 54 per cent stated this was because promotion was 'automatic' for white-collar workers. The kinds of responses which they made included such statements as 'white-collar workers get promoted as they get older', 'you just sit there and go up', 'it's automatic for them', and so on. But of the 43 English respondents who evaluated their chances in this way, only 16 per cent gave similar reasons. At the same time, 81 per cent of the 37 English workers who claimed that their own opportunities for promotion were 'better' or 'much better' said this was because there were more opportunities available on the shop floor than in the office. They made statements like 'chances are always cropping up on the factory floor, but you have to wait for dead men's shoes in the office', 'there are always chances' and 'jobs are always coming up'. Consequently, these figures tend to indicate that the Swedish workers had more 'realistic' assessments of their career prospects compared with those of white-collar workers employed in the same organisation, than the English workers. Indeed, the Swedish workers perceived that white-collar employment provided a built-in career structure which was not available to manual workers. The English workers, by contrast, felt that there was much more opportunity in the factory than in the office and they seemed to be unaware of the structural differences which existed between manual and non-manual employment.

Both samples were asked: 'What about your working conditions compared with those of white-collar workers? Would you say that they were 'much better', 'better', 'about the same', 'worse', or 'much worse'?' Among the Swedish workers, 89 per cent claimed that their working conditions (meaning physical working conditions) were either 'worse' or 'much worse' than those of white-collar workers and a further 10 per cent felt that they were 'about the same'; only one respondent said they were 'better'. Among the English sample, by contrast, 58 per cent considered their working conditions to be 'worse' or 'much worse' and 34 per cent thought that they were 'about the same'; 7 per cent held they were either 'better' or 'much better'. The English sample seems to have felt more deprived in terms of working conditions than in terms of earnings but they still felt less deprived on that score than the Swedes; 31 per cent fewer of the English workers considered their working conditions to be either 'worse' or 'much worse' than those of white-collar workers. The difference is particularly noticeable in view of the fact that *actual* differences in the working conditons of manual workers and white-collar workers were less in the Swedish factory than in the

English.

The evidence clearly suggests that the Swedish sample demonstrated a greater awareness of the inequalities which existed between themselves and white-collar workers than the English. Indeed, there was a tendency for this to be reflected in heightened feelings of resentment. Both samples were asked: 'How do you feel about all these things — earnings, conditions of work, etc.?' The responses were then coded according to those expressing sentiments of 'approval' and 'disapproval'. Table 5.3 presents the data relating to attitudes to earnings analysed in this way.

Among the 77 Swedish workers who claimed that their earnings were either 'worse' or 'much worse' than those of white-collar workers, 26 per cent 'approved' and 72 per cent 'disapproved'. By contrast, of the 30 English workers who thought their earnings were either 'worse' or 'much worse', 43 per cent 'approved' and only a small majority — 53 per cent — 'disapproved'. This suggests that among those workers of both samples who felt they were relatively deprived, the Swedish respondents were more resentful than the English.

But what is more surprising is that 'disapproval' was also expressed by very high proportions of the Swedish sample who felt their earnings were 'much better', 'better', or 'about the same' as white-collar workers. For the first two of these categories the numbers are so small that it is difficult to make further interpretation. However, among the 37 Swedish workers who felt their earnings were 'about the same', as many as 95 per cent 'disapproved', compared with only 25 per cent of the 32 English respondents. Why did such a high proportion of the Swedish sample 'disapprove'? Was it because they felt that their earnings should have been higher or lower than those of white-collar workers? Their responses to other questions suggest that they felt their earnings should have been higher; for example, 91 per cent of these 35 Swedish workers claimed that white-collar workers had a number of advantages over themselves and felt that this was 'a bad state of affairs'. In view of this, the overall interpretation of Table 5.3 is that a far higher proportion of the Swedish workers than the English felt relatively deprived and resentful about their earnings.

This pattern was reflected in responses to the very general, open-ended question: 'What are the major differences, as you see them, between factory workers and white-collar workers these days?' This question was formulated in order to obtain respondents' opinions about the relative rewards accruing to white-collar and manual workers in society rather than within the two factories.

As Table 5.4 suggests, a majority of both samples stressed advantages

Table 5.3: 'How do you feel about all these things — earnings?'

| Earnings compared with those of white-collar workers | Swedish Workers | | | | | | | | English Workers | | | | | | | |
|---|---|---|---|---|---|---|---|---|---|---|---|---|---|---|---|---|
| | 'Approval' | | 'Disapproval' | | D.K. | | Total | | 'Approval' | | 'Disapproval' | | D.K. | | Total | |
| | Nos. | % | Nos. | % | Nos. | % | Nos. | % | Nos. | % | Nos. | % | Nos. | % | Nos. | % |
| Much better | — | — | 1 | 100.0 | — | — | 1 | 100.0 | 5 | 83.3 | 1 | 16.7 | — | — | 6 | 100.0 |
| Better | — | — | 4 | 100.0 | — | — | 4 | 100.0 | 39 | 76.5 | 11 | 21.6 | 1 | 1.9 | 51 | 100.0 |
| About the same | 2 | 5.4 | 35 | 94.6 | — | — | 37 | 100.0 | 22 | 68.8 | 8 | 25.0 | 2 | 6.2 | 32 | 100.0 |
| Worse | 20 | 29.0 | 48 | 69.5 | 1 | 1.5 | 69 | 100.0 | 13 | 46.4 | 14 | 50.0 | 1 | 3.6 | 28 | 100.0 |
| Much worse | — | — | 8 | 100.0 | — | — | 8 | 100.0 | — | — | 2 | 100.0 | — | — | 2 | 100.0 |
| Don't know | — | — | — | — | 2 | 100.0 | 2 | 100.0 | — | — | — | — | 8 | 100.0 | 8 | 100.0 |
| Not recorded | — | — | — | — | — | — | 1 | 100.0 | — | — | — | — | — | — | 1 | 100.0 |
| Total | | | | | | | 122 | 100.0 | | | | | | | 128 | 100.0 |

for white-collar workers, but the Swedish workers did so to a far greater degree than the English. Furthermore, the two samples differed considerably in the extent to which they held that there were *no* differences between white-collar workers and manual workers.

Table 5.4: 'What are the major differences, as you see them, between factory workers and white-collar workers these days?'

|  | Swedish Workers | | English Workers | |
|---|---|---|---|---|
|  | Nos. | % | Nos. | % |
| Responses suggesting advantages for white-collar workers | 109 | 89.4 | 73 | 57.0 |
| Responses suggesting advantages for manual workers | — | — | 5 | 3.9 |
| Claims that there were no differences | 11 | 9.0 | 44 | 34.4 |
| Claims that they were 'just different' | — | — | 5 | 3.9 |
| Don't know | 1 | 0.8 | 1 | 0.8 |
| Not recorded | 1 | 0.8 | — | — |
| Total | 122 | 100.0 | 128 | 100.0 |

The responses to this question were then coded according to the reasons workers gave for suggesting that white-collar workers had advantages. There were important differences between the two groups in the reasons given by those people who thought that white-collar workers were advantaged. As Table 5.5 shows, almost three-quarters of the Swedish sample mentioned economic advantages compared with about one-third of the English workers; the latter tended to mention economic factors with the same frequency as 'status' factors and working conditions. The reasons given for suggesting the advantages of white-collar workers included comments such as they were 'better paid' and acquired 'higher earnings'; for 'intrinsic' job factors, that 'their work is more interesting' and that 'they have more responsibility'; and for 'status' factors, that white-collar workers are 'looked up to', 'they have more prestige' and generally 'have better reputations in the community'.

Furthermore, feelings of resentment stimulated by this question, asking for their opinions about the major differences between factory and white-collar workers, were not the same for both samples. Both groups of workers who perceived advantages for white-collar workers were asked: 'Do you think that this is a good state of affairs? — "Yes" or "No"?' Only 6 per cent of the Swedish respondents claimed that it was a good state of affairs, while 93 per cent disapproved. On the other hand, 47 per cent of the English workers approved, while only 48 per cent held that it was a bad state of affairs.

Table 5.5: Reasons for suggesting the advantages of white-collar workers*

| Reason | Swedish Workers | | English Workers | |
|---|---|---|---|---|
| | Nos. | % | Nos. | % |
| Economic factors | 80 | 73.4 | 25 | 34.3 |
| Working conditions — | | | | |
| noise, lighting, ventilation, etc. | 25 | 22.9 | 29 | 39.7 |
| 'Intrinsic' job factors | 18 | 16.5 | 5 | 6.9 |
| 'Status' factors | 20 | 18.4 | 25 | 34.3 |
| Other and non-classifiable responses | 13 | 11.9 | 18 | 24.7 |

*109 Swedish and 73 English workers said that there were advantages for white-collar workers but some people gave more than one reason, so the answers total more than 100 per cent.

The two samples were then asked a number of general questions about the economic rewards accruing to different social classes. As stated in Chapter 4, 118 and 119 of the Swedish and English samples respectively recognised the existence of social classes. Having named the classes[12] and then described the composition of these,[13] the respondents were asked, 'Which class do you think has done best economically over the past few years?' Their replies to this question are shown in Table 5.6.

In Table 5.6, column (1) gives the number of respondents of each sample that described the class structure by reference to various labels; this column, in fact, repeats the figures listed in Chapter 4, Table 4.3. Column (2) specifies which class, of those which they mentioned in describing the class structure, they considered to have done best economically over the past few years. The final column then calculates the percentage of workers who, having mentioned a specific class, considered it 'to have done best'.

From Table 5.6 it is clear that the two samples had very different conceptions about which classes had made the most financial gains recently. For example, among those respondents that mentioned 'upper', 'top', or 'higher' in their descriptions of the class structure, 54 per cent of the Swedish but only 17 per cent of the English considered this class to have experienced the greatest economic gains. There is a

Table 5.6 'Which class do you think has done best economically over the past few years?'[14]

| 'Labels' mentioned by respondents in describing the class structure | Nos. of respondents mentioning specific classes in their description of the class structure (1) | | Nos. of respondents stating that a specific class 'had done best' (2) | | Percentage of respondents mentioning a specific class and who also stated it 'had done best' $\frac{(2)}{(1)} \times 100$ | |
|---|---|---|---|---|---|---|
| | Swedish Workers | English Workers | Swedish Workers | English Workers | Swedish Workers | English Workers |
| 1. 'Upper', 'top' 'higher classes' | 24 | 89 | 13 | 15 | 54.2 | 16.9 |
| 2. 'The wealthy', 'rich', 'those with plenty of money' | 14 | 19 | 9 | 4 | 64.3 | 21.1 |
| 3. 'Social Group I' | 57 | — | 33 | — | 57.9 | — |
| 4. 'Middle class' | 19 | 90 | 5 | 29 | 26.3 | 32.2 |
| 5. 'White-collar people' | 20 | 1 | 10 | — | 50.0 | — |
| 6. 'Educated people' | 5 | 1 | 3 | 1 | 60.0 | 100.0 |
| 7. 'Social Group II' | 56 | — | 16 | — | 28.6 | — |
| 8. 'Social Group III' | 47 | — | 7 | — | 14.9 | — |
| 9. 'Working class' | 46 | 89 | 12 | 51 | 26.1 | 57.3 |
| 10. 'Ordinary', 'average people' | 2 | 2 | — | — | — | — |
| 11. 'Lower class' | 2 | 21 | 1 | 3 | 50.0 | 14.3 |
| 12. 'The poor', 'the lower paid' | 7 | 8 | — | 3 | — | 37.5 |
| 13. Negative evaluation ('Those who don't want to work', etc.) | 10 | 1 | — | — | — | — |
| Don't know | — | — | 9 | 13 | — | — |
| Total | — | — | 118 | 119 | — | — |

similar magnitude in the differences between the responses of the two samples among those who mentioned 'the wealthy', 'rich' and 'those with plenty of money'; 64 per cent and 21 per cent of the Swedish and English samples respectively considered this class to 'have done best economically'. In addition, among those Swedish respondents who mentioned 'Social Group I' – which in many ways is comparable with the English 'upper class' – 58 per cent considered it to have made the greatest economic gains. On the other hand, among those respondents referring to 'working class' in their descriptions of the class structure, only 26 per cent of the Swedish respondents, compared with 57 per cent of the English, claimed that it 'had done best'. Consequently, the major interpretation to be taken from Table 5.6 is that the Swedish workers were much more likely than their English counterparts to believe that, over recent years, the greater economic gains had been enjoyed by the more dominant groups in society. The English respondents, by contrast, were more inclined to think that these had been achieved by the working class.

Although Table 5.6 describes the classes respondents mentioned in their conceptions of the class structure and those which they felt had done best economically over recent years, it does not specify their own self-placements. Consequently, it fails to show whether they felt their own economic position or that of some other group had enjoyed the greatest economic gains. This is analysed in Table 5.7, where respondents' own class self-placements are cross-tabulated with their comments about which class 'has done best economically over the past few years'. For the purpose of classification, these opinions have been re-coded in terms of whether respondents referred to their 'own class' or to 'another class'.

As Table 5.7 demonstrates, a far higher proportion of the Swedish workers considered that 'another class' had done best than the the English; 71 per cent compared with 41 per cent. Conversely, only 29 per cent of the Swedish workers, but as many as 59 per cent of their English counterparts, felt their 'own class' to have acquired the highest economic gains. In view of these differences, it is interesting to enquire whether or not there were variations between the two samples in terms of feelings of resentment. It could, of course, be entirely possible that the Swedish workers approved of 'other classes' achieving greater economic rewards than themselves. In order to investigate this possibility, the two samples were asked: 'How do you feel about this?', the responses to which were coded according to whether opinions of 'approval' or 'disapproval' were expressed. The results are presented in Table 5.8.

It is clear from Table 5.8 that for both the Swedish and the English workers, 'approval' was expressed by virtually 100 per cent of those claiming their 'own class' to have done best. However, there was a striking difference between the responses of the two groups when 'another class' was mentioned. Of the 84 Swedish respondents who mentioned 'another class', 82 per cent 'disapproved' and only 12 per cent 'approved'. Among the comparable 49 English workers, only 25 per cent 'disapproved' and as many as 55 per cent (27) 'approved'.

Table 5.7: Respondents' conceptions of whether their 'own class' or 'another class' 'has done best economically over the past few years'

| Respondents' own class self-placement | Class which 'has done best' | | | | | | | | | | | |
|---|---|---|---|---|---|---|---|---|---|---|---|---|
| | Swedish Workers | | | | | | English Workers | | | | | |
| | 'Own' | | 'Another' | | Total | | 'Own' | | 'Another' | | Total | |
| | Nos. | % | Nos. | % | Nos. | % | Nos. | % | Nos. | % | Nos. | % |
| 'Middle class' | 3. | 27.3 | 8 | 72.7 | 11 | 100.0 | 14 | 60.9 | 9 | 39.1 | 23 | 100.0 |
| 'Social Group II' | 12 | 40.0 | 18 | 60.0 | 30 | 100.0 | – | – | – | – | – | – |
| 'Social Group III' | 6 | 24.0 | 19 | 76.0 | 25 | 100.0 | – | – | – | – | – | – |
| 'Average people' | – | – | 2 | 100.0 | 2 | 100.0 | – | – | 2 | 100.0 | 2 | 100.0 |
| 'Working class' | 12 | 26.1 | 34 | 73.9 | 46 | 100.0 | 49 | 59.0 | 34 | 41.0 | 83 | 100.0 |
| 'Lower class' | 1 | 50.0 | 1 | 50.0 | 2 | 100.0 | 3 | 50.0 | 3 | 50.0 | 6 | 100.0 |
| 'The poor' | – | – | – | – | – | – | 3 | 75.0 | 1 | 25.0 | 4 | 100.0 |
| Other and non-classifiable responses | – | – | 2 | 100.0 | 2 | 100.0 | 1 | 100.0 | – | – | 1 | 100.0 |
| Total | 34 | 28.8 | 84 | 71.2 | 118 | 100.0 | 70 | 58.9 | 49 | 41.1 | 119 | 100.0 |

Table 5.8: Respondents' opinions about the economic gains acquired by their 'own class' and 'another class' (in absolute numbers)*

| Respondents' own class Self-placement | Swedish Workers | | | | | | | English Workers | | | | | | |
|---|---|---|---|---|---|---|---|---|---|---|---|---|---|---|
| | 'Own Class' | | | 'Another Class' | | | | 'Own Class' | | | 'Another Class' | | | |
| | 'Approve' | 'Disapprove' | 'Don't Know' | 'Approve' | 'Disapprove' | 'Don't Know' | Total | 'Approve' | 'Disapprove' | 'Don't Know' | 'Approve' | 'Disapprove' | 'Don't Know' | Total |
| 'Middle class' | 3 | — | — | 1 | 5 | 2 | 11 | 14 | — | — | 4 | 2 | 3 | 23 |
| 'Social Group II' | 12 | — | — | 4 | 14 | — | 30 | — | — | — | — | — | — | — |
| 'Social Group III' | 6 | — | — | 3 | 15 | 1 | 25 | — | — | — | — | — | — | — |
| 'Average people' | — | — | — | — | 2 | — | 2 | — | — | — | 2 | — | — | 2 |
| 'Working class' | 12 | — | — | 2 | 30 | 2 | 46 | 48 | — | 1 | 20 | 8 | 6 | 83 |
| 'Lower class' | 1 | — | — | — | 1 | — | 2 | 2 | 1 | — | 1 | 2 | — | 6 |
| 'The poor' | — | — | — | — | — | — | — | 3 | — | — | — | — | 1 | 4 |
| Other and non-classifiable responses | — | — | — | 2 | 2 | — | 2 | 1 | — | — | — | — | — | 1 |
| Total | 34 | — | — | 10 | 69 | 5 | 118 | 68 | 1 | 1 | 27 | 12 | 10 | 119 |

*In view of the small numbers involved, no percentage figures are given.

Among these 27 English respondents, the classes most frequently mentioned were the 'upper' and 'middle' classes; these were specified by 41 per cent and 33 per cent of the workers respectively.

Table 5.8 clearly suggests that the Swedish workers were much more likely than the English to resent the greater economic gains which they perceived had been acquired by other classes in society. In sharp contrast to these feelings, the English workers expressed such opinons as 'best of luck to them', 'I would do the same if I were them', 'it doesn't make any difference to me', 'it doesn't bother me', etc.; indeed, statements which indicated that they perceived little or no social link between their own position and that of other groups in society. Accordingly, by comparison with the Swedish workers, they experienced little resentment.

These results, when taken together, suggest that there was a greater awareness of inequalities of economic condition among the Swedish workers than among the English. Furthermore, this awareness tended to be associated with heightened feelings of resentment. Indeed, the differences between the two samples are so striking that it is necessary to consider the degree to which the attitudes of the English respondents were atypical for those of English workers in general. As emphasised in Chapter 3, the samples cannot be regarded as representative of either the national populations or of industrial workers in the two countries. But the attitudes of the English respondents were such that they suggest rather more acquiescence than that which has been found among workers in many other industrial situations in Britain.[15] Since there was no attempt in this study to ascertain the representativeness of the English sample, it is only possible to speculate about some of the reasons for this. Labour-management relations, for example, according to both senior management and local union officials, were considered to be good. Thus, the 'culture' of the factory was not conducive to the generation of feelings of resentment among employees. Indeed, this was probably reinforced by the community in which the factory was situated: a town of 28.000 people with no tradition of industrial conflict. Furthermore, at the time when the interview survey was undertaken, spring 1970, there seems to have been a low level of socio-political involvement in Britain; demonstrated, that is, by the relatively low turnout of voters in the general election of that year.[16] These are but some of the factors which would need to be taken into account in any attempt to relate the attitudes of the English respondents to the study of manual workers in general; if only because the findings of various studies suggest that there are marked contrasts within the English working class in terms of feelings of resentment and levels of articulated protest.[17] But even if the differences between the attitudes of the English and the Swedish samples were greater than those which would be produced by a comparative study of national samples, it does seem that Swedish manual workers tend to be more aware of large-scale economic inequalities than their English counterparts. This is particularly striking in view of the fact that the Swedish respondents in the present enquiry were comparable to the English workers in a number of important respects, and especially since they were *also* chosen from a factory in which management-worker relations were good, and located in a relatively small community of only 25,000 inhabitants with no tradition of industrial conflict. Why, then, as far as the two samples of workers are concerned, were the Swedish respondents more aware of economic inequalities than the English?

Runciman has argued that in order to explain the experience of relative deprivation, it is necessary to take into account the reference groups which people adopt for the purpose of comparison. Consequently, he suggests that the resentment of class inequality in Britain is slight because individuals, particularly manual workers, tend to adopt highly restricted reference groups.[18] However, this does not appear to be the case in Sweden because, as the results of the interview survey demonstrated, the respondents adopted more broadly based reference groups incorporating both manual and non-manual workers. Thus, a factor to take into account is the degree to which the respondents of the two samples had immediate experiences of white-collar 'worlds'. If there were differences in these, it could be conducive to variations in their knowledge of economic inequalities as they exist between manual workers and other occupational groups. In order to investigate this, the two samples were compared in terms of criteria which would be likely to lead them to experience white-collar influences; namely, patterns of social mobility as measured in terms of the occupations of their sons and fathers, the social origins of their wives, as represented by the occupations of their fathers-in-law when they were first married, and the occupations of working wives.

The two samples were first compared in terms of the mobility patterns of their sons. But as the evidence in Chapter 4 suggested, for both groups of respondents, similar numbers of sons were engaged in non-manual employment; only 7 and 6 of the Swedish and English samples respectively. Consequently, intergenerational upward mobility cannot be seen to account for the differences in their awareness of inequality. The two samples were then compared according to the occupations of their fathers in order to find out whether the Swedish workers were more likely to have been exposed to white-collar norms by virtue of their fathers' occupations. Both samples were asked: 'What was the title of your father's job when you left school?' The coded responses are given in Table 5.9:

Table 5.9: 'What was the title of your father's job when you left school?'

| Father's Occupation | Swedish Workers | | English Workers | |
|---|---|---|---|---|
| | Nos. | % | Nos. | % |
| Manual | 89 | 73.0 | 98 | 76.6 |
| Non-manual | 8 | 6.5 | 4 | 3.1 |
| Self-employed (not farmer) | 7 | 5.7 | 7 | 5.5 |
| Farmer | 11 | 9.0 | 1 | 0.8 |
| Farm worker | 3 | 2.5 | 11 | 8.6 |
| Military (conscription and regular) | 1 | 0.8 | 3 | 2.3 |
| Don't know | 3 | 2.5 | 4 | 3.1 |
| Total | 122 | 100.0 | 128 | 100.0 |

From Table 5.9 it is clear that there are no large differences between the two groups in terms of their fathers' occupations; 73 per cent of the Swedish sample were the sons of manual workers compared with 76 per cent of the English. The only major difference is in the proportion who were the sons of farmers. Although this was higher among the Swedish workers, it is unlikely to have provided a white-collar or middle-class 'experience' for respondents since with one exception, they were the sons of farmers working smallholdings without the use of employed labour.[19] Clearly, a home background of this kind is unlikely to generate an awareness, and even less a resentment, of inequalities as they exist between manual and white-collar workers in society. It thus seems reasonable to assume that the Swedish workers were no more likely than the English to have encountered white-collar life-styles during their childhood. Consequently, their heightened awareness of economic inequalities, together with their more intense feelings of resentment, cannot be explained by a more frequent experience of intergenerational, downward mobility. In view of this, it is worth while to consider the source of a further possible white-collar influence: the wives — their social origins and, if they are at work, their occupations.

The married respondents were asked: 'What was your father-in-law's job when you got married?' Among the English workers there was a large number who claimed that they did not know; this was stated by no less than 19 per cent of the 111 married respondents. By comparison, only 8 per cent of the 104 married Swedish workers gave a similar response. In view of this, the figures in Table 5.10 are for only those workers who were able to name the occupations of their wives' fathers; that is, for 96 and 90 of the Swedish and English respondents respectively.

Table 5.10: 'What was your father-in-law's job when you got married?'

| Father-in-law's Occupation | Swedish Workers | | English Workers | |
|---|---|---|---|---|
| | Nos. | % | Nos. | % |
| Manual | 56 | 58.3 | 53 | 58.9 |
| Non-manual | 13 | 13.5 | 10 | 11.1 |
| Self-employed (not farmer) | 12 | 12.5 | 9 | 10.0 |
| Farmer | 14 | 14.6 | 4 | 4.4 |
| Farm worker | 1 | 1.0 | 12 | 13.4 |
| Military (conscription and regular) | – | – | 2 | 2.2 |
| Total | 96 | 100.0 | 90 | 100.0 |

Table 5.10 shows that there are close similarities between the two samples in terms of the social origins of their wives. The only major differences are the proportions from different types of farming background; a higher percentage of the Swedish wives were the daughters of farmers while among the English respondents more wives came from the homes of agricultural workers. But only two of these 14 Swedish farmers employed workers and so it is difficult to regard these wives as coming from middle-class homes in terms of life-styles and normative influences. Consequently, it is reasonable to assume that the social origins of the respondents' wives cannot explain the different attitudes expressed by the two groups of workers.

But an alternative method by which the respondents' wives could bring white-collar influences into their homes is by their employment. If, for example, they had clerical, secretarial and other white-collar occupations, they would witness the privileges and rewards of professional managerial and other non-manual workers. Of the 104 Swedish and the 111 English wives, 67 per cent and 61 per cent respectively held some kind of employment. But among these, there were important differences between the two groups in the proportions employed in white-collar jobs. No less than 80 per cent (56) of the Swedish working wives were ngaged in white-collar occupations compared with only 35 per cent (24) of the English wives. Similarly, only 20 per cent (14) of the Swedish wives were in manual employment by comparison with as many as 65 per cent (44) of their English counterparts. This does suggest, then, that a higher proportion of the Swedish respondents, through the employment of their wives, were more likely to be exposed to influences conducive to a heightened awareness of inequality as it existed between manual and non-manual occupational groups. Therefore, in order to test whether this was the case, the Swedish sample's responses to the question 'Are there any people you can think of who are better off than workers like yourself?'[20] were cross-tabulated with the experience of having wives employed in non-manual and manual occupations. The results are given in Table 5.11:

Table 5.11: Swedish respondents' awareness of inequality related to wives' occupations

| 'Are there any people better off than workers like yourself?' | Wife's Occupation | | | |
|---|---|---|---|---|
| | Manual | | Non-Manual | |
| | Nos. | % | Nos. | % |
| Yes | 10 | 71.5 | 42 | 75.0 |
| No | 1 | 7.1 | 6 | 10.7 |
| Don't know | 3 | 21.4 | 8 | 14.3 |
| Total | 14 | 100.0 | 56 | 100.0 |

Table 5.11 suggests that the occupations of wives do not affect in any fundamental manner the Swedish respondents' awareness of economic inequality. Only 3 per cent more of those workers with wives in non-manual employment could think of 'people better off than themselves' than those with wives in manual jobs; 75 per cent compared with 72 per cent. Therefore, it appears that wives' experiences of 'white-collar worlds' had little impact upon the Swedish workers' conceptions of inequality.

    Thus, the evidence seems to show that the Swedish respondents were no more likely than the English to be 'exposed' to white-collar influences within the family; the two samples differ only in terms of the occupations of their wives — a factor which does not seem to have been conducive to generating experiences of relative deprivation. Therefore, in order to understand the differences in attitudes of the two samples, it is necessary to consider influences other than those located within the immediate structural experiences of the respondents.[21]

Parkin has suggested that the awareness of inequality in capitalist societies is closely related to the relative influence of different ideologies.[22] He claims that there are at least three kinds of *meaning systems,* each of which has as part of its function the interpretation of social and economic ineqaualities. These are (1) the *dominant* value system, which endorses existing structures of inequality and becomes internalised by members of the 'under-class' in either 'aspirational' or 'deferential' terms;[23] (2) the *subordinate* value system, generated by the working-class community which promotes an *accommodative* response to inequality; this is often reflected as fatalism, resignation, limited aspirations, and an acceptance of existing inequalities as legitimate;[24] (3) the *radical* value system, with its source in the mass political party based on the working class which promotes an *oppositional* interpretation of class inequality.[25]

Empirical studies conducted in Britain have suggested that of these meaning systems, the *radical* has been the least influential. Investigations have shown, for example, that not only the Labour Party, but large sectors of the trade union movement have given little emphasis to the grass-roots participation of rank-and-file members and to political socialisation.[26] As a result, the *radical* value system is largely ineffective among many sectors of manual workers in Britain in providing an *oppositional* interpretation of social inequality, with a consequence that inequality has been interpreted according to ideas inherent in either the *dominant* or *subordinate* value systems. Accordingly, the existing structure of inequality has remained fundamentally unquestioned.[27]

In Sweden, on the other hand, has the development of working-class institutions been more influential in providing *oppositional* interpretations of social and economic inequalities? Variations in the frequency of relative deprivation, the adoption of reference groups and attitudes of resentment between the two samples could then be seen as a consequence of the differential degree to which they have been exposed to *radical* values. Of course, the reverse is also possible; there could be a more radical labour movement in Sweden simply because workers are more radical. Which, then is cause and which is effect? This is a difficult relationship to unravel and perhaps it is inappropriate to pose the problem in this way. A better way to conceive of it is in terms of mutual feedbacks; the attitudes of rank-and-file members will impose certain constraints upon the policies of their leaders but at the same time, leaders will shape the attitudes of rank-and-file members. In most circumstances, however, the latter is more likely to occur if only because of the highly bureaucratised structure of working-class institutions.[28] Certainly the evidence lends support to this contention.

In both samples union membership was 100 per cent, but there were striking differences between the two groups in terms of their opinions about the aims of labour unions. Respondents were asked the open-ended question: 'What do you think should be the major aim of trade unions?'

Table 5.12: 'What do you think should be the major aim of trade unions?'

| Major Aim | Swedish Workers | | English Workers | |
|---|---|---|---|---|
| | Nos. | % | Nos. | % |
| Responses suggesting improved social justice, socialism | 52 | 42.6 | 2 | 1.6 |
| 'To represent workers' interests' | 3 | 2.5 | 17 | 13.4 |
| Economic factors | 48 | 39.4 | 72 | 55.9 |
| Improved working conditions | 12 | 9.8 | 30 | 23.6 |
| 'To protect the individual' | 2 | 1.6 | 4 | 3.1 |
| Other and non-classifiable responses | 5 | 4.1 | 2 | 1.6 |
| Not recorded | — | — | 1 | 0.8 |
| Total | 122 | 100.0 | 128 | 100.0 |

Whereas substantial minorities of the Swedish sample stated either 'socialist' or economic factors, the former were hardly mentioned by the English workers; even if respondents who made the general statement 'to represent workers' interests' are taken into account. Instead, the English workers tended to stress the need for unions to improve pay and working conditions, factors which suggested that they perceived trade unions in instrumental and economic ways rather than in ideological terms.[29] The Swedish workers, by contrast, when they mentioned 'socialist' factors, tended to stress such things as the need to 'increase equality', to 'improve social justice' and 'to remove social injustices at the workplace'; sentiments which were not evident in the responses of the English sample.

As stated in earlier chapters, Swedish labour unions have adopted as an explicit objective the need to increase equality. Particularly since the war, LO has pursued a policy of 'wage solidarity', the objective of which has been to negotiate with employers wage increases which would, at the same time, reduce differentials between different groups of manual workers. Although this policy has had little consequence in fundamentally narrowing differentials, it has remained a desirable and a central goal of labour union policy. In Britain, by contrast, despite the trade union movement's frequent expression of concern about the earnings of low wage groups and the desirability of establishing a national minimum wage, it has never seriously pursued an explicit policy of 'wage solidarity' in the Swedish sense.[30] But not only have Swedish labour unions attempted to narrow differentials between various categories of manual workers, they have also questioned differentials in the wages, fringe benefits, conditions of employment and general working conditions as they exist between white-collar and manual workers. Because these groups belong to unions which are affiliated to separate national confederations, manual and non-manual differentials are generally more salient in industrial bargaining than they are in Britain. LO can, therefore, pursue policies of 'equality' between white-collar and manual workers in a more explicit manner than is available to the TUC in Britain, with its affiliation of both white-collar and manual unions.[31]

All this has created in Sweden a general awareness of differences in the economic conditions of manual and non-manual workers; a situation which has led to the adoption of broadly based, cross-class reference groups among manual workers and a consciousness of relative deprivation.[32] In fact, this has been reinforced by the activities of the Social Democratic Party which, over recent years, has questioned the legitimacy of manual/non-manual differentials.[33]

Both samples of workers were asked if they had voted in the last election; 98 per cent of the Swedish workers claimed they had, compared with 88 per cent of the English sample. These respondents were then asked: 'If a General Election were to be held in the near future, which party would you vote for?'[34] Among these Swedish workers 81 per cent declared their allegiance to the Social Democratic Party and 68 per cent of the English respondents said they would vote for Labour. These respondents were then asked: 'Why would you vote in this way?'

For both samples there was a 'generalised' working-class identification with the political party. But as Table 5.13 shows, although they were a small minority of both samples, more than three times as many Swedish workers as English mentioned 'socialist' policies; these included such statements as 'they are more likely to increase equality', 'they are more likely to make a more just society', 'we haven't achieved equality yet.' At the same time more than 70 per cent of the Swedish respondents perceived the Social Democrats as the party most likely to improve social benefits and to develop the welfare state; factors mentioned by less than one-third of the English workers.

Table 5.13: 'Why would you vote in this way?'*

| Reasons | Swedish Workers | | English Workers | |
|---|---|---|---|---|
| | Nos. | % | Nos. | % |
| General 'working class' identification with Labour/Social Democrats | 64 | 66.7 | 50 | 64.9 |
| Family traditions | 5 | 5.2 | 8 | 10.4 |
| Economic factors | 42 | 43.8 | 15 | 19.5 |
| 'Socialist' policies | 17 | 17.7 | 4 | 5.2 |
| 'Welfare' policies | 69 | 71.9 | 23 | 29.9 |
| Other and non-classifiable responses | 26 | 27.1 | 18 | 23.4 |

*Asked of those people who said that they had voted in the last general election and who also claimed that they would vote for the Social Democratic or Labour Party in the next. Some people gave more than one answer so that the numbers add to more than 100 per cent.

Since the late 1960s, issues of equality and social justice have been at the centre of political debate in Sweden, to the extent that in the 1970 General Election, the Social Democratic Party adopted 'Increased Equality' ('Ökad Jämlikhet') as its election slogan. This was supported by other statements, many of which were financed by specific labour unions and by LO, and included 'We shall remove social injustices at work' and 'Dangers at work will be removed.' The British Labour Party, on the other hand, has not stressed issues of inequality when it has been in government, nor has it made them the centre of its electoral campaign.[35] In presenting itself as the champion of social justice, the Social Democratic Party has generated a sense of relative deprivation among manual workers which exists to a greater degree than among large sectors of the working class in England.

Furthermore, Social Democracy in Sweden has led to the development of an achievement-orientated, 'open' and egalitarian ideology, which has had important implications for the experience of relative deprivation. As Lipset and Trow have suggested,

An egalitarian, 'open class' value system with its less rigid social

structures may actually engender more immediate discontent among
low socio-economic groups, than does a more rigidly stratified
structure. An open-class value system leads workers to define inequalities in income and status between themselves and others as
illegitimate more frequently than do workers in countries which
have more sharply and rigidly defined social structures.[36]

But as the evidence in Chapter 2 suggested, economic inequalities and
mobility chances are much the same in Sweden as they are in England
and the social structure of the former is no less rigid than the latter. As
a result, differences in the frequency of relative deprivation between
the two samples of workers must be seen to be more a consequence of
differences in *meaning systems* than to any structural variations
between either the immediate situations of the two samples or of the
two countries.

However, it is appropriate at this point to refer to an apparent contradiction in the attitudes of the Swedish workers. Considerable
emphasis has been given to the labour movement's ideology of egalitarianism and the degree to which this has shaped attitudes. But why
should this have created an awareness of inequalities in economic
rewards but not of mobility chances? A possible explanation is that,
according to Social Democratic appeals, equality of opportunity has
been achieved to a large extent, especially by the reforms of the educational system undertaken during the 1960s.[37] The introduction of a
non-streamed comprehensive system of education, together with the
debate which this has generated, appears to have created a public ethos
of equal opportunity.[38] However, the Swedish working-class movement
has made no such claims about the structure of economic rewards. The
Social Democratic Party, particularly since the late 1960s, has emphasised the need to *increase* economic equality and in doing so it has
stressed the persistence of inequalities in contemporary Sweden.[39]
Thus, in order to retain rank-and-file allegiance, it has presented itself
as the only movement in Sweden capable of reducing existing differentials; an argument which has been supported by the appeals of LO.
In this way, an awareness of existing inequalities has been created
among industrial manual workers. This has been reinforced by the
structure of Swedish unionism which, during national wage negotiations,
illuminates differences in the economic rewards accruing to different
occupational categories.[40] Therefore, although there appears to have
been a paradox in the attitudes of the Swedish respondents in the
sense that they were aware of inequalities in economic rewards but not

in mobility chances, this is explained by the specific policies pursued by the labour movement within the context of its ideological commitment to egalitarianism.

This chapter suggests, then, that contrasts in the awareness of economic inequalities between the two samples were, if only partly, a function of variations in the *meaning systems* to which they were exposed. The greater knowledge of economic inequalities among the Swedish workers appears to have been a consequence of the impact of *radical* values, as expressed by working-class institutions. If this interpretation is correct, it highlights a dilemma for Social Democratic governments in capitalist countries. It seems that aspirations are heightened and the experience of relative deprivation among rank-and-file supporters increases. But the institutions of capitalism generate structures of economic and social inequality. Accordingly, it may be appropriate to consider Social Democracy in capitalist societies as a 'temporary' phenomenon so that over the long term, two possible developments could be expected. Disillusionment could become so widespread among manual workers that there is a shift in support for more 'right-wing' political parties; indeed there were strong indications of this in the mid-1970s. Alternatively, there could be increased government intervention in the economy so that ultimately the means of production are publicly owned and a socialist society established. If this were to occur then the whole process could be regarded as one in which, in the initial stages, Social Democratic and union leaders generate heightened experiences of relative deprivation in order to command and later maintain the support of the rank and file, but at a later stage they are forced by their members to adopt more 'radical' policies. But irrespective of these alternatives it seems that, at present, an ideology of egalitarianism and the persistence of structural inequalities has generated inevitable tensions in Sweden. The extent to which these have affected the legitimacy of the labour movement among industrial workers and particularly among the Swedish respondents is investigated in the next chapter.

## Notes

1. W.G. Runciman, *Relative Deprivation and Social Justice,* London, 1966.
2. Westergaard, however, in a re-interpretation of Runciman's findings, has suggested that the awareness of inequality, together with feelings of discontent, were probably greater than Runciman claimed. See J. Westergaard, 'The Rediscovery of the Cash Nexus', *Socialist Register,* London, 1970.
3. J. Goldthorpe, D. Lockwood, F. Bechhofer and J. Platt, *The Affluent Worker in the Class Structure,* Cambridge, 1969, Ch. 5.

4.  See, for example, R. Miliband, *The State in Capitalist Society*, London, 1969. For a discussion of the development of industrialisation in different capitalist societies and how this has affected forms of working-class consciousness in Europe, the United States and Japan, see A. Giddens, *The Class Structure of the Advanced Societies*, London, 1973.
5.  W.G. Runciman, op. cit., p. 192.
6.  As in Chapter 4, only rounded-up percentages are given in the text.
7.  See Chapter 2.
8.  In ranking the earnings of male wage-earners in 13 industries for a number of West European countries, a United Nations enquiry found that construction workers came 'first' in Sweden and 'sixth' in Britain. See United Nations, *Incomes in Post-War Europe*, Geneva, 1967, Table 5.2.
9.  W.G. Runciman, op. cit., Ch. 10. Table 20.
10. For data on the two countries, see Chapter 2; and for the two factories, Chapter 3.
11. For the relevant data, see Chapter 4.
12. See Table 4.3.
13. See Table 4.6.
14. For the ways in which respondents defined the classes which they mentioned, see Table 4.6.
15. For a comprehensive discussion of sources of acquiescence and dissent within the English working class, see J. Westergaard and H. Resler, *Class in a Capitalist Society*, London, 1975, Part Five.
16. See R. Rose, 'Voting Trends Surveyed' in *The Times, Guide to the House of Commons 1970*, London, 1970.
17. See the studies reviewed in J. Westergaard and H. Resler, op. cit.
18. W.G. Runciman, op. cit.
19. If a respondent mentioned his father was a farmer he was asked whether or not he had any employees. This was in order to differentiate crudely between 'large' and 'small' farmers.
20. See Table 5.1.
21. Of course, this analysis has not discussed all of the possible structural influences. It has not, for example, considered the social composition of the neighbourhoods in which the respondents lived; a factor which could have affected their awareness of economic inequalities. Thus, if they lived in socially 'mixed' residential areas in which there were both non-manual and manual workers, it is possible they would have been more aware of inequalities than if they had lived in neighbourhoods consisting of only manual workers.
22. F. Parkin, *Class Inequality and Political Order*, London, 1971. Ch. 3.
23. Parkin defines 'aspirational' as 'a view of the reward structure which emphasises the opportunities for self-advancement and social promotion', and 'deferential' as 'a view of the social order as an organic entity in which each individual has a part to play, however humble. Inequality is seen as inevitable as well as just, some men being inherently fitted for positions of power and privilege.' F. Parkin, op. cit., p. 85.
24. 'Insofar as it is possible to characterise a complex set of normative arrangements by a single term, the subordinate value system could be said to be essentially *accommodative;* that is to say its representation of the class structure and inequality emphasises various modes of adaptation, rather than either full endorsement of, or opposition to, the *status quo.'* F. Parkin, op. cit., p. 88.
25. 'The radical value system purports to demonstrate the systematic nature of class inequality and attempts to reveal a connectedness between man's

personal fate and the wider political order.' F. Parkin, op. cit., p. 97.

26. See, for example, J. Goldthorpe, D. Lockwood, F. Bechhofer and J. Platt, *The Affluent Worker: Political Attitudes and Behaviour,* Cambridge, 1968; and B. Hindess, *The Decline of Working Class Politics,* London, 1971.

27. Although Westergaard and Resler have suggested that the level of radicalism is probably greater than that suggested by several sociological studies. See J. Westergaard and H. Resler, op. cit.

28. Michels was one of the first to stress that the bureaucratisation of organisations leads to the development of oligarchic tendencies. See R. Michels, *Political Parties,* New York, 1962. For a summary of the structure of the Swedish trade union movement, see T. Johnston, *Collective Bargaining in Sweden,* London, 1962.

29. This finding is consistent with the results reported in J. Goldthorpe, D. Lockwood, F. Bechhofer and J. Platt, *The Affluent Worker: Industrial Attitudes and Behaviour,* Cambridge, 1968, Ch. 5.

30. The £6-a-week flat rate increase negotiated between the TUC and the Labour government in 1975 had an egalitarian effect. However, this was introduced more by a concern to curb inflation than to erode occupational differentials.

31. This is discussed in Chapter 1.

32. The role of political and labour union leaders in defining the reference groups of rank-and-file members is discussed by S. Lipset and M. Trow, 'Reference Group Theory and Trade Union Wage Policy', in M. Komarovsky (ed.), *Common Frontiers of the Social Sciences,* Glencoe, 1957.

33. See Chapter 2.

34. In fact, general elections were held in both countries in 1970, the year when the social survey was conducted. The interviewing was completed before the respective 'campaigns' had begun.

35. Until, that is, the two elections of 1974, when it gave rather more attention to issues of equality and social justice than in the elections of 1964, 1966 and 1970.

36. S. Lipset and M. Trow, op. cit., p. 401.

37. See, for example, the statements in A. Myrdal, *Towards Equality,* Stockholm, 1971.

38. See Chapter 5.

39. In doing this it has made extensive use of the findings of the *Commission on Low Incomes* which has demonstrated the magnitude of economic inequalities in Sweden. See, for example, Statens Offentliga Utredningar (SOU), *Svenska Folkets Inkomster (The Income of the Swedish Population),* Stockholm, 1970.

40. See Chapter 1 for a discussion of this point.

# 6 CONCEPTIONS OF THE CLASS STRUCTURE: (3) INEQUALITIES OF POWER

The previous chapters have emphasised how the labour movement in Sweden enjoys a greater degree of legitimacy among industrial workers than in Britain. It was suggested that the Swedish respondents' conceptions of the class structure, together with their opinons about the possibilities for individual upward mobility, were largely the result of a 'meritocratic' ideology put forward by the Social Democratic Party. At the same time, it was claimed that the egalitarian objectives of the Party and the trade union movement had heightened the general awareness of economic inequalities. It was argued that in Britain, by contrast, the labour movement had been less influential in shaping workers' attitudes with the consequence that the English respondents had a limited awareness of class inequalities. Furthermore, it was suggested that the power structure of Sweden probably incorporates the interests of industrial manual workers to a greater extent than in Britain, if only because the activities of dominant economic groups are more 'constrained' by the labour movement. The present chapter considers this further by reference to the samples' conceptions of the exercise of power. More specifically, it investigates whether there are differences between the two groups of respondents in terms of their perceptions of the influence exercised by the respective labour movements.

Although membership was not obligatory, 100 per cent of both samples belonged to trade unions. Despite this, they were asked: 'Is it compulsory for you to belong to a trade union in your job?' In reply to this question, 66 per cent (81) of the Swedish and 78 per cent (100) of the English workers claimed that it was.[1] These respondents were then asked: 'Do you think that it is a good thing or a bad thing?' There was an interesting difference between the two groups in their answers; whereas no less than 96 per cent (78) of the Swedish workers said that it was 'a good thing', this opinion was expressed by 68 per cent (68) of the relevant English respondents. Conversely, only 4 per cent (3) of the Swedish workers claimed it was a 'bad thing' compared with as many as 32 per cent (32) of the English. Both samples were then asked: 'Why do you think it is a good (or bad) thing?' Their coded replies to this question are reproduced in Table 6.1.

As Table 6.1 suggests, 86 per cent of the Swedish sample who

Table 6.1: 'Why do you think it is a good (or bad) thing?' (that it is compulsory to belong to a trade union)*

| Responses suggesting that: | Swedish Workers | | | | English Workers | | | |
| | 'Good' | | 'Bad' | | 'Good' | | 'Bad' | |
| | Nos. | % | Nos. | % | Nos. | % | Nos. | % |
|---|---|---|---|---|---|---|---|---|
| It strengthens the bargaining power of workers | 67 | 85.9 | – | – | 13 | 19.1 | – | – |
| Everyone should belong because they all receive the benefits | 9 | 11.5 | – | – | 49 | 72.1 | – | – |
| It restricts individual freedom | – | – | 3 | 100.0 | – | – | 31 | 96.9 |
| Other and non-classifiable responses | 1 | 1.3 | – | – | 6 | 8.8 | 1 | 3.1 |
| Don't know | 1 | 1.3 | – | – | – | – | – | – |
| Total | 78 | 100.0 | 3 | 100.0 | 68 | 100.0 | 32 | 100.0 |

*Asked of the 81 and 100 Swedish and English workers respectively who considered that union membership was compulsory.

thought that union membership was compulsory considered it to be 'a good thing' because they felt it strengthened the negotiating position of workers. Consequently, they made such statements as 'solidarity gives strength', 'if you all stick together, things can be done', 'it strengthens our position against managers', etc. Among the comparable English workers, by contrast, only 19 per cent made comments of this kind, while a further 72 per cent said it was 'a good thing' because everybody took advantage of the benefits. Hence, they stated that 'everyone should belong and pay their dues because they all reap the rewards', 'why should some pay for the benefit of others?' and 'everybody gets the benefits of a wage increase.' In other words, whereas the Swedish workers stressed the positive advantages of 'collective action' and 'solidarity', the English workers were more concerned about colleagues enjoying the rewards achieved by the efforts of others. Indeed, the Swedish workers seemed to be stating opinions about the position of trade unions *in relation* to other groups in society while the English tended to be more concerned about unionism among manual workers. Of the 32 English workers who considered that compulsory union membership was 'a bad thing', no less than 97 per cent made comments suggesting they felt it infringed individual freedom in some way. Consequently, these respondents often said that it 'restricts individual choice', 'it limits individual freedom', 'it takes away the liberty of the individual', and so on. In fact, expressed as a proportion of the total sample, no less than 24 per cent of the 128 English workers were opposed to the idea that union membership should be compulsory; by comparison, this opinion was shared by only 2 per cent of the 122 Swedish respondents. Thus, the evidence suggests, if only indirectly, that the legitimacy of union membership was better established among the Swedish workers than their English counterparts. At the same time, the Swedish respondents were more interested in union affairs. This was reflected in attendance at local meetings and the proportion holding positions within the local branch.

Both samples were asked: 'How often do you go to union meetings? Would you say that you went regularly, occasionally, rarely, or never?' Among the Swedish workers, 15 per cent claimed that they attended 'regularly' and a further 30 per cent 'occasionally'. For the English respondents, only 8 per cent and 20 per cent gave similar replies. Furthermore, whereas 15 per cent of the Swedish sample said that they never attended meetings, this was claimed by no less than 39 per cent of the English workers.[2] The greater involvement of the Swedish workers in union affairs was confirmed by the higher proportion who were union officials. The respondents were asked: 'Do you hold any position in your present trade union?' In their replies, twice as many of the Swedish than the English workers claimed that they did; 15 per cent compared with 7 per cent. Consequently, the 'density' of active union members, measured in terms of the proportion who were local officials and the frequency of attendance at branch meetings, was far greater in the Swedish workplace. Thus, the national union in Sweden was in a potentially better position to generate a greater degree of involvement among its 'grass-roots' members; it had greater possibilities to influence the attitudes of workers and to reinforce their commitment to the organisation. In other words, the higher proportion of union 'influentials' in the Swedish workplace meant that they could be used in order to publicise official policies among rank-and-file members and to act as agents of political socialisation. In fact, these local officials appear to have been more highly regarded by the Swedish respondents than by their English counterparts. The two samples were asked: 'Do you think that local union officials represent the interests of the ordinary members?' For the purposes of this question, it was explained to respondents that 'local union officials' referred to shop stewards as well as to branch officials.[3] Among the 104 Swedish workers who were not

officials, 76 per cent claimed that they did, compared with 64 per cent
of the English respondents. Only 22 per cent of the Swedish compared
with 33 per cent of the English workers considered that local union
officials did not represent their interests and a further 2 per cent and 3
per cent of the Swedish and English samples claimed they did not know.
The respondents who were not local officials and felt that these did not
represent the interests of ordinary members were asked: 'Why is this?'
The coded responses are shown in Table 6.2:

Table 6.2: 'Why is this?' (that local union officials do not represent the
interests of the ordinary members)*

| Responses suggesting that: | Swedish Workers | | English Workers | |
|---|---|---|---|---|
| | Nos. | % | Nos. | % |
| They only think of themselves | 10 | 43.5 | 16. | 41.0 |
| They are too closely allied with management | 1 | 4.3 | 15 | 38.5 |
| Other and non-classifiable responses | 6 | 26.1 | 8 | 20.5 |
| Don't know | 6 | 26.1 | — | — |
| Total | 23 | 100.0 | 39 | 100.0 |

*Asked of the 23 Swedish and the 38 English workers who were not local
officials and felt that officials did not represent the interests of ordinary members.

Table 6.2 suggests that similar proportions of these respondents in both
samples considered that local union officials did not represent their
interests because of 'selfish' reasons. A number of workers felt, for
example, that local officials were only interested in 'working their way
up the union', 'advancing their own interests' and 'looking after number
one'. But a far smaller proportion of the Swedish respondents claimed
that local union officials did not represent their interests because they
were too closely identified with management. A number of English
workers, for instance, stated that 'they always side with management',
'they are too much with the managers', 'they're more concerned with
the managers' interests than with ours.'
      The inference to be drawn from these results is that a far higher
proportion of the English sample were 'estranged' from the local union.
They were more likely to be suspicious of local officials and as a result,
the national union could hardly use them as effective agents of political
socialisation, as they were regarded as suspect by a substantial minority
of rank-and-file members. Among the Swedish workers, on the other
hand, there was a greater belief that they did represent the interests of

ordinary members; even when officials were regarded as pursuing their
own self-interests, they were not considered to be 'taking the side of
management' in the same way as they were regarded by the English
sample. All this suggests, then, that in terms of participation at branch
meetings, the 'density' of active union members and the general level of
legitimacy enjoyed by local officials, that the Swedish respondents were
more involved in union affairs than their English counterparts. As a
result, the Swedish union was in a better position to influence members'
attitudes and beliefs. Alternatively, of course, this could have constituted a source of opposition to the national union and its policies.[4] But
this was not the case, as confirmed by two factors. First, the workers
had never been involved in an unofficial strike. Secondly, the extent to
which LO's policies of wage solidarity and of greater economic equality
between the earnings of manual and non-manual occupational groups
had been accepted by rank-and-file members. As stated in Chapter 5,
when asked, 'What do you think should be the major aim of trade
unions?', no less than 43 per cent of the Swedish compared with only
2 per cent of the English workers gave replies suggesting the need for
greater social justice and more equality.[5] In other words, they appeared
to be expressing opinions presented to them by the trade union
leadership and, to some extent, the Social Democratic Party.[6] Furthermore, as many as 48 per cent of these particular Swedish workers felt
that trade unions had been either 'extremely successful' or 'successful'
in achieving this aim; a surprisingly high percentage in view of their
general awareness of inequality as it existed between manual workers
and other groups in society.[7] This is indicative of the extent to which
the respondents accepted the legitimacy of trade unionism; although
they recognised the existence of inequalities, a substantial proportion
felt that trade unions were playing an active role in reducing them.

The Social Democratic Party also seems to have attained a higher
level of support among the Swedish respondents than the Labour Party
among the English sample. Both groups of respondents were asked
about their voting behaviour in the most recent general elections held in
the two countries before the interview survey was conducted; elections,
that is, held in Sweden in 1968 and in Britain in 1966. Of the total
sample of Swedish workers, 84 per cent voted for the Social Democratic Party compared with only 63 per cent of the English workers.[8]
Since both samples consisted of industrial manual workers – the basis
for 'solid' Social Democratic and Labour support – it is clear that the
Swedish party had achieved a greater degree of penetration among this
group; whereas the Social Democratic Party had succeeded in acquiring

more than four-fifths of the votes of the Swedish sample, the Labour
Party had obtained little more than sixty per cent. Furthermore, the
Social Democratic voters of the 1968 election appeared to be far more
loyal to the party than the Labour voters of the 1966 general election.
When asked about their voting intentions for the general elections to be
held in 1970, as many as 95 per cent of the 1968 Social Democratic
supporters said they would vote for the party again, compared with 79
per cent of the 1966 Labour voters. Thus, the evidence suggests that
commitment to the Social Democratic Party, as measured in terms of
voting behaviour, was greater among the Swedish workers than that of
the English sample to the Labour Party. This was confirmed by respondents' attitudes about improvements in employment conditions and
standards of living.

Both samples were asked a number of questions to find out whether
they felt the respective working-class movements had exercised influence in society to produce benefits for industrial manual workers. They
were asked: 'Do you think that employment conditions have improved
for factory workers since the war?'[9] An overwhelming majority of the
workers in both samples claimed that they had: 93 per cent and 98 per
cent of the total Swedish and English samples respectively. These respondents were then asked: 'In what ways do you think they have
improved?' The coded responses are shown in Table 6.3.

Among those of the Swedish sample who felt that employment
conditions had improved, 57 per cent mentioned 'work tasks', making
such comments as 'the new machinery has made work easier', 'the jobs
are not so tiring now', and 'you don't have to carry things about so
much today.' A further 33 per cent referred to improvements in the
physical conditions of the factory — lighting, heating, and ventilation —
while 35 per cent mentioned improvements in wage rates. But as many
as 23 per cent suggested that there was now more 'social justice' and
'equality' in the workplace. Among these responses there were a number of statements which suggested that 'the individual has more rights
now than before', 'managers treat the workers more on equal terms,'
'there is less of a division between white-collar workers and the rest of
us.' By contrast, 82 per cent of the English workers referred to improvements in the physical conditions of the workplace, 35 per cent to
better 'work tasks', 21 per cent to shorter working hours, and only 3
per cent to 'social justice' and 'equality'. It is interesting that such a
high proportion of the English workers should have referred to
'physical' improvements since, as shown in Chapter 4, they tended to
be more discontented about these in their comparisons with white-

Table 6.3: 'In what ways do you think they (employment conditions) have improved?'*

| Improvements in: | Swedish Workers | | English Workers | |
|---|---|---|---|---|
| | Nos. | % | Nos. | % |
| Physical conditions — noise, lighting, ventilation | 37 | 32.7 | 103 | 81.8 |
| Work tasks | 64 | 56.6 | 44 | 34.9 |
| Manager/worker relationships | 5 | 4.4 | 11 | 8.7 |
| Welfare benefits | 17 | 15.0 | 3 | 2.4 |
| Shorter working hours | 30 | 26.5 | 27 | 21.4 |
| Wage rates | 39 | 34.5 | 13 | 10.3 |
| 'Social justice' and 'equality' | 26 | 23.0 | 4 | 3.2 |
| Other and non-classifiable responses | 9 | 7.9 | 9 | 7.1 |

*Asked of those 113 Swedish and 126 English respondents who claimed that employment conditions had improved. Since most workers mentioned more than one factor, the figures add to more than 100 per cent.

collar workers than about earnings and chances for promotion. This, on the face of it, suggests a possible contradiction in the attitudes of the respondents. However, it is quite possible for the respondents to have been aware of improvements in physical working conditions and still regard these as inferior to those enjoyed by white-collar workers.

The respondents who considered that employment conditions had improved since the war were then asked: 'What do you think is the major factor which has brought this about?' The coded answers are presented in Table 6.4:

Table 6.4: 'What do you think is the major factor which has brought this about?' (Improvements in the employment conditions of factory workers)*

| Major Factor | Swedish Workers | | English Workers | |
|---|---|---|---|---|
| | Nos. | % | Nos. | % |
| Trade unions | 55 | 48.7 | 59 | 46.8 |
| Social Democratic/Labour Party | 23 | 20.4 | 1 | 0.8 |
| Management | 7 | 6.2 | 36 | 28.6 |
| Technological change | 13 | 11.5 | 19 | 15.1 |
| Other and non-classifiable responses | 14 | 12.3 | 10 | 7.9 |
| Don't know | 1 | 0.9 | 1 | 0.8 |
| Total | 113 | 100.0 | 126 | 100.0 |

*Asked of the 113 and 126 Swedish and English workers who considered that employment conditions had improved since the war.

Although both samples gave equal significance to the role of trade unions, there were other important differences in their responses. Whereas one-fifth of the Swedish respondents claimed that improvements in employment conditions had been brought about by the efforts of the Social Democratic Party, only one of the English workers mentioned the Labour Party. At the same time, as many as 29 per cent of the English, but as few as 6 per cent of the Swedish workers, attributed improvements to the efforts of management. Consequently, Table 6.4 suggests that more than two-thirds of the Swedish workers compared with less than one-half of the English respondents attributed improvements in their conditions of employment to the activities of the labour movement; that is to the efforts of trade unions and the Social Democratic Party. In other words, it appears as though the Swedish workers were more likely to regard the labour movement as a force for reform in the workplace; they perceived that it was this which had brought about improvements rather than the 'goodwill' of management.

The greater legitimacy of the labour movement among the Swedish respondents, particularly of the Social Democratic Party, was confirmed by their answers to questions about their standard of living. Enquiries conducted during the 1950s found that Swedish workers tend to attribute improvements in this to the efforts of the labour movement. Dahlström, for example, when he asked: 'What factors do you think explain the increase in living standards over the last 50 years?' found that approximately one-half of all the manual workers in his sample claimed they were a consequence of the activities of labour unions.[10] Similarly, Segerstedt and Lundquist found that almost 23 per cent of their respondents attributed improvements in the living conditions of workers to the role of the Social Democratic Party, and a further 44 per cent to the efforts of labour unions; they found that these institutions were mentioned to the same extent by both manual and non-manual workers.[11] In the present enquiry, the respondents were asked: 'Do you think that the standard of living for people like yourself has improved in this country since the war?' In both samples, an overwhelming majority of workers stated that it had; 96 per cent and 98 per cent of the Swedish and English respondents respectively. These workers were then asked: 'What do you think has brought this about?' Their coded replies are shown in Table 6.5.

As Table 6.5 suggests, a far higher proportion of the Swedish workers mentioned the Social Democratic Party as the major reason for the increase in the standard of living than of the English respondents who referred to the Labour Party; 52 per cent compared with 6 per

Table 6.5: 'What do you think has brought this about?' (the increase in the standard of living)*

| Factor Mentioned: | Swedish Workers | | English Workers | |
|---|---|---|---|---|
| | Nos. | % | Nos. | % |
| General improvements in trade and business | 11 | 9.4 | 12 | 9.5 |
| Social Democratic/Labour Party | 61 | 52.1 | 8 | 6.4 |
| Trade unions | 10 | 8.6 | 37 | 29.4 |
| 'Worker demands' | — | — | 10 | 7.9 |
| 'Full employment' | 16 | 13.7 | 13 | 10.3 |
| 'Higher wages' | 8 | 6.8 | 26 | 20.6 |
| Other and non-classifiable responses | 11 | 9.4 | 19 | 15.1 |
| Don't know | — | — | 1 | 0.8 |
| Total | 117 | 100.0 | 126 | 100.0 |

*Asked of the 117 Swedish and 126 English respondents who claimed that the standard of living had improved.

cent. Even when the figures are combined for those workers who mentioned the Social Democratic/Labour parties, trade unions and 'worker demands', it is clear that these accounted for as many as 61 per cent of the replies of the Swedish sample, but for 44 per cent of the English respondents. But it is interesting that only 9 per cent of the Swedish, compared with as many as 30 per cent of the English workers, referred to trade unions. One possible explanation for this, as suggested in Chapter 4, could be that the Swedish workers tended to make a distinction between 'work' and 'society' as normative and institutional orders. Consequently, when they referred to the working-class movement in their replies, they tended to mention trade unions in their comments about the factory, employment and working conditions, and the Social Democratic Party in their attitudes about society. In other words, they regarded the Social Democratic Party and the labour unions as interrelated institutions and to refer to either of these according to the institutional context about which they were being invited to comment. In Sweden, with a long tradition of Social Democratic governments and an economy which is overwhelmingly privately owned, the division between 'industry' and 'society' becomes pronounced. But it is clear from Table 6.5 that the English workers, despite recognising the importance of trade unions, attached little importance to the role of the Labour Party in improving the standard of living. Among the Swedish workers, by contrast, the legitimacy of the Social Democratic

Party was strengthened by the fact that it was seen to be the major force which had brought this about. Indeed, the Social Democratic Party has emphasised this in successive general elections; it has stressed that since coming to power in 1932, the Swedish standard of living has risen from the lowest in Northern Europe to among the highest in the world.[12]

Clearly, the Swedish respondents were more likely than the English to regard the working-class movement as an agent of reform, bringing about improvements in living and working conditions. In view of this, did they conceive of themselves as members of an influential social force in the manner suggested in the enquiry by Segerstedt and Lundquist? In their study they asked: 'Which class do you think is the most influential in Sweden?' Among male manual workers, 46 per cent of those identifying themselves as 'working class' stated their 'own' social class, while only 37 per cent mentioned 'another' class.[13] In order to investigate this, those workers of both samples who recognised the existence of social classes – 118 and 119 of the Swedish and English respondents – were asked: 'Which class, do you think, has the most influence over things today?' The responses are shown in Table 6.6.

From Table 6.6 it is clear that a majority of both samples who mentioned the 'upper class' considered it to exercise the most influence in society. At the same time, 83 per cent of the Swedish workers claimed 'Social Group I' had the greatest degree of influence, together with 79 per cent of those who referred to 'the rich' in their descriptions of the class structure. By contrast, only 37 per cent of the English respondents who mentioned 'the rich' shared the same opinion. They were more likely to mention the 'working class'; no less than 42 per cent of the English workers who had used this 'label' considered that it exercised the most influence compared with only 13 per cent of their Swedish counterparts. In fact, of the 47 Swedish workers who mentioned 'Social Group III' in their descriptions of the class structure, as few as 9 per cent felt it was the most influential group in society.

The respondents were then asked: 'Why is this?' (that this class has the most influence over things today). Since some of the classes were mentioned by only a very small number of respondents, those considered to be most influential were allocated, for the purposes of this analysis, to three categories – (A), (B) and (C) in the manner shown in Table 6.7.

Table 6.8 indicates that 75 per cent of the Swedish respondents attributed the influence exercised by category (A), that is the 'upper',

Table 6.6: 'Which class do you think has the most influence over things today?'[14]

| Labels mentioned by respondents in describing the class structure | Nos. of respondents mentioning specific classes in their descriptions of the class structure (1) | | Nos. of respondents stating that a specific class 'had the most influence' (2) | | Percentage of respondents mentioning a specific class and who also stated it 'had the most influence' $\frac{(2)}{(1)} \times 100$ | |
|---|---|---|---|---|---|---|
| | Swedish Workers | English Workers | Swedish Workers | English Workers | Swedish Workers | English Workers |
| 1. 'Upper', 'top', 'higher classes | 24 | 89 | 15 | 49 | 62.5 | 55.1 |
| 2. 'The wealthy', 'rich', 'those with plenty of money' | 14 | 19 | 11 | 7 | 78.6 | 36.8 |
| 3. 'Social Group I' | 57 | — | 47 | — | 82.5 | — |
| 4. 'Middle class' | 19 | 90 | 5 | 18 | 26.3 | 20.0 |
| 5. 'White-collar people' | 20 | 1 | 9 | — | 45.0 | — |
| 6. 'Educated people' | 5 | 1 | 5 | — | 100.0 | — |
| 7. 'Social Group II' | 56 | — | 6 | — | 10.7 | — |
| 8. 'Social Group III' | 47 | — | 4 | — | 8.5 | — |
| 9. 'Working class' | 46 | 89 | 6 | 37 | 13.0 | 41.6 |
| 10. 'Ordinary people' | 2 | 2 | — | 1 | — | 50.0 |
| 11. 'Lower class' | 2 | 21 | — | 1 | — | 4.8 |
| 12. 'The poor', 'the lower paid' | 7 | 8 | — | 1 | — | 12.5 |
| 13. Negative evaluation | 10 | 1 | — | — | — | — |
| Don't know | — | — | 10 | 5 | — | — |
| Total | — | — | 118 | 119 | — | — |

Table 6.7:   The allocation of social classes to categories (A), (B) and (C).

| | | |
|---|---|---|
| 'Upper', 'top', 'higher class'<br>'The wealthy', 'the rich'<br>'Social Group I' | ) ) ) | (A) |
| 'Middle class'<br>'White-collar people'<br>'Educated people'<br>'Social Group II' | ) ) ) ) | (B) |
| 'Social Group III'<br>'Working class'<br>'Ordinary people'<br>'Lower class'<br>'The poor' | ) ) ) ) ) | (C) |

'the rich' and 'Social Group I', to economic factors.[15] Hence they claimed that 'money talks', 'those with the money take the decisions,' 'it's their wealth which makes them powerful.' Among the English workers 52 per cent referred to economic factors of this kind in their comments about the classes grouped in category (A). But there was a far greater tendency for them to give examples of 'influence' which were often unconnected with economic factors; they often made statements such as 'they are the born leaders,' 'they have always taken the decisions' and 'they occupy the powerful positions.'[16] The Swedish workers, by contrast, seem to have regarded the 'influence' exercised by these groups to be determined by the economics of the market-place. If a high proportion of the English respondents (42 per cent) considered the 'working class' to exercise the most influence in society, it is evident from Table 6.8 that they felt this to be a consequence of the activities of trade unions. Thus, these were mentioned by no less than 60 per cent of those workers who claimed that the classes in category (C) exercised the most influence.[17] At the same time, a further 23 per cent felt the classes in category (C) were the most influential because they were 'the majority of people', 'most people in the country' and 'the greater proportion of the country'.[18]

Although Tables 6.6 and 6.8 describe the samples' beliefs about social classes and the exercise of influence in society, they do not specify the respondents' own class self-placements. Consequently, they fail to disclose whether the respondents perceived their 'own class' or 'another class' to be the most influential. Such an analysis is presented in Table 6.9.

As Table 6.9 suggests, more than twice as many of the English

Table 6.8: 'Why is this?' (that this class has the most influence over things today)

| Responses suggesting: | Category mentioned as the 'Most Influential' | | | | | | | | | | | |
| | Swedish Workers | | | | | | English Workers | | | | | |
| | Category (A) (N = 73) | | Category (B) (N = 25) | | Category (C) (N = 10) | | Category (A) (N = 56) | | Category (B) (N = 18) | | Category (C) (N = 40) | |
| | Nos. | % | Nos. | % | Nos. | % | Nos. | % | Nos. | % | Nos. | % |
|---|---|---|---|---|---|---|---|---|---|---|---|---|
| Economic factors | 55 | 75.4 | 5 | 20.0 | — | — | 29 | 51.8 | 2 | 11.1 | — | — |
| Activities of trade unions | — | — | 2 | 8.0 | 2 | 20.0 | — | — | — | — | 24 | 60.0 |
| 'Majority of people' | — | — | 4 | 16.0 | 4 | 40.0 | — | — | 3 | 16.7 | 9 | 22.5 |
| Specific examples of influence | 9 | 12.3 | 6 | 24.0 | — | — | 24 | 42.9 | 7 | 38.9 | 1 | 2.5 |
| Other and non-classifiable responses | 9 | 12.3 | 8 | 32.0 | 4 | 40.0 | 2 | 3.6 | 4 | 22.2 | 4 | 10.0 |
| Don't know | — | — | — | — | — | — | 1 | 1.7 | 2 | 11.1 | 2 | 5.0 |
| Total | 73 | 100.0 | 25 | 100.0 | 10 | 100.0 | 56 | 100.0 | 18 | 100.0 | 40 | 100.0 |

Table 6.9: Respondents' conceptions of whether their 'own class' or 'another class' exercised the most influence over things

| Respondents' own class self-placement | Class mentioned as the 'Most Influential' | | | | | | | | | | | |
| --- | --- | --- | --- | --- | --- | --- | --- | --- | --- | --- | --- | --- |
| | Swedish Workers | | | | | | English Workers | | | | | |
| | 'Own' | | 'Another' | | Total | | 'Own' | | 'Another' | | Total | |
| | Nos. | % | Nos. | % | Nos. | % | Nos. | % | Nos. | % | Nos. | % |
| Middle class | 3 | 27.3 | 8 | 72.7 | 11 | 100.0 | 7 | 30.4 | 16 | 69.6 | 23 | 100.0 |
| Social Group II | 6 | 20.0 | 24 | 80.0 | 30 | 100.0 | – | – | – | – | – | – |
| Social Group III | 4 | 16.0 | 21 | 84.0 | 25 | 100.0 | – | – | – | – | – | – |
| Average people | – | – | 2 | 100.0 | 2 | 100.0 | 1 | 50.0 | 1 | 50.0 | 2 | 100.0 |
| Working class | 6 | 13.0 | 40 | 87.0 | 46 | 100.0 | 35 | 42.2 | 48 | 57.8 | 83 | 100.0 |
| Lower class | – | – | 2 | 100.0 | 2 | 100.0 | 1 | 16.7 | 5 | 83.3 | 6 | 100.0 |
| The poor | – | – | – | – | – | – | 1 | 25.0 | 3 | 75.0 | 4 | 100.0 |
| Other and non-classifiable responses | 1 | 50.0 | 1 | 50.0 | 2 | 100.0 | 1 | 100.0 | – | – | 1 | 100.0 |
| Total | 20 | 16.9 | 98 | 83.1 | 118 | 100.0 | 46 | 38.7 | 73 | 61.3 | 119 | 100.0 |

workers compared with the Swedish considered their 'own class' exercised the most influence; 39 per cent compared with 17 per cent. At the same time, of those respondents defining themselves as 'working class', no less than 42 per cent of the English workers in contrast to only 13 per cent of the Swedish felt their 'own class' exercised the most influence. In other words, it is clear that the Swedish workers were much less likely than their English counterparts to regard themselves as members of the 'most influential' group in society. This is a surprising result in view of Segerstedt and Lundquist's conclusions. How, then, can the difference between their findings and those of the present study be explained?

The major factor could be the development of feelings of relative deprivation which seems to have occurred among Swedish manual workers since the Segerstedt and Lundquist study conducted in the 1950s. As discussed in Chapter 5, the Social Democratic Party and the labour unions have emphasised the persistence of economic inequalities and the need for these to be reduced. It would, then, be surprising if feelings of deprivation which these policies appear to have generated did not affect attitudes towards the distribution of power in society; particularly in view of the fact that the Swedish respondents overwhelmingly attributed the influence of the 'upper class', 'the rich', and 'Social Group I' to economic factors. Furthermore, it is possible to suggest that the Swedish respondents' awareness of the influence exercised by these groups was a function – if only partly – of their greater commitment to the Social Democratic Party; certainly, by comparison with the English workers' attachment to the Labour Party. In successive general elections, the Social Democratic Party, with the support of the labour unions, has stressed the need for the election of Social Democratic governments so that wage earners can be protected against the interests of 'Big Business'. Hence, the Swedish labour movement has emphasised the importance of its role in society as a 'check' against the economic self-interests of modern capitalism. Consequently, if 'democracy' is to be preserved, according to Social Democratic electoral appeals, it is necessary for the political apparatus of the state to be 'isolated' from the control of financial and industrial interests; this can only be achieved by electing Social Democratic governments.[19] In other words, the appeals that have been put forward by the party and trade union leadership have emphasised the class basis of political power and possibly, if only partly as a result of this, Swedish manual workers, as illustrated by the attitudes of the respondents, have become more aware, not only of economic inequalities, but also of power differentials as they exist in contemporary Sweden.

The interview survey, unfortunately, did not enquire into the attitudes of those English respondents who felt they were members of the most influential group in society. Did they approve or disapprove of this? Their responses relating to feelings about their 'own' class acquiring the greatest economic gains during recent years would indicate they approved.[20] On the other hand, various investigations have shown that a substantial proportion of English manual workers disapprove of the influence of working-class institutions such as trade unions.[21] Thus, whether or not the English workers approved of the perceived influence exercised by the 'working class' is a matter of conjecture. But what the evidence of the present enquiry does suggest is that the Swedish workers were more aware of the influence exercised by economically dominant groups in society than their English counterparts. Indeed, this appears to have been a consequence of their membership in a working-class movement with an ideological commitment to egalitarianism. However, if existing power differentials continue to persist, this could have implications for rank-and-file commitment to the leadership of the movement as well as for the future development of Social Democracy in Sweden. Resentful attitudes could develop so that allegiance to the leadership declines. That this has been recognised by the leadership is confirmed by the fact that both LO and the Social Democratic Party have recently proposed a number of far-reaching reforms intended to strengthen the influence of workers in the decision-making process of industry.[22] But at the time of the enquiry, the Swedish labour movement enjoyed a level of support which was far greater than that experienced by its counterpart in Britain.

This, then, concludes the discussion of the samples' conceptions of the two class structures. Having considered patterns of inequality in Britain and Sweden and the respondents' interpretations of them, the next chapter makes some concluding observations about the labour movements in the two countries.

## Notes

1. As in previous chapters, only rounded-up percentages are given in the text.
2. Goldthorpe and his associates found among their sample of manual workers that 7 per cent attended union meetings 'regularly' and 14 per cent 'occasionally'. As many as 60 per cent 'never' attended a meeting. It

seems that union involvement among the English sample was greater than for Goldthorpe *et al.'s* respondents. See J. Goldthorpe, D. Lockwood, F. Bechhofer, J. Platt, *The Affluent Worker: Industrial Attitudes and Behaviour*, Cambridge, 1968, Table 40.

3. In retrospect, this was a badly formulated question. It would have been more useful to have asked separate questions about respondents attitudes towards shop stewards and local union officials in order to investigate whether they held different sets of opinions.

4. In Britain, highly organised local unionism has often constituted a source of opposition to national union policies. For a discussion of this, see T. Lane and D. Roberts, *Strike at Pilkingtons*, London, 1971, and T. Lane, *The Union Makes Us Strong*, London, 1974.

5. See Table 5.12.

6. For a discussion of this point, see Chapter 5.

7. Respondents were asked, 'How successful do you think they have been in achieving this aim? Do you think they have been "extremely successful", "successful", "not so successful" or "completely unsuccessful"?'

8. All the workers in both samples were eligible to vote.

9. 'Employment conditions' were defined to refer to all aspects of the employment relationship – the work tasks, the physical environment of the workplace, and relationships with fellow workers and management. In other words, to all of the economic, social and physical aspects of work.

10. E. Dahlström, *Tjänstemännen, Naringslivet och Samhället, (Management, Unions and Society)*, Stockholm, 1954, pp. 97-9.

11. T. Segerstedt and A. Lundquist, *Människan i Industrisamhället, (Man in Industrialised Society)* Stockholm, 1955, Pt. II, pp. 335-6.

12. In 1972 the national income *per capita,* as expressed in US dollars, was 4,032 in Sweden compared with 4,573 in the United States, 3,769 in Canada, 3,168 in West Germany and 2,218 in the United Kingdom. See United Nations, *Yearbook of National Accounts Statistics 1972, Pt. III – International Tables*, New York, 1974. Thus, in 1972, as measured in terms of *per capita* income, Sweden had the second highest standard of living in the world (second only to the United States) and almost double that of the United Kingdom.

13. T. Segerstedt and A. Lundquist, op. cit., Pt. II, pp. 287-93.

14. For the ways in which respondents defined the social classes, see Table 4.6.

15. 'Economic factors' were mentioned by 93 per cent, 82 per cent and 68 per cent of those who referred to the 'upper class', 'the rich' and 'Social Group I' respectively.

16. Of those who referred to the 'upper class', 49 per cent mentioned economic factors, while 45 per cent gave specific examples of influence.

17. Of those who specifically mentioned the 'working class', 65 per cent referred to the activities of trade unions.

18. These factors were mentioned by 22 per cent of those who claimed that the 'working class' exercised the most influence.

19. These appeals were particularly emphasised in the party's campaigns in the 1970 and 1973 general elections. But they have always been central to party policy. See, for example, G. Adler-Karlsson, *Functional Socialism*, Stockholm, 1967; A Myrdal, *Towards Equality*, Stockholm, 1971; and H. Tingsten, *The Swedish Social Democrats*, New Jersey, 1973.

20. See Chapter 5.

21. A number of these studies are mentioned in Chapter 1. See, for example, J. Goldthorpe *et al.,* op. cit.; R. McKenzie and A. Silver, *Angels in Marble*, London, 1968; and D. Butler and D. Stokes, *Political Change in*

*Britain,* Harmondsworth, 1971.
22.  In 1975 a Government Commission produced a 961-page report which is
    to provide the basis for these reforms. See, Statens Offentliga Utredningar
    (SOU), *Demokrati på Arbetsplatsen (Democracy at the Workplace),* Stock-
    holm, 1975.

# 7 CONCLUSIONS

One of the objectives of this study has been to identify the effects of Social Democratic policies upon patterns of social and economic inequality. This was undertaken by comparing industrial and political developments in Sweden and Britain. However, it is important to emphasise that there was no attempt to assess the effects of these policies for many other aspects of society; for example, economic growth and the development of the welfare state.[1] Indeed, only limited dimensions of class inequality have been studied; in any comprehensive assessment of the Swedish labour movement it would have been necessary to have investigated the economic and social welfare of such groups as the retired, the long-term ill and the unemployed, as well as of those gainfully employed in the labour market. In this way it would have been possible to have estimated whether or not various welfare policies have been redistributive. This and many other dimensions of class inequality have been neglected, with the result that this study has focused almost exclusively upon economic, social and power differentials, as they exist between manual and non-manual workers.[2] The major reason for this is that the Swedish Social Democratic Party has always stated one of its major aims to be the creation of an egalitarian society in which the economic, social and political interests of industrial manual workers would be better represented.

Despite this, the labour movement in Sweden seems to have accomplished little in changing the reward structure in any fundamental manner. Thus, the evidence suggests that the economic conditions of managerial, professional and higher white-collar groups are much better than those enjoyed by industrial manual workers. Within the constraints of a capitalist economy it is not difficult to understand why this is the case. Although there has been direct government intervention in various sectors of the economy and further 'indirect' influence by the adoption of various fiscal policies, the price of labour in Sweden continues to be overwhelmingly determined by the forces of capital accumulation. Thus, it is difficult to envisage how policies of equality and 'wage solidarity' can have their desired effects without much more direct governmental control over the ownership of industrial and commercial resources. Without this, it seems highly likely that the forces of Swedish and international capitalism will continue to impose severe constraints upon Social Democratic and trade union policies. However, the present enquiry suggests that the Social Democratic Party and LO, in the pursuit of egalitarian goals, have brought about some changes in Swedish society. The more important of these are in terms of the structure of power and workers' consciousness.

Although Sweden and Britain are both capitalist countries it is not to be assumed that they have exactly comparable power structures. In Sweden, the development of an influential working-class movement has increased the representation of industrial manual workers in the governmental decision-making process and thus restricted the emergence of a national power structure in which political and economic interests are closely interrelated in pursuing the objectives of private capital. In other words, the state is less dominated by the interests of the privately owned economy than it is in Britain. One of the most systematic empirical studies of the relationship between the political state and private capital in modern Western societies has been undertaken by Miliband.[3] He argues that in such countries economic elites are interconnected so that they constitute a dominant economic class. This class, he claims, has more influence than any other class and exercises a *decisive* degree of political power. Although the structure of power in Britain may be of the kind described by Miliband, it is difficult to argue that such circumstances prevail to a similar degree in Sweden. Most certainly there is a dominant economic class which primarily represents the interests of private property, but it is doubtful whether it can be regarded as a ruling class in the sense of dominating the formal state political apparatus. If successive Social Democratic governments have, as yet, done little to destroy the parameters and mechanisms of contemporary capitalism, they have restricted the degree to which privately owned economic interests have dominated the exercise of political power. Indeed, the Social Democratic Party has always emphasised the need to separate 'the state' and 'the economy' in order to preserve the 'pluralism' of Swedish society. In recent elections, for example, it has been argued that only the continuation of Social Democratic governments will prevent the development of a power structure in which economic and political interests are united in a capitalist-based élite. Such appeals are, of course, an important form of political legitimation for the Social Democratic Party, but they can also be supported by a certain amount of evidence. Therefore, since the war — and particularly during the 1960s and early 1970s — Social Democratic governments have passed legislation which has not only protected the interests of employees but also increased their representation in formally prescribed decision-making processes. For example, legislation has been introduced which has increased the job security of workers and restricted traditional managerial prerogatives in relation to hiring and firing, while other laws have increased the participation of manual workers in decision-making at industrial, company and plant levels. Similarly, legislation has been enacted which has been aimed at protecting the interests of consumers and clients against the potential abuses of private and public bureaucracies. Although Labour governments in Britain have often pursued comparable policies, they have been less comprehensive than in Sweden. In these ways, Social Democratic governments have represented the interests of industrial manual workers to a far greater degree than has been the case in Britain. If, then, both countries are to be regarded as similar types of capitalist society in the sense that they are both dominated by economic classes which overwhelmingly own and control the means of production, they must also be seen as different to the extent to which the self-interests of these classes are 'restrained' by the representation of labour movements within their respective political decision-making processes. In other words, the development of the working-class movement in Sweden has tended to reduce the degree to which economic domination has been 'converted' into political control. Thus, a comparison of political developments in Britain and Sweden would suggest that although they possess a number of features common to all capitalist countries, they also have a number of differences. As Runciman has argued,[4] it is possible to categorise societies in terms of whether they are 'capitalist' or 'socialist', but this should not lead to the assumption that there are no differences between countries within these socio-economic systems.[5] Consequently it can be argued that in Sweden, the labour movement has led the state to exercise a greater degree of control over privately owned institutions than in Britain although it has not, as yet, fundamentally transformed the dynamics of Swedish capitalism. However, because the growth of a well-organised working-class movement in Sweden has led to the development of a power structure which represents the interests of industrial manual workers to a greater extent than in Britain, it does mean it is in a better position to alter existing patterns of ownership and the relations of production. The distribution of income, earnings and wealth in Sweden has been, and continues to be, primarily determined by the private ownership of the means of production, and by national and international forces of supply and demand. But in the long term, the legitimacy of Swedish capitalism could be undermined because of the way in which the labour movement's ideological commitment to egalitarianism has affected workers' attitudes.

The social survey demonstrated that the Swedish respondents were more aware of economic inequalities than their English counterparts. It was suggested that there were three major reasons for this: first, the egalitarian ideology of the Social Democratic Party; secondly, LO's policy of wage solidarity; and thirdly, the structure of Swedish trade unionism, closely linked to divisions within the occupational structure emphasising differences in the economic and employment conditions of manual and non-manual workers. Whereas Social Democratic policies have created a heightened awareness of class differences, political developments in Britain, together with the structure of trade unionism, have been conducive to the formation of attitudes reinforcing sources of differentiation *within* the working class.[6] Indeed, one of the more striking features of wage negotiations in Britain has been the emphasis by large sectors of industrial workers upon differentials between various categories of manual employees, rather than upon the structure of income differences in society as a whole.[7] Consequently, the earnings of higher-paid groups such as managerial and professional workers have not been subject to the degree of public scrutiny as those of miners, assembly-line workers and other categories of manual employees. Thus, the policies and fragmented structure of British trade unionism reinforce the privileges of more highly paid groups.[8]

Although the Swedish respondents had a greater awareness of economic inequalities this does not seem, as yet, to have generated demands for a drastic restructuring of society according to principles which would be more favourable to the industrial working class. At the most it seems to have heightened feelings of resentment. Why, then, have there not been greater rank-and-file pressures for a radical restructuring of society and for the abolition of the institutions of private property? In order to offer some kind of answer to this question it is necessary to consider changes in the ideological themes of the Social Democratic Party during different periods of the twentieth century.

Since its inception in the latter part of the nineteenth century, the primary objective of the Social Democratic Party has been to create a more egalitarian society.[9] But, the *means* whereby this could be achieved has been subject to considerable debate within the party and the basis for the revision of policies at different points of time. Thus, it is possible to identify phases in the history of the party when the abolition of private property was considered essential if egalitarian goals were to be achieved, while at other times it has been argued that such goals were compatible with capitalism and attainable within the para-

meters of such a society. The first period can be considered to have
lasted until the end of the First World War, when the public ownership
of the forces of production was seen to be the only means whereby
greater economic and political equality could be attained.[10] The second
phase can be regarded as lasting from this time until the early 1930s
when, during a decade of minority governments, the Party pursued
'pragmatic' and short-term policies which were more concerned with
solving current economic crises rather than pursuing long-range radical,
socialist objectives. It was in the 1920s, according to Tingsten, that the
predominant ideology of the Social Democratic Party became deradicalised, rejecting the necessity for socialising the means of production for
the attainment of egalitarian goals. The Party was then elected to office
in 1932 and during a third period – which lasted for approximately
thirty years – reformist-welfare policies almost completely dominated
the objectives as formulated by the leadership of the working-class
movement. Thus, it was considered by the leadership of the Social
Democratic Party that the development of the welfare state, the appli-
cation of Keynesian economics and the regulation of economic activity
by systems of government controls were sufficient to guarantee that the
wealth created by capitalism would be distributed according to criteria
of social justice and equality. However, during the early 1960s there
was a further shift in Social Democratic thought when there were re-
appraisals of the degee to which party goals could be achieved within
the parameters of capitalist society. Consequently, it is possible to de-
lineate a fourth stage in the development of Social Democratic thinking
which has lasted until the present. Therefore, more radical measures
have been contemplated and the party has re-adopted a more positive
attitude towards state ownership of the means of production.[11] In this
way, it has again recognised that public ownership provides an important instrument whereby the traditional ideological goals of the party
can be achieved.

Thus, the development of the Swedish Social Democratic Party
suggests that a process of deradicalisation, in the sense of rejecting the
extension of state ownership and control, and the representation of
working-class interests in society, cannot be seen as an inevitable feature
of working-class parties in capitalist societies in the manner suggested
by Michels.[12] At certain stages in their development, it may be
necessary for such parties to pursue less radical policies for the purposes
of obtaining widespread electoral support, but at a later period the
heightened expectations of the rank and file may force the leadership
to adopt more radical objectives. Whether such shifts in ideological

parameters are initiated by changes in the attitudes of leaders, or by the leadership responding to perceived changes in the attitudes of its supporters is problematic. Michels, for example, suggested it was the attitudes of the leadership which determined the policies of working-class parties while Tingsten, on the other hand, has claimed that the rejection of policies advocating the public ownership of the means of production by the Swedish Social Democratic Party during the 1920s was primarily a consequence of the leadership responding to the immediate demands of rank-and-file members.[13] He claims that during this period the party membership was more concerned with immediate policies which would reduce the level of unemployment, raise real wages and provide a minimum of social security than with restructuring owernship and control in society. Consequently, it is difficult to identify the bases for changes in Social Democratic policies in terms of whether they originated from the leadership or the mass-based supporters. But it does seem that once party objectives have been formulated, the working-class movement in Sweden has enjoyed a considerable degree of success in retaining the commitment of its membership. Whether this allegiance will continue in the future will largely depend upon the extent to which rank-and-file supporters perceive the leadership to be successful in achieving the movement's explicitly stated goals. The ideological commitment to egalitarianism by the party appears to have been conducive to the generation of attitudes which could have important implications for the long-term development of the Swedish working-class movement, particularly in generating feelings of relative deprivation and resentment. These attitudes could – if they are indicative of wider patterns in Sweden – lead to an increased recognition among workers of the inherent contradictions between the movement's goals and the existing socio-economic structure. So far, these contradictions have been successfully accommodated by the Social Democratic Party, by adopting a number of tactics for the purposes of legitimation, of which the following are but two of the more important.

In the first place, the party claims to be equalising opportunities for workers' children by reforming the educational system, and to be pursuing policies which will ultimately break down existing economic inequalities. But at the same time, it has legitimated its relationship with industrial manual workers by emphasising the improvements in the standard of living which have occurred since the 1930s. This argument has been strengthened by the adoption of the two sets of comparisons which are frequently used in Social Democratic debate – one historical,

the other cross-national. In terms of the first, the party has always presented itself as an instrument of progress and change. Thus, for the
purposes of political rhetoric, history has often been categorised in
terms of two eras – the 'old' and the 'new' Sweden.[14] 'Old' Sweden is
described as consisting of widespread and acute inequalities, injustices
and deprivations which have only been removed as a result of the
achievements of the working-class movement. According to many of
the arguments, the Social Democratic Party and the labour movement
have contributed to the development of a 'new' society in which remaining inequalities and social injustices are finally being abolished. The
second set of comparisons emphasises the advantages of industrial
manual workers in Sweden over those of workers in other countries.[15]
For these purposes, Britain and the United States are the two countries
which are most frequently chosen. Britain is used in order to demonstrate the relative equality of Swedish society and the socio-economic
advantages of Swedish manual workers. Journalists in newspapers, radio
and television emphasise the inequalities of British society and the
poor living conditions of the industrial working class. At the same
time, the United States is often used to emphasise the high standard
of the Swedish urban environment, the 'progressive' attitude of
Sweden towards developing countries and the lack of 'corruption' in
Swedish political life. If, then, to put the matter crudely, Britain, the
United States and other Western countries are characterised by glaring
social, political and economic injustices and if, at the same time, East
European state socialist countries fail to protect individual and civil
liberties then, according to the arguments, Swedish workers must live
in one of the most egalitarian and democratic countries in the world;
an achievement, so it is claimed, which has been brought about by the
policies pursued by the leadership of the working-class movement.

   These are but two examples of the rhetoric used by the Social Democratic Party in order to maintain its legitimacy with rank-and-file supporters. In these ways it has been possible for leaders of the Swedish
labour movement to conceal – if not completely successfully – some
of the inherent contradictions between an ideological commitment to
egalitarianism and a capitalist productive system. By the use of cross-
national comparisons, the attempt has been to demonstrate that the
labour movement has, indeed, achieved a considerable degree of equality.
If there are persisting inequalities in Sweden these will be removed, according to the appeals of the leadership, provided that continued support
to the movement by rank-and-file supporters is forthcoming. But such
appeals tend to reinforce the tensions that exist between ideology and

material infrastructure. If efforts by the leadership to accommodate these strains become less successful in the future, then the Social Democratic Party may either lose its broadly based support among industrial workers or be increasingly forced to adopt radical policies towards existing patterns of ownership and control. If the latter occurs, there is a greater likelihood that the original egalitarian goals of the Social Democratic Party, as formulated during the late decades of the nineteenth century, will be achieved.

In Britain, by contrast, the Labour Party and the trade unions have not created such an acute tension between ideology and institutional structure. Unlike its counterpart in Sweden, the British labour movement is not a coherent ideological force in society. Consequently, it does not have an explanatory framework within which its policies can be interpreted and understood by rank-and-file members. Thus, the introduction of such measures as comprehensive education and nationalisation of sectors of the economy are often seen to be unrelated and even irrelevant by a large proportion of the working class, simply because they are not explained within the context of a coherent, well-defined ideology. The result is that the labour movement is rarely regarded by the rank-and-file as a force introducing specific reforms for the long-term purposes of creating a *new social order*. Indeed, as the responses of the English sample suggested, the Labour Party and trade unions are not conceived as part and parcel of a *movement* by large sectors of the working class. The failure to regard these institutions as interrelated parts of a *movement* is reinforced by two further characteristics of labour organisations in contemporary Britain. First, compared with the Swedish labour movement, there is little emphasis upon active rank-and-file participation and grass-roots political socialisation. Secondly, the more decentralised structure of British unionism is conducive to division and cleavage *within* the working class; thus, there is the persistence of strong occupational, craft and skill ideologies. In the absence of a coherent class-based *movement* which is capable of transcending these divisions, the English working class continues to be characterised by a diversity of attitudes towards the dominant institutional order, ranging from deference and acquiescence to militant protest and radicalism.[16] The latter can have little effect so long as they are located *within* the working class, among those working in particular occupations, crafts and industries. The British labour movement, then, has been unable to develop a class-based ideology capable of transcending such divisions. Consequently, despite its continuing commitment to nationalisation, it has never constituted a coherent social force with an explicit ideology for a long-term development of society that can be interpreted and understood by rank-and-file supporters. Thus, in the absence of an institutional and normative base of the kind enjoyed by the Social Democratic Party and the Swedish labour unions, the British Labour Party is unable to act as the ideological spearhead of a broadly supported *movement*. The fact that the Labour Party and the trade unions in Britain do not integrate and represent the working class as a *movement* constitutes one of the major differences between British Labourism and Swedish Social Democracy.

Finally, what is the relevance of this analysis for the debate about the convergence of industrial societies?[17] While some writers have stated that changing institutional structures are leading to increasing similarities, others have emphasised the role of ideology for persisting differences. A conclusion of this study must be that, both analytically and empirically, it is difficult to make any kind of clear distinction between the respective effects of ideology and social institutions in shaping long-term developments in different industrial countries. Hence, there are both persisting differences and similarities in the social structures of Britain and Sweden which have been brought about by the interplay of various ideological and institutional influences in each of the two countries. More specifically, this study has suggested that the emergence of an influential working-class movement in Sweden has led to the development of an egalitarian ideology, creating strains which could, in the long term, lead to changes in patterns of economic and social inequality as they have been generated by the institutions of contemporary capitalism. However, should a non-social democratic government be elected — which in early 1976 seems to be a possibility — it is difficult to envisage how it could stay in office for any length of time in view of the ideological and institutional influence of the labour movement. Thus, although Britain and Sweden are similar in that they are both capitalist countries, there are important differences between them in terms of the degree to which their respective institutional structures are legitimated among industrial manual workers.

## Notes

1. For a discussion of the development of welfare systems in Britain and Sweden see H. Heclo, *Modern Social Politics in Britain and Sweden*. New Haven, 1974.
2. It is important to emphasise that the welfare system of any capitalist country constitutes an important dimension of class inequality if only because social policies are important for determining the economic con-

dition of such groups as the retired, the sick, the unemployed and those workers who acquire low earnings in the labour market. Thus, in a capitalist society, the development of an *egalitarian* welfare system could 'compensate' for inequalities generated by participation (or non-participation) in the market economy.

3. R. Miliband, *The State in Capitalist Society*, London, 1969.
4. W.G. Runciman, 'Towards a Theory of Social Stratification' in F. Parkin (ed.), *The Social Analysis of Class Structures*, London, 1974.
5. Giddens, for example, devotes little attention to differences between capitalist countries in his analysis of contemporary class structure. He does, however, discuss variations in the characteristics of working-class movements in France, Italy, Britain and the United States. See A. Giddens, *The Class Structure of the Advanced Societies*, London, 1973.
6. There is probably a wider diversity of attitudes in terms of acquiescence, resentment and protest among industrial workers in Britain than in Sweden, fostered by the development of a variety of different forms of occupational and trade consciousness.
7. For example, in wage negotiations during the 1970s the National Union of Mineworkers has argued that the earnings of its members have not kept pace with those of many other categories of *manual* workers.
8. Compared, that is, to the situation in Sweden.
9. For a detailed discussion of this, see H. Tingsten, *The Swedish Social Democrats*, New Jersey, 1973; and J. Lindhagen, *Social Democratins Program (The Social Democrats' Programme)*, Stockholm, 1972.
10. The evidence for this and the following statements is mainly derived from Tingsten's and Lindhagen's excellent accounts. See H. Tingsten, op. cit., and J. Lindhagen, op. cit.
11. Policies in this direction have been pursued, for example, in terms of using the financial resources of the State Pension Fund to buy stocks and shares in privately owned companies and to build state-owned factories and manufacturing processes. In 1976, furthermore, it is considering the possibility of adopting LO's policy that trade unions should acquire company stocks, ultimately making them the major shareholders in Swedish industry. See Chapter 2.
12. R. Michels, *Political Parties*, New York, 1962.
13. H. Tingsten, op. cit.
14. Often expressed in terms of *förr i tiden* and *nuförtiden*. Although these terms have a general meaning and refer to 'past' and 'present', they have acquired the more specific meaning in political debate.
15. This and the following comments are derived from the author's personal experience of the interpretation of news and current affairs by party spokesmen in the Swedish mass media over the past ten years; particularly in the radio, television and the press as represented by reports in *Dagens Nyheter, Expressen* and *Aftonbladet* — the largest selling daily newspapers in Sweden. Although there was no attempt to undertake a systematic content analysis, such an investigation would almost certainly confirm the present observations.
16. See, for example, M. Bulmer (ed.), *Working-Class Images of Society*, London, 1975; and J. Westergaard and H. Resler, *Class in a Capitalist Society*, London, 1975, Part. 5.
17. As briefly stated in the Introduction.

# REFERENCES

Adler-Karlsson, G., *Functional Socialism: A Swedish Theory for Democratic Socialisation,* Stockholm, 1967.

Anderson, B., 'Opinion Influentials and Political Opinion Formation in Four Swedish Communites', *International Social Science Journal,* Vol. 14 (1962).

Anderson, B., 'Some Problems of Change in the Swedish Electorate', *Acta Sociologica,* Vol. 6 (1962).

Bain, G., *The Growth of White-Collar Unionism,* London, 1972.

Bain, G. and Price, R., 'Union Growth and Employment Trends in the United Kingdom, 1964-1970', *British Journal of Industrial Relations,* Vol. 10 (1972).

Barratt Brown, M., 'The Controllers of British Industry', in J. Urry and J. Wakeford (eds.), *Power in Britain,* London, 1973.

Bauer, R., Inkeles, A. and Kluckhohn, C., *How the Soviet System Works,* Cambridge (Mass.), 1956.

Bell, C. and Newby, H., 'The Source of Variation in Agricultural Workers' Images of Society', *Sociological Review,* Vol. 21 (1973). Reprinted in M. Bulmer (ed.), *Working-Class Images of Society,* London, 1975.

Bendix, R., *Work and Authority in Industry,* New York, 1956.

Bentzel, R., *Inkomstfördelningen i Sverige (The Distribution of Income in Sweden),* Stockholm, 1952.

Beynon, H. *Working for Ford,* Harmondsworth, 1973.

Birnbaum, N., *The Crisis of Industrial Society,* London, 1969.

Blake, D., 'Swedish Trade Unions and the Social Democratic Party; The Formative Years', *Scandinavian Economic History Review,* Vol. 8 (1960).

Bolinder, E., Magnusson E. and Nyren, L., *Risker I Jobbet (Risk at Work),* Stockholm, 1970.

Bulmer, M. (ed.), *Working-Class Images of Society,* London, 1975.

Butler, D., *British Political Facts, 1900-1967,* (2nd ed.), London, 1968.

Butler, D. and Kavanagh, D., *The British Election of February 1974,* London, 1974.

Butler, D. and Stokes, D., *Political Change in Britain,* Harmondsworth, 1971.

Bäckström, K., *Arbetarrörelsen i Sverige,* Vols. I and II *(The Labour*

*Movement in Sweden)*, Stockholm, 1971.

Carlson, B., *Trade Unions in Sweden,* Stockholm, 1969.

Carlsson, G., *Social Mobility and Class Structure,* Lund, 1958.

Carlsson, S., *Bonde-Präst-Ämbetsman (Farmer, Priest and Official),* Stockholm, 1962.

Central Bureau of Statistics, *Historical Statistics for Sweden,* Vol. 1, Stockholm, 1955.

Central Bureau of Statistics, *Historical Statistics of Sweden* (Statistical Survey), Stockholm, 1960.

Central Bureau of Statistics, *Statistical Abstract of Sweden,* Stockholm, 1971.

Central Bureau of Statistics, *Statistical Abstract of Sweden,* Stockholm, 1973.

Central Bureau of Statistics, *Swedish Survey on Relative Income Differences, 1972,* Stockholm, 1974.

Central Statistical Office, *Social Trends,* London, Vol. I (1970).

Chapman, R., *The Higher Civil Service in Britain,* London, 1970.

Christoffersson, U., Molin, B., Månsson, L. and Strömberg, L., *Byråkrati och Politik (Bureaucracy and Politics),* Stockholm, 1972.

Clark, D., *The Industrial Manager: His Background and Career Pattern,* London, 1966.

Clegg, H., Fox, A.and Thompson, A., *A History of British Trade Unionism Since 1889,* Oxford, 1964.

Clements, R., *Managers: A Study of their Careers in Industry,* London, 1958.

Committee on Higher Education, (The Robbins Report), *Higher Education,* London, 1963.

Comte, A., *Cours de Philosophie Positive,* Paris, 1830-42.

Copeman, G., *Leaders of British Industry,* London, 1955.

Dahlström, E., *Tjänstemännen, Näringslivet och Samhället, (Management, Unions and Society),* Stockholm, 1954.

Davis, K., 'The Urbanisation of the Human Population', in *Scientific American,* Vol. 213 (1965).

Davis, K. and Moore, W., 'Some Principles of Social Stratification', *American Sociological Review,* Vol. 10 (1945).

Deane, P. and Cole, W., *British Economic Growth 1688-1959* (2nd ed.), Cambridge, 1967.

Dunning, E. and Hopper, E., 'Industrialisation and the Problem of Convergence: A Critical Note', *Sociological Review,* Vol. 14 (1966).

Durkheim, E., *The Rules of Sociological Method,* Chicago, 1958.

Elvander, N., *Intresseorganisationerna i Dagens Sverige (Interest Groups in Contemporary Sweden),* Lund, 1969.

Erikson, R., *Uppväxtförhallånden och Social Rörlighet) Childhood Living Conditions and Social Mobility),* Stockholm, 1971.

Faris, R., *Chicago Sociology, 1920-1932,* California, 1967.

Faunce, W. and Form, W., 'The Nature of Industrial Society', in W. Faunce and W. Form (eds.), *Comparative Perspectives on Industrial Society,* Boston, 1969.

Feldman, A. and Moore, W., 'Industrialisation and Industrialism; Convergence and Differentiation', *Transactions of the Fifth World Congress of Sociology,* Vol. 2 (1962).

Fletcher, R., *The Making of Sociology,* Vol. I, London, 1971.

Fulcher, J., 'Class Conflict in Sweden', *Sociology,* Vol. 7 (1973).

Giddens, A., *The Class Structure of the Advanced Societies,* London, 1973.

Glass, D., *Social Mobility in Britain,* London, 1967.

Glennerster, H., 'Education and Inequality', in P. Townsend and N. Bosanquet, *Labour and Inequality,* London, 1972.

Goldthorpe, J.H., 'Social Stratification in Industrial Society', *Sociological Review Monograph,* No. 8 (1964).

Goldthorpe, J.H. and Lockwood, D., 'Affluence and the British Class Structure', *Sociological Review,* Vol. 11 (1963).

Goldthorpe, J.H. Lockwood, D., Bechhofer, F., and Platt, J., *The Affluent Worker: Industrial Attitudes and Behaviour,* Cambridge, 1968.

Goldthorpe, J.H., Lockwood, D., Bechhofer, F. and Platt, J., *The Affluent Worker: Political Attitudes and Behaviour,* Cambridge, 1968.

Goldthorpe, J.H., Lockwood, D., Bechhofer, F. and Platt, J., *The Affluent Worker in the Class Structure,* Cambridge, 1969.

Guttsman, W., 'The British Political Elite and the Class Structure' in P. Stanworth and A. Giddens (eds.), *Elites and Power in British Society,* London, 1974.

Halsey, A. and Trow, M., *The British Academics,* London, 1971.

Hancock, M.D., *Sweden: The Politics of Post-Industrial Change,* Hinsdale (Ill.), 1972.

Härnqvist, K., *Reserverna For Högre Utbildning (Reserves of Talent for Higher Education),* Stockholm, 1958.

Hart, H. and V-Otter, C., 'The Determination of Wages in Swedish Industry' in R. Scase (ed.), *Readings in the Swedish Class Structure,* Oxford, 1976.

Heckscher, E., *An Economic History of Sweden,* Cambridge (Mass.), 1954.

Heclo, H., *Modern Social Politics in Britain and Sweden,* New Haven,

1974.

Henkel, R. and Morrison, D. (eds.), *The Significance Test Controversy*, London, 1970.

Hindess, B., *The Decline of Working Class Politics*, London, 1971.

Hobsbawm, E., 'The British Standard of Living 1790-1850', *Economic History Review* (2nd Series), Vol. 10 (1957-8).

Holmberg, P., *Arbete och Löner i Sverige (Work and Wages in Sweden)*, Solna, 1963.

Hoselitz, B. and Moore, W. (eds.), *Industrialisation and Society*, Paris, 1963.

Huntford, R., *The New Totalitarians*, London, 1971.

Ingham, G., *Size of Industrial Organisation and Worker Behaviour*, Cambridge, 1970.

Inkeles, A., 'Industrial Man: The Relation of Status to Experience, Perception and Values', *American Journal of Sociology*, Vol. 66 (1960-1).

Inkeles, A. and Bauer, R., *The Soviet Citizen*, Cambridge (Mass.), 1959.

International Labour Office, *Yearbook of Labour Statistics*, Geneva, 1967.

International Labour Office, *Yearbook of Labour Statistics*, Geneva, 1975.

Israel, J., 'Uppforstran och Utbildning' ('Socialisation and Education') in E. Dahlström (ed.), *Svensk Samhällsstruktur i Sociologisk Belysning (Sociological Perspectives in the Swedish Social Structure)*, Stockholm, 1969.

Janson, C.-G., 'Urbanisering och Flyttning' ('Urbanisation and Migration') in E. Dahlström (ed.), *Svensk Samhällsstruktur i Sociologisk Belysning (Sociological Perspectives in the Swedish Social Structure)*, Stockholm, 1969.

Johansson, L., *Utbildning – Empirisk Del (Education – Some Empirical Data)*, Stockholm, 1971.

Johansson, S., 'Inkomstutvecklingen, 1966-1969', ('The Development of Incomes, 1966-1969'), mimeo., 1972.

Johnston, T., *Collective Bargaining in Sweden*, London, 1962.

Karlbom, T., *Arbetarnas Fackföreningar (Workers' Trade Unions)*, Helsinki, 1969.

Kelsall, R., *Higher Civil Servants in Britain*, London, 1955.

Kelsall, R., 'Recruitment to the Higher Civil Service: How has the Pattern Changed?' in P. Stanworth and A. Giddens (eds.), *Elites and Power in British Society*, London, 1974.

Kerr, C., Dunlop, J., Harbison, F. and Myers, C., *Industrialism and Industrial Man*, Cambridge (Mass.), 1960.

Klein, J., *Samples From English Cultures*, Vol. I, London, 1965.

Kälvesten, A.-L., *The Social Structure of Sweden*, Stockholm, 1966.

Landauer, C., *European Socialism*, Vol. I and II, Berkeley, 1959.

Landström, S., 'Svenska Ämbetsmäns Sociala Ursprung' ('The Social Background of Higher Civil Servants in Sweden'), *Statsvetenskapliga Föreningen i Uppsala*, Vol. 34 (1954).

Lane, T., *The Union Makes Us Strong*, London, 1974.

Lane, T. and D. Roberts, *Strike at Pilkingtons*, London, 1971.

Lenski, G. *Power and Privilege*, New York, 1966.

Leonard, R., *Elections in Britain*, London, 1968.

Lerner, D., *The Passing of Traditional Society*, New York, 1958.

Levy, M. Jr., *Modernisation and the Structure of Societies*, Princeton, 1966.

Lindbom, T., *Den Svenska Fackföreningsrörelsens Uppkomst och Tidigare Historia (The Growth and Early History of Swedish Trade Unions)*, Stockholm, 1938.

Lindhagen, J., *Social Democratins Program (The Social Democrats' Programme)*, Stockholm, 1972.

Lipset, S. and Bendix, R., *Social Mobility in Industrial Society*, California, 1959.

Lipset, S. and Trow, M., 'Reference Group Theory and Trade Union Wage Policy' in M. Komarovsky (ed.), *Common Frontiers of the Social Sciences*, Glencoe, 1957.

Lipset, S., Trow, M. and Coleman, J., *Union Democracy*, Illinois, 1956.

LO (Landorganisation), *Demokrati i Företagen (Democracy in Companies)*, Stockholm, 1971.

LO (Landorganisation), *Kollektiv Kapital Bildning genom Löntagarfonder (Capital Formation through the Wage Earners' Fund)*, Lund, 1976.

Lockwood, D., 'Sources of Variation in Working-Class Images of Society', *Sociological Review*, Vol. 14 (1966). Reprinted in M. Bulmer (ed.), *Working-Class Images of Society*, London, 1975.

Malmeström, G., and Widenborg, B., '245 Svenska Företagsledare' ('245 Swedish Business Leaders'), *Studier och Debatt* (1958).

Mathias, P., 'The Social Structure in the Eighteenth Century: A Calculation by Joseph Massie', *Economic History Review* (2nd Series), Vol. 10 (1957-8).

McKenzie, R. and Silver, A., *Angels in Marble*, London, 1968.

Michels, R., *Political Parties*, New York, 1962.

Meidner, R., 'Samordning och Solidarisk Lönepolitik under Tre Decennier' ('Co-ordination and Policy of Wage Solidarity'), in LO (Landorganisation), *Tvärsnitt (Cross-Section)*, Stockholm, 1973.

Meyer, A., 'Theories of Convergence', in C. Johnson (ed.), *Change in Communist Systems*, Stanford, 1970.

Miliband, R., *Parliamentary Socialism*, London, 1961.

Miliband, R., *The State in Capitalist Society*, London, 1969.

McMiller, S., 'Comparative Social Mobility', *Current Sociology*, Vol. 9 (1960).

Mills, C. Wright, *The Sociological Imagination*, New York, 1959.

Mitchell, G., *A Hundred Years of Sociology*, London, 1968.

Moore, R., 'Religion as a Source of Variation in Working-Class Images of Society', in M. Bulmer (ed.), *Working-Class Images of Society*, London, 1975.

Moore, W., *Social Change*, Englewood Cliffs, 1963.

Moore, W., *The Impact of Industry*, Englewood Cliffs, 1965.

Moorhouse, H., 'The Political Incorporation of the British Working Class: An Interpretation', *Sociology*, Vol. 7 (1973).

Mouly, J., 'Wages Policy in Sweden', *International Labour Review*, Vol. 95 (1967).

Myrdal, A., *Towards Equality*, Stockholm, 1971.

Newby, H., 'Paternalism and Capitalism', in R. Scase (ed.), *Industrial Society: Class, Cleavage and Control*, London, 1977.

Nichols, T., *Ownership. Control and Ideology*, London, 1969.

Noble, T., 'Social Mobility and Class Relations in Britain', *British Journal of Sociology*, Vol. 23 (1972).

Otley, C., 'The Public Schools and the Army', in J. Urry and J. Wakeford (eds.), *Power in Britain*, London, 1973.

Otter, C.V., 'Arbetarnas Fackliga Organisationsgrad' ('The Strength of Trade Unions'), *Arkiv för Studier i Arbetarrörelsens Historia (Journal for the Study of the History of Labour Movements)*, No. 4 (1973).

Parkin, F., 'Working Class Conservatives: A Theory of Political Deviance', *British Journal of Sociology*, Vol. 18 (1967).

Parkin, F., *Class Inequality and Political Order*, London, 1971.

Parry, N. and J., 'Collective Social Mobility and Social Closure', in R. Scase (ed.), *Industrial Society: Class, Cleavage and Control*, London, 1977.

Pelling, H., *A Short History of the Labour Party*, London, 1961.

PEP (Political and Economic Planning), *Trade Union Membership* (Planning 463), London, 1962.

Petersson, O. and Särlvik, B., 'The 1973 Election', *General Elections 1973, Vol. 3*, Central Bureau of Statistics, Stockholm, 1975.

Petrén, G., *Några Uppgifter om Proffessorskåren i Uppsala och Lund under 1800 Talet och Första Hälften av 1900 Talet (Some Information* on *Professors at Uppsala and Lund during the Nineteenth and the First Half of the Twentieth Centuries)*, Lund, 1952.

Pulzer, P., *Political Representation and Elections in Britain*, London, 1972.

Reuterberg, S.-E., 'Val av Teoretisk Utbildning i Relation till Sociala och Regionala Bakgrundsfaktorer' ('Choice of "Academic" Education in Relation to Social and Regional Background'), mimeo, Gothenburg, 1968.

Rex, J., *Discovering Sociology*, London, 1973.

Richardson, G., *Kulturkamp och Klasskamp: Ideologiska och Sociala Motsättningar i Svensk Skol och Kulturpolitik Under 1880-Talet (Cultural Struggle and Class Conflict: Ideological and Social Disputes in Swedish School and Cultural Politics during the 1880s)*, Gothenburg, 1963.

Rose, R., 'Voting Trends Surveyed' in *The Times, Guide to the House of Commons 1970*, London, 1970.

Rostow, W., *The Stages of Economic Growth*, Cambridge, 1961.

Roth, A., *The Business Background of M.P.s*, London, 1972.

Routh, G., *Occupation and Pay in Great Britain*, Cambridge, 1965.

Royal Commission on the Distribution of Income and Wealth, *Report No. I*, London, 1975.

Runciman, W.G., *Relative Deprivation and Social Justice*, London, 1966.

Runciman, W.G., 'Towards a Theory of Social Stratification', in F. Parkin (ed.), *The Social Analysis of Class Structures*, London, 1974.

Samuelsson, K., *From Great Power to Welfare State*, London, 1968.

Schiller, B., 'LO Paragraph 32 och Företagsdemokratin' (LO, Paragraph 32 and Company Democracy), in LO (Landorganisation), *Tvärsnitt, (Cross-Section)*, Stockholm, 1973.

Seeman, M., 'On the Personal Consequences of Alienation in Work', *American Sociological Review*, Vol. 32 (1967).

Segerstedt, T. and Lundquist, A., *Människan i Industrisamhället (Man in Industrialised Society), Society)*, Stockholm, 1955.

Sköld, L. and Halvarson, A., 'Riskdagens Sociala Sammansättning under Hundra År', ('The Social Composition of Parliament during 100 Years'), in *Samhället och Riksdag*, Del. I (*Society and Parliament*, Part I), Stockholm, 1966.

Smelser, N., 'Mechanisms of Change and Adjustment to Change', in W. Faunce and W. Form (eds.), *Comparative Perspectives on Industrial Society*, Boston, 1969.

Spiegelberg, R., 'Parliamentary Business', *The Times*, 3 July 1970.

Spånt, R., *Den Svenska Inkomstfördelningens Utveckling (The Development of the Distribution of Income in Sweden)*, Uppsala, 1976.

Stanworth, P. and Giddens, A., 'An Economic Elite: A Demographic Profile of Company Chairmen', in P. Stanworth and A. Giddens (eds.)., *Elites and Power in British Society*, London, 1974.

Statens Offentliga Utredningar (SOU), *Ägande och Inflytande inom det Privata Näringslivet (Ownership and Influence in the Private Economy)*, Stockholm, 1968.

Statens Offentliga Utredningar (SOU), *Svenska Folkets Inkomster (The Income of the Swedish Population)*, Stockholm, 1970.

Statens Offentliga Utredningar (SOU), *Val Av Utbildning och Yrke (Choice of Education and Work)*, Stockholm, 1971.

Statens Offentliga Utredningar (SOU), *Demokrati på Arbetsplatsen (Democracy at the Workplace)*, Stockholm, 1975.

Thompson, K., 'Church of England Bishops as an Elite', in P. Stanworth and A. Giddens (eds.), *Elites and Power in British Society*, London, 1974.

Tingsten, H., *The Swedish Social Democrats*, New Jersey, 1973.

Tomasson, R., 'The Extraordinary Success of the Swedish Social Democrats', *Journal of Politics*, Vol. 31 (1969).

Tomasson, R.,*Sweden: Prototype of Modern Society*, New York, 1970.

Tumin, M., 'Some Principles of Stratification: A Critical Analysis', *American Sociological Review*, Vol. 18 (1953).

Ullenhag, J., *Den Solidariska Lönepolitiken i Sverige (The Policy of Wage Solidarity in Sweden)*, Stockholm, 1971.

United Nations, *Economic Survey of Europe*, Geneva, 1957.

United Nations, *Incomes in Post-War Europe*, Geneva, 1967.

United Nations, *Yearbook of National Accounts Statistics 1972, Pt. III – International Tables*, New York, 1974.

Utton, M., *Industrial Concentration*, Harmondsworth, 1970.

Weber, M., *The Methodology of the Social Sciences*, Chicago, 1949.

Wedderburn, D. and Craig, C., 'Relative Deprivation in Work', in D. Wedderburn (ed.), *Poverty, Inequality and Class Structure*, London, 1974.

Weinberg, I., 'The Problem of Convergence of Industrial Societies. A Critical Look at the State of a Theory', in *Comparative Studies in Society and History*, Vol. II (1969).

Westergaard, J., 'The Rediscovery of the Cash Nexus', *Socialist Register*, London, 1970.

Westergaard, J. and Resler, H., *Class in a Capitalist Society*, London, 1975.

Whitely, R., 'The City and Industry: the directors of large companies, their characteristics and connections', in P. Stanworth and A. Giddens (eds.), *Elites and Power in British Society,* London, 1974.

Wilensky, H., 'Work as a Social Problem' in H. Becker (ed.), *Social Problems: A Modern Approach,* London, 1966.

Wilensky, H., *The Welfare State and Equality,* London, 1975.

# INDEX